Arrest, Search, and Seizure

GLENCOE PRESS CRIMINAL JUSTICE SERIES

General Editor:

G. DOUGLAS GOURLEY

Inspector (Ret.), LA Police Department
Chairman, Department of Criminal Justice
California State University at Los Angeles
Los Angeles, California

Arrest, Search, and Seizure

Lawrence C. Waddington

Judge of the Municipal Court
Los Angeles, California

GLENCOE PRESS
A division of Benziger Bruce & Glencoe, Inc.
Beverly Hills
Collier Macmillan Publishers
London

Glencoe Press
A division of Benziger Bruce & Glencoe, Inc.
8701 Wilshire Boulevard
Beverly Hills, California 90211
Collier-Macmillan Canada, Ltd.

Library of Congress Catalog Card Number: 73-7366

First printing, 1974

Contents

Preface

Until recently, a comprehensive text on the law of search and seizure for peace officers would have been difficult to write. Only since the U.S. Supreme Court's landmark decision in *Mapp* v. *Ohio*,[1] in 1961, did all peace officers employed by state and local agencies require any instruction on search and seizure. But the courts, and particularly the U.S. Supreme Court, could provide adequate guidelines only when a sufficient number of cases had been decided. Now, twelve years later, court decisions have outlined basic principles that can be summarized with a fair degree of certainty. Perfect stability can never be achieved, doubtless, but the major landmarks are clear.

Although fifty state appellate courts can arguably reach fifty different opinions on a given point of search and seizure, the decisional supremacy of the U.S. Supreme Court narrows the range of options available to state courts. For these reasons, each chapter of this text relies principally on the U.S. Supreme Court decisions, supplemented by important state court opinions. Necessarily, the more urbanized states render a prolific number of opinions, and references to decisions from larger jurisdictions predominate. But any law librarian can assist the student in determining whether his/her own state has decided a point of law referred to in the text. The text outlines the basic law of search and seizure, however, and any marked variance therefrom would be surprising.

---

1. 367 U.S. 643, 81 S. Ct. 1684, 6 L. Ed. 2d 1081.

This volume attempts to achieve several goals: first, to serve as a basic text on the law of arrest, search, and seizure useful for the teacher, student, and peace officer on the job; second, to provide a source of reference materials to facilitate quick research on search and seizure; and third, to provide the serious student with legal problems that require more complex analysis. Several chapters conclude with cases and materials for further reference and study.

Introduction

Despite the general consensus that a trial should be a quest for truth, all state and federal jurisdictions have imposed limitations on the admissibility of evidence in court. Certain kinds of evidence are excluded because of their inherently untrustworthy character. Hearsay is the most conspicuous example. Evidence is also excluded when its probative value is outweighed by the potential prejudicial effect on the jury. Generally speaking, these rules of evidence are found in statutes or judicial decisions of state and federal courts.

Within the last several years a new body of law has developed: limitations on the admissibility of evidence as required by the U.S. Constitution. Courts have imposed restrictions on admitting evidence at trial, not because of the traditional rules of evidence but, rather, for constitutional principles as stated in the Bill of Rights. These constitutional limitations on the admissibility of evidence, as contained particularly in the Fourth, Fifth, and Sixth amendments, are imposed regardless of the reliability or truthworthiness of the evidence. Evidence is excluded in these cases—even though relevant and material to the issue on trial—out of respect for constitutional guarantees.

For example, relevant evidence seized pursuant to a search of a suspect is excluded because of the Fourth Amendment, which prohibits unreasonable searches and seizures; a voluntary confession may be excluded because the arrestee was not informed of his right to remain silent as required by the Fifth Amendment; a robbery victim's testimony is excluded because police conducted a lineup of the defendant in the absence of his counsel as required by the Sixth Amendment. In each case, otherwise reliable evidence is excluded because constitutional rights of the suspect were ignored or abridged.

The authors of the Bill of Rights necessarily painted with a broad brush. It was impossible to extensively detail basic concepts of liberty, and so they drafted only a general statement of democratic principles. Although the Bill of Rights is a ringing endorsement of individual freedoms, it includes no constitutional provision to enforce compliance with the commands inherent in these first ten amendments. It did not specifically authorize judges to enforce obedience to the Constitution. In order to compel respect for these constitutional principles, the courts fashioned the only legal weapon available to them—that of excluding evidence obtained in their violation. In that context, respect for constitutional principles is compelled.

Of course this discussion assumes that the courts have interpreted the Constitution in harmony with the broad principles announced in the Bill of Rights. Yet there has never been universal agreement on whether the judicially created constitutional limitations on the admissibility of evidence are sound. And nowhere does the Constitution authorize the courts to exclude relevant evidence. In fact, the current debate over court decisions rages as hot as the day the key cases interpreting the Constitution were pronounced. Moreover, the Bill of Rights itself applies to the federal government. Only by holding that the due process clause of the Fourteenth Amendment incorporates by implication some of the Bill of Rights has the U.S. Supreme Court imposed constitutional limitations on the admissibility of evidence in state courts.

This volume focuses on the Fourth Amendment to the United States Constitution. From this amendment has developed all the constitutional rules respecting the arrest of suspects and the search of their person, cars, or houses. Arrest and search are awesome governmental powers. History records a vivid legacy of oppression facilitated by indiscriminate arrest and search. Indeed the Fourth Amendment itself is a restatement of the basic principle that people are to be free from unreasonable searches and seizures. Yet the Constitution never intended to confer license for anarchy by fettering governmental agents. The question is: Where do we draw the line between the right of the citizen to live in security and privacy and the duty of governmental agents to maintain an ordered society in which all may live with reasonable security?

Arrest, Search, and Seizure

Chapter One

The Fourth Amendment

History

The Fourth Amendment to the U.S. Constitution provides: "The right of the people to be secure in their persons, houses, papers, and effects, against unreasonable searches and seizures, shall not be violated, and no warrants shall issue, but upon probable cause, supported by oath or affirmation, and particularly describing the place to be searched, and the persons or things to be seized."

The Fourth Amendment is the source of all the rules that govern the arrest, search, and seizure of persons and/or property. Despite state and federal statutes that define arrest and search authority, the Fourth Amendment is the ultimate yardstick. Because the issue of arrest and search emerges almost exclusively in criminal trials, or in proceedings of an essentially criminal nature, judges must determine whether governmental agents obtained evidence in violation of the provisions of the Fourth Amendment. Without any statute to refer to, judges must resort to previous decisions of state and federal courts that interpret the constitutional language. These cases, which are reported and published, articulate the rules of arrest, search, and seizure.

The Fourth Amendment was written against a background of colonial rage against indiscriminate searching practices of British officers. Widespread use of blank warrants—to be filled in with unlimited discretion—substantially contributed to American grievances culminating in the Revolutionary War. For a people imbued with a heritage of individual freedom, warrantless arrests and forcible intrusions into homes were intolerable. To prevent the fledgling U.S. Government from continuing previous British practices, authors of the Bill of Rights sought to draft language that would forever prevent indiscriminate arrest and search power. That decision is reflected in the language of the Fourth Amendment.

Although the Fourth Amendment is frequently characterized as the chief protection against arbitrary arrest and search, judicial interpretation of the amendment was not considered until almost a century after adoption of the Bill of Rights. In a case involving an alleged customs violation, the U.S. Supreme Court interpreted the language of the Fourth Amendment as expressing constitutional protection for the sanctity of a man's home and the privacies of life. In subsequent cases, the justices reaffirmed this rationale and reasoned that the Fourth Amendment protects *people* and assures them a right of *privacy*. Although the protection of privacy is perhaps the core of the Fourth Amendment, such a term is elusive at best. In a more recent judicial expression, the U.S. Supreme Court held that the Fourth Amendment's objective is to protect personal security. Indeed the language of the Fourth Amendment itself asserts "the right of the people to be secure in their persons, houses, papers and effects."

Yet the promise of personal security cannot be absolute. The Fourth Amendment prohibits only unreasonable breaches of personal security. Determination of "reasonableness" inevitably invites subjective evaluation, and often courts disagree. Nonetheless, measuring the governmental agents' conduct against an objective standard of reasonableness is the judicial goal. The boundaries of that standard will be the subject of this book.

The Exclusionary Rule

Despite the constitutional endorsement of individual personal security and the corresponding prohibition against unreasonable searches, the Fourth Amendment contains no enforcement clause. The Fourth Amendment nowhere provides a penalty for violation of its provisions. Nor is any governmental agency empowered to supervise the actions of those whose conduct allegedly trespasses on Fourth Amendment freedoms. Not even civil lawsuits to recover damages are authorized. How then could the constitutional command of the Fourth Amendment be enforced?

The Bill of Rights, as originally enacted in 1789, applied only to the federal government and its agents acting on its behalf. Accordingly, the applicability of the Fourth Amendment to federal officers first arose in a federal criminal trial. In 1914, the U.S. Supreme Court ruled that any evidence seized by federal officers in violation of the Fourth Amendment would be inadmissible in a federal trial. This judicial doctrine became known as the *exclusionary rule*. The exclusionary rule was a judicially created rule of evidence barring judges and juries from considering any evidence seized in violation of the Fourth Amendment—no matter how relevant and material to the issue on trial—in determining guilt or innocence. Although the exclusionary rule has been criticized as not constitutionally required, it remains today as a judicial technique for excluding evidence seized in violation of the Fourth Amendment.[1]

Despite the formulation of the exclusionary rule as an implementation of the Fourth Amendment, federal courts could still admit evidence seized by state officers if no federal agents were involved. This rule, known as the "silver platter" doctrine, was originally conceived because of the unique federal-state relationship existing in the United States. At the time the "silver platter" doctrine was current, federal courts had held that the Fourth Amendment applied only to federal officials. This interpretation of the Bill of Rights was consistent with constitutional theory in that the first ten amendments had been drafted as applicable to the federal government only. Constitutional regulation of state officers was embraced only by the due process and equal protection clauses of the Fourteenth Amendment. Therefore, state officers acting within their own sphere of enforcement were immune from the provisions of the Fourth Amendment. Because state officers were acting lawfully within their respective states, the federal courts held that it would be improper to penalize state officers merely because the forum for criminal proceedings against an accused arose in a federal court.

As time passed and the U.S. Supreme Court articulated new constitutional theory, the "silver platter" doctrine came under attack. The Supreme Court had ruled, in a series of cases, that the due process and equal protection clauses of the Fourteenth Amendment of the Constitution incorporated the broad principles of the Bill of Rights. In 1949, the Court ruled specifically that unreasonable searches and seizures conducted by state officers violated the due process clause of the Fourteenth Amendment. But the Court stopped short of imposing the exclusionary rule on the states. As a consequence, even though a state officer conducted an unreasonable search, the evidence he seized could still be admitted in a state or federal court. But the "silver platter" was becoming tarnished.

---

1. For example, in 1904 this doctrine was almost repudiated (*Adams* v. *New York*, 192 U.S. 585, 24 S. Ct. 48 L. Ed. 575), but was reaffirmed ten years later; *Weeks* v. *United States*, 232 U.S. 383, 34 S. Ct. 341, 58 L. Ed. 2d 652.

Then, during the following decade, the U.S. Supreme Court considered two major cases involving serious intrusions of privacy by state officials into the home and person of the respective arrestees. In *Irvine* v. *California,* the Court reviewed evidence that reflected indiscriminate forcible entry and search of a personal residence by police in order to conceal a microphone for purposes of recording conversations. In *Rochin* v. *California,* the Court reviewed a conviction based on evidence extracted from an arrestee's stomach by a stomach pump. Despite the flagrant intrusions of personal security and the right of privacy in each case, the Supreme Court could review the convictions only under the broad protection of the Fourteenth Amendment because state officers alone were involved.

These and other cases ultimately led the federal courts to repudiate the "silver platter" doctrine. In 1960, the U.S. Supreme Court held that evidence seized by state officers would be inadmissible in federal courts if seized in noncompliance with the provisions of the Fourth Amendment.

In 1961, in *Mapp* v. *Ohio,* the Supreme Court held that the Fourth Amendment, as incorporated by the Fourteenth Amendment, was enforceable against state officers and that the exclusionary rule would be imposed in state courts. The Court concluded that the exclusionary rule was indeed of constitutional origin and not a mere rule of evidence. It directed state courts to enforce the Fourth Amendment against state officers in state trials. Thus one hundred seventy years after the adoption of the Constitution, the U.S. Supreme Court ultimately ruled that the Fourth Amendment applied to all governmental agents, state or federal, and that the constitutional protection was enforceable by judicially excluding from evidence any materials seized in violation of an individual's personal security.

Both the Fourth and the Fourteenth Amendments apply to "state action," i.e., action by governmental officials. Evidence obtained by private parties who are not working in conjunction with, or under the direction of, a governmental agency is not subject to constitutional exclusion. But nongovernmental employees who provide essentially law enforcement services, i.e., security guards, could arguably be subject to Fourth Amendment standards.

By the time of the Supreme Court's decision in the *Mapp* case, several states had already judicially imposed the exclusionary rule on their own officials. California, the nation's most populous state, was a notable example. California had earlier adopted the common-law rule that if otherwise competent evidence was offered to prove the truth or falsity of a charge, it should be admitted regardless of how the evidence was obtained. In a 1955 case, the California Supreme Court rejected the argument that the only issue regarding the admissibility of evidence in trial was its relevance and materiality to the cause. In *People* v. *Cahan,* the California Supreme Court reviewed its previous decisions and concluded that it was persuaded to adopt the exclusionary rule because all other means of securing compliance with constitutional provisions prohibiting unlawful searches and seizures had failed. The Court stated that those who had been subjected to an unreasonable search and seizure by state agents were remediless; that prosecutors were reluctant to file criminal charges against police officers with whom they worked daily; and that juries refused to award damages to complainants whose criminal record impaired the validity of their contentions. All other measures having failed, said the Court, the judiciary should not lend its aid to illegal methods of obtaining evidence. This conclusion was restated in a different form by the U.S. Supreme Court in *Mapp* when it held that respect for the Fourth Amendment could only be compelled by removing the incentive to disregard it.

Although the Fourth Amendment had now been applied to the states, a final question remained: Who would determine the standard of "reasonableness" required by the Amendment in determining whether evidence had been seized reasonably or not? Some state courts held that such a decision was their own prerogative, but the U.S. Supreme Court held in *Ker* v. *California* that the standard of reasonableness was the same under the Fourth and Fourteenth amendments. As a consequence, the decisions of the U.S. Supreme Court on Fourth Amendment issues are authoritative and binding on state courts. It is these decisions that will form the nucleus of this study.

Because the exclusionary rule was fashioned to compel respect for the Fourth Amendment, the courts have not limited the scope of constitutional protection to criminal trials only. Many proceedings which may be labeled *civil,* rather than *criminal,* are essentially criminal in nature. These quasi-criminal proceedings, such as the revocation of probation or outpatient status, narcotic commitment proceedings, or revocation of parole, involve potential breaches of personal security subject to constitutional scrutiny.

In another context, courts will exclude not only evidence seized incidental to an unreasonable search, but the "fruits" of an unreasonable search as well. Evidence seized as the direct product of a Fourth Amendment violation cannot be insulated from judicial scrutiny.

Although the rationale of the exclusionary rule presumes that its enforcement will deter lawless law enforcement, recent critics contend that it fails to achieve this goal. The exclusionary rule serves only to prevent admissibility of evidence in a trial; it imposes no controls on allegedly unlawful arrests and searches that do not result in a criminal prosecution. Police officers have been known to arrest and search

people for purposes unrelated to prosecution. Motivation for indiscriminate arrest and search can include harassment, destruction of
evidence, or the removal of particular persons from a specific area.
Or police can invoke other policy considerations in which trial and
punishment are not the goal.

Recent commentators have also noted that the exclusionary rule
is imposed months later—sometimes years later if an appeal is filed—
on a police officer who is often unaware of the final court decision;
that the rules have become so complex and unsettled that officers cannot proceed with certainty prior to an arrest or search; that judges
and prosecutors entertain widely differing theories in applying the rule.
Out of all this, contend the critics, has emerged a procedural legal
jungle that obscures the presumed object of a trial, i.e., determining
the truth or falsity of the criminal charge. Arguments over the admissibility of evidence and the lawfulness of police conduct often are the
only critical issues. Guilt or innocence of the suspect becomes subordinate, contend the critics.

Supporters of the exclusionary rule acknowledge its defects, but
maintain that the rule remains as the only procedure, however ineffective, against unbridled governmental authority. Until an alternative
policy can be found that will more effectively regulate lawless law
enforcement, they argue, the exclusionary rule should remain.

It is not the purpose here to debate the merits of the exclusionary rule. Everyone agrees that it is deplorable that an otherwise guilty
suspect escapes conviction because of an error in arrest and search
procedures. Society pays a heavy price for the exclusionary rule, but
arguably this is the cost of democracy. Most observers would probably prefer that the exclusionary rule be abolished and that a better
method of enforcing the commands of the Fourth Amendment be
adopted. As yet, no one has suggested a procedure that seems reasonably adequate to that goal and that simultaneously enlists the support
of critics and supporters of the rule.

The Two Clauses

Dividing the language of the Fourth Amendment into two clauses
is the first step in its analysis. The first clause ("The right of the people
to be secure in their persons, houses, papers and effects against unreasonable searches and seizures . . .") may be denominated the
unreasonable search and seizure clause. The second clause ("and no
warrants shall issue but upon probable cause . . .") may be called the
warrant clause. The courts have held that the Fourth Amendment requires all searches to be conducted under the authority of a warrant

issued by a judicial officer, unless an "exception" can be demonstrated. Absent evidence justifying a warrantless search, any invasion of personal security must be authorized by a detached and neutral magistrate rather than exercised at the discretion of an officer enforcing the law. Perhaps the best expression of this ideal was written by Justice Jackson in the case of *Johnson* v. *United States*:

> The point of the Fourth Amendment, which often is not grasped by zealous officers, is not that it denies law enforcement the support of the usual inferences which reasonable men draw from evidence. Its protection consists in requiring that those inferences be drawn by a neutral and detached magistrate instead of being judged by the officer engaged in the often competitive enterprise of ferreting out crime. Any assumption that evidence sufficient to support a magistrate's disinterested determination to issue a search warrant will justify the officers in making a search without a warrant would reduce the Amendment to a nullity and leave the people's homes secure only in the discretion of police officers. . . . When the right of privacy must reasonably yield to the right of search is, as a rule, to be decided by a judicial officer, not by a policeman or government enforcement agent.

Not only are search warrants judicially preferred, but their issuance presumes that a search has been authorized as "reasonable" within the meaning of the Fourth Amendment. Evidence seized pursuant to a search warrant may be offered by the prosecutor at a subsequent trial with a corresponding presumption of legality that the defendant must rebut. On the other hand, searches conducted without a warrant must be justified as an exception to the warrant requirement, and the burden is on the prosecutor to establish the validity of the search.

Despite judicial preference for search warrants, and despite the burden of proof imposed on the prosecutor to justify warrantless searches, the vast majority of searches are conducted without a warrant. This is attributable partly to the untold number of police searches conducted on streets and roads throughout the nation where obtaining a warrant is impractical; partly also to the excessive time necessary for a law enforcement agent to obtain a search warrant—particularly in busy metropolitan courts. As a consequence, most courts have reviewed the admissibility of evidence within the confines of the "unreasonable search and seizure clause" rather than the "warrant clause."

Even so, the theory behind both clauses is similar. In cases involving the Fourth Amendment, the central inquiry is into the reasonableness of all aspects of a particular governmental invasion of a citizen's personal security. In determining "reasonableness," the courts focus on the governmental interest that allegedly justifies official intrusion on constitutionally protected interests of private citizens. There is no mathematical test for determining reasonableness other than balancing the need to arrest or search against the invasion that is entailed.

The inquiry as to reasonableness is twofold: Was the action justified at the inception? If so, was it reasonably related in scope to the circumstances that justified the interference? Another way to restate this principle would be: Was there a legitimate basis for invading a citizen's personal security and right of privacy? If so, was the scope of the invasion related to the reasons that justified the initial invasion? In succeeding chapters, this broad principle will be sketched in more detail.

A quick reading of the Fourth Amendment might lead to the conclusion that only *searches* are within the ambit of constitutional protection. The courts have held, however, that the Fourth Amendment's prohibition against unreasonable *seizures* applies to an arrest as well. An arrest is a seizure within the meaning of the Fourth Amendment, and consequently every arrest must be based on a constitutionally adequate ground regardless of state or local statutes defining *arrest*. Thus, the same judicial inquiry that is made into the reasonableness of a search must also be made into the reasonableness of an arrest, or seizure. In applying the *unreasonable search and seizure* clause of the Fourth Amendment to any inquiry into the validity of a warrantless search or arrest, one must begin with the issue of whether either kind of invaded personal security was reasonable.

To complement the logic of the *unreasonable search and seizure* clause, the courts have held that the *warrant* clause in the Fourth Amendment requires that a reasonable basis must be provided to a judicial officer that will authorize him to sanction a search warrant, which, in turn, authorizes the police to enter the "place to be searched," or a warrant commanding the arrest of the "person to be seized." What is the standard that governs a magistrate when he issues a warrant authorizing an invasion of the place to be searched or jailing the person to be seized? The standard is a judicially formulated rule entitled *Probable Cause*. A warrant may be issued only upon probable cause, i.e., a sufficient quality of evidence to justify a breach of personal security. *Probable cause is crucial to the discussion of arrest warrants and search warrants* (see chapter 5, Search Warrants).

Just as probable cause is required for the issuance of a search warrant, any arrest and search without a warrant must also be based on probable cause. In determining whether there has been any breach of the "right of the people to be secure against unreasonable searches and seizures," the courts measure that invasion against the standard of probable cause. Was there probable cause to arrest (or seize) without a warrant? Was there probable cause to search without a warrant? If probable cause to breach personal security existed, the ensuing seizure or search will be reasonable within the meaning of the Fourth Amendment unless the search could legally be accomplished only by warrant. Probable cause, then, is the legitimate basis for the invasion of personal security.

If a "reasonable" basis to invade personal security can be established, governmental officers are constitutionally sanctioned to arrest or search. But how extensively, or intensively, may they search? The issue then becomes the scope of the search, i.e., the degree and extent of the search. If the warrantless arrest (seizure) of a person is based on probable cause, does the act of arrest authorize a search of his person? his car? his house? his effects? If a person's house is searched pursuant to a warrant, are officers authorized to seek evidence in the basement? the attic? the garage? inside a medicine cabinet? under rugs? The test is: Is the scope of the search reasonably related to the circumstances that justified the original intrusion. In analyzing this question, it is important to determine the nature of these intrusions of personal security. When the circumstances that justify the original invasion are outlined, the scope of the invasion can be ascertained.

The analysis of all search and seizure issues requires a twofold inquiry into "reasonableness": Was the initial invasion of personal security justified, i.e., was there probable cause? If so, was the invasion limited to satisfying the original need for the breach? Put another way, was there a right to invade personal security and, if so, was the exercise of the right limited to satisfying the original cause for invasion?

Cases and Materials

Bivens v. *Agents*, 403 U.S. 388, 91 S. Ct. 1999, 29 L. Ed. 2d 619.

Caleb Foote, "The Fourth Amendment: Obstacle or Necessity in the Law of Arrest?" 51 *Journal of Criminal Law, Criminology and Police Science,* p. 402 (1961).

Charles Alan Wright, "Must the Criminal Go Free if the Constable Blunders?" 50 Texas Law Review, 736 (1972).

Comment, "The Decline of the Exclusionary Rule: An Alternative to Injustice," 4 *Southwest University Law Review*, 68 (1972).

Dallin H. Oaks, "Studying the Exclusionary Rule in Search and Seizure," 37 *University of Chicago Law Review*, 665 (1970).

Elkins v. *United States*, 364 U.S. 206, 80 S. Ct. 1437, 4 L. Ed. 2d 1669.

Irvine v. *California*, 347 U.S. 128, 74 S. Ct. 381, 98 L. Ed. 561.

Johnson v. *United States,* 333 U.S. 10, 68 S. Ct. 367, 92 L. Ed. 436.

Katz v. *United States,* 389 U.S. 347, 88 S. Ct. 507, 19 L. Ed. 2d 576.

Ker v. *California,* 374 U.S. 23, 83 S. Ct. 1623, 10 L. Ed. 2d 726.

Kingsley A. Taft, "Protecting the Public from Mapp v. Ohio, without Amending the Constitution," 50 American Bar Association Journal, 815 (1964).

Mapp v. *Ohio,* 367 U.S. 643, 81 S. Ct. 1684, 6 L. Ed. 2d 1081.

Marcus v. *Search Warrant,* 367 U.S. 717, 81 S. Ct. 1708, 6 L. Ed. 2d 1127.

Other articles are collected in an appendix to Chief Justice Burger's dissent in *Bivens* v. *Agents* at page 426.

People v. *Cahan,* 44 Cal. 2d 434, 282 P. 2d 905.

President's Commission on Law Enforcement and Administration of Justice, *Task Force Reports.*

Robert E. Burns, "Mapp v. Ohio: An All-American Mistake," 19 *DePaul Law Journal* 80 (1969).

Rochin v. *California,* 342 U.S. 165, 72 S. Ct. 205, 96 L. Ed. 183.

Weeks v. *United States,* 232 U.S. 383, 34 S. Ct. 341, 58 L. Ed. 652.

Wolfe v. *Colorado,* 338 U.S. 25, 69 S. Ct. 1359, 93 L. Ed. 1782.

Chapter Two

Detention and Arrest

Detention—the Stop

Confrontations between citizens and peace officers are manifold in variety and purpose. The spectrum fluctuates from the casual friendly conversation between beat officer and shopkeeper to the violence incident to the arrest of an armed-robbery suspect. In some cases the initial meeting may begin routinely enough, but erupt quickly in violence. To the officer who reads about or is aware of public hostility to law enforcement, every confrontation contains the seeds of violence. The routine inquiry addressed to a pedestrian on the street, the familiar traffic stop, the service of a traffic warrant—any of these daily minor acts may suddenly become hazardous. Law enforcement's concern for personal welfare is a relevant factor and an important consideration in measuring the reasonableness of the steps officers take under these circumstances. On the other hand, to assume that every citizen is potentially hostile is unreasonable.

What have the courts to do with police-citizen confrontations? Although various state and federal statutes authorize civil suits for money damages against peace officers for alleged violations of civil rights, in an ensuing criminal trial the courts will rule on the admissibility of any evidence seized as a consequence of the confrontation. If the confrontation violates a person's Fourth Amendment right to personal security, the court will exclude evidence seized as a consequence of the violation. Accordingly, it becomes extremely important to focus on the initial contact between citizen and police officer. If that contact is incompatible with Fourth Amendment requirements, any subsequent arrest or search may be tainted and important evidence excluded. For example, a search otherwise valid under the Fourth Amendment may become unlawful if the seized evidence was a product of an earlier unlawful detention.

Right to Detain—Forcible Detention

Police attention is drawn to a person for any number of reasons, some quite evident and others dependent on intuition. Whatever factors alert the officer's suspicion, the issue is whether he has any right to stop the person and possibly question him. The officer may not have seen sufficient evidence to justify an arrest for a specific crime, but he may have seen enough to alert him to the possibility of a recently committed crime or to an act that suggests the preparation of a crime. How does the Fourth Amendment come into play in such instances?

In 1968, the U.S. Supreme Court decided *Terry* v. *Ohio*. In *Terry*, a veteran police officer testified that he had been assigned to patrol a location in downtown Cleveland. He observed standing on the corner of an intersection two men whom he had never seen before. He saw one of the men leave the other and walk past some stores. "The man paused for a moment and looked into a store window, then walked a short distance, turned around and walked back toward the corner, pausing once again to look into the same store window. He rejoined his companion at the corner, and the two conferred briefly. Then the second man went through the same series of motions, strolling down the same street, looking in the same window, walking on a short distance, turning back, peering in the store window again, and returning to confer with the first man at the corner. The two men repeated this ritual alternately between five and six times apiece— in all roughly a dozen trips. At one point while the two were standing together on the corner, a third man approached them and engaged them briefly in conversation. This man then left the two others and walked away. The first two men resumed their measured pacing, peering, and conferring. After this had gone on for several minutes, the two men walked off together following the path taken earlier by the third man." Believing the two men to be "casing" the store, the officer approached the three men, identified himself, grabbed Terry, spun him around, and commenced a cursory search of his clothing. His search yielded a concealed weapon, whereupon the officer arrested Terry. Subsequently, Terry was convicted of carrying a concealed weapon.

After his conviction, Terry appealed. He contended that his detention was a "seizure" in the sense of the Fourth Amendment and therefore had to be based on a quality of evidence that would constitute probable cause to arrest. Further, he contended that in the absence of evidence justifying an arrest, no invasion of personal security could be judicially approved.

The State of Ohio responded that the thrust of the Fourth Amendment is "reasonableness" and that, even if a detention is a "seizure" in the constitutional sense, the act should be measured in terms of balancing the personal security of the citizen against the need to investigate possible criminal activities.

Support of the latter rule prevailed. The Supreme Court held that indeed the forcible detention of a citizen by an officer constituted an invasion of personal security and was therefore a "seizure" within the meaning of the Fourth Amendment. Consequently, any such intrusion must be compatible with the Fourth Amendment command that people are to be free from unreasonable searches and seizures. Using the balancing test of reasonableness, the Court held that the detection of crime and its prevention were obvious governmental interests. And if the facts, objectively viewed, revealed that the detention was reasonably related to achieving that objective, the invasion would be constitutionally sanctioned. The Court in *Terry* ruled that "a police officer may in appropriate circumstances and in an appropriate manner approach a person for the purpose of investigating possible criminal behavior even though there is no probable cause to make an arrest."

In a later case decided in 1972 (*Adams* v. *Williams*), the Court stated that the Fourth Amendment does not require a policeman to shrug his shoulders and allow a crime to occur or a criminal to escape simply because he lacks the precise level of information necessary to establish probable cause to arrest. On the contrary, continued the Court, "it may be the essence of good police work to adopt an intermediate response. A brief stop of a suspicious individual in order to determine his identity, or to maintain the status quo momentarily while obtaining more information, may be most reasonable in light of the facts known to the officer at the time."

Terry and *Adams* thus confirm the right of police to stop, i.e., "seize" citizens short of actually effecting an arrest. The right to "stop" was approved; the "frisk," which the Court held was a "search," was also approved—under proper circumstances (see section entitled Limited Search—the Frisk).

Most states authorize arrests by statute, but, until *Terry,* few jurisdictions statutorily authorized officers to forcibly detain citizens. The practice of detention, short of sufficient evidence to justify arrest, was widespread throughout the United States, however. *Terry* held that these confrontations were subject to the Fourth Amendment guarantee of personal security and that any evidence seized as a consequence of the detention must be measured against that standard. The court approved the detention of citizens based on a quality of evidence less than the "probable cause" required for arrest. (See chapter 3, Arrest.) As a shorthand phrase, the Court approved a doctrine of "probable cause to detain."

Many police contacts with citizens have nothing to do with suspected criminal activity. Neighborhood noise, domestic quarrels, lost children—all occupy a substantial portion of police time. Just as frequently, officers routinely stop motorists for moving traffic violations or defective vehicular equipment. If an officer encounters possible criminal activity in either of these contexts of apparently noncriminal activity, he may escalate his response from investigation to forcible detention. And further investigation may lead to arrest. Because police contact with citizens is so diverse, the Supreme Court in *Terry* constitutionally approved a range of flexible police responses reasonably related to the incident at hand. When an arrest ensues as the result of the contact, the court will scrutinize the officer's entire conduct to determine if his acts were reasonably related to the perceived objective. If a person was detained on evidence insufficient to establish that his conduct merited investigation for criminal activity, his detention will be held constitutionally unlawful and any evidence seized as a consequence thereof will be excluded.

Right to Detain—Investigative Detention

In *Terry,* the Supreme Court reviewed facts that reflected an officer's forcible detention of a suspect without prior questioning. The officer had seen enough to justify a reasonable suspicion that an armed robbery was about to take place. Suppose an officer observes suspicious activity that appropriately merits investigation, but he only wants to ask the person questions. *Terry* apparently confirms the right of officers to detain for questioning—often called an investigative seizure, although the Court did not specifically discuss this issue since the case involved forcible detention based on facts that clearly evidenced possible criminal activity. Where observed conduct is equivocal, and not so clearly criminal, officers may merely want to question without necessarily physically detaining the person and subjecting him to a search.

The *Terry* rule, however, suggests that officers do possess the right to detain a person involuntarily and to subject him to questioning, even if probable cause to arrest for a specific crime is lacking. For example, both California and New York grant officers this right constitutionally to detain a suspect for questioning if the circumstances would indicate to a reasonable man in a like position that the detention is necessary to the proper discharge of the officers' duties. Of course this right to detain is measured against an objective standard and must be based on articulated facts and circumstances—not on a hunch. The California rule appears in *People* v. *Mickelson*:

> In this state, however, we have consistently held that circumstances short of probable cause to make an arrest may still justify an officer's stopping pedestrians or motorists in the streets for questioning. If the circumstances warrant it, he may in self-protection request a suspect to alight from an automobile or to submit to a superficial search for concealed weapons. Should the investigation then reveal probable cause to make an arrest, the officer may arrest the suspect and conduct a reasonable incidental search.

Standard of Detention

The right to detain without necessarily arresting has a salutary effect: it wards off pressure on officers to make an arrest when only an investigation is required. Through such an investigation, the officer may dispel or corroborate his suspicions without haste. Detention permits him reasonable investigation commensurate with the circumstances that confront him and allows him legal flexibility to dispose of a bewildering variety of street encounters. At the same time, officers are required to articulate facts that distinguish the innocent citizen from the possibly guilty one, thereby insuring all citizens that the judiciary will scrutinize the detention and demand that it pass constitutional muster before any evidence seized is permitted in court. Court decisions sanctioning or disapproving a particular detention frequently present a kaleidoscopic pattern. Although this fact is disconcerting, the average observer of court opinions understands that any attempt to write an undeviating rule of "stop and frisk" is inherently inconsistent. First, the English language is not equal to the task for writer or reader; second, the very flexibility that the rule is designed to accommodate necessarily precludes any other result. What the courts seek from officers is a clear articulation of their observation and knowledge sufficient to validate their judgment objectively.

In *Terry* the Court stated that the test for a lawful detention was: "Would the facts available to the officer at the moment of seizure . . . warrant a man of reasonable caution in the belief that the action taken was appropriate?" Although this standard is not altogether free from vagueness, it requires a threefold test:

1. a rational suspicion by a peace officer that some activity out of the ordinary is or has been taking place;

2. some evidence to connect the person under suspicion with the unusual activity;

3. some suggestion that the activity is related to crime.

It is the last requirement that probably is most crucial and on which a peace officer must focus his attention.

In attempting to meet the requirement that the observed activity is related to crime, officers can use evidence obtained by any of their senses, evidence obtained from other sources, relevant surrounding circumstances known to them, as well as their expertise and experience. All these factors, which, incidentally, are identical with those that justify an arrest, may be relied on to establish a reasonable basis for detention, i.e., probable cause to detain. Since probable cause to detain rests on the same kind of factors that provide probable cause to arrest, but to a lesser degree, these factors will be considered in the section on Probable Cause to Arrest. (See chapter 3, Arrest.)

Although each case must ultimately depend on the specific facts involved, common sense dictates that some consideration be allotted to the gravity of the crime under investigation. Balancing the interest of personal security against the social need for protecting or detecting crime is more than an academic exercise. Approaching an armed robber differs substantially from arresting the possessor of marijuana cigarettes. Courts have said as much, and a general judicial consensus recognizes the need for instant and flexible police response to danger.

Most cases involving the detention of a person for suspected criminal activity arise from personal observation by the officer. In *Terry*, for example, the defendant was observed by the officer while he walked along a public sidewalk in front of a commercial store. His conduct was ambiguous at best, but clearly suspicious. Contrast Terry's action with that of the defendants in the following cases:

Police officers were sent to the airport to investigate a telephoned report from an airline that an employee had discovered what appeared to be marijuana in a passenger's baggage. When the passenger (Cauwels) came to the storage room to claim his package, he was arrested. One of the officers observed the number on the baggage tag attached to the arrestee's package. After the arrest, the officer left the storage room in the baggage area to see whether the arrestee was accompanied by anyone else. He observed the defendant (Irwin) "just standing" in the lobby about fifteen feet outside a glass door separating the baggage area from the lobby, which led to the sidewalk. "The defendant was standing next to three pieces of baggage, consisting of two pieces of luggage and a paper bag. Attached to one piece of luggage was a baggage tag bearing the next sequential number to the tag of the arrestee's cardboard box.

"[The officer] asked the defendant to accompany him to the storage room in the baggage claim area. In response to the officer's question, the defendant said he had no baggage. After leaving the defendant where his partner could 'keep an eye on him,' the officer went back to the lobby 'to examine the baggage.' He picked up the paper bag and detected an odor similar to the odor which came from the arrestee's baggage. He then took the bag and the two pieces of luggage back to the storage room, where he examined the bag, and found clothing, an envelope with defendant's name, and 'six paper-wrapped packages . . . each containing a green, plant material.'" The officer then arrested the defendant.

The Court said: "Although the discovery that the arrestee (Cauwels) had shipped a box of marijuana showed criminal activity, there was nothing *unusual in the activity* of the defendant who was standing close to baggage near the baggage area in the airport. The basis of [the officer's] initial decision to see if the arrestee was accompanied by anyone else did not appear in the record; the court had to assume that the officer had a "hunch" that marijuana shippers might be traveling in pairs. Certainly there was nothing in the defendant's activity to distinguish him from any other embarking or debarking passenger at the airport.

"Nor does the circumstance that one of the pieces of luggage near where [the defendant] was standing contained the next-numbered tag to the arrestee's baggage tag rationally suggest criminal activity by [the defendant], or provide a *rational connection to* [the arrestee's] *criminal activity*. The most that can be said of this circumstance, in isolation, is that the defendant was the next passenger in line at the baggage check-in counter.

"Even assuming that it could be inferred that [the defendant] stood behind [the arrestee] in line and further inferred that [the defendant] knew [the arrestee], the next inference that [the defendant] was *involved in* [the arrestee's] *criminal activity* is based on nothing more substantial than inarticulate hunches. There is no evidence that the officer had any additional information about [the arrestee] or [the defendant], or had any tip that persons traveling in pairs were shipping marijuana." (*Irwin* v. *Superior Court.*)

Compare this example: "An experienced narcotic officer responded to the call of a private citizen who had discovered a kit containing apparatus used in administering narcotics. The kit was found in a flower planter box adjacent to the sidewalk in front of his place of business, and had not been there 24 hours prior to the report. The officer . . . proceeded to examine the premises, and while at the back thereof [the defendant] Reulman was observed driving a Cadillac through the alleyway at the rear of the building. The officer 'felt' that [the defendant] was out of place in the Cadillac and the alleyway and for that reason gave particular attention to his movements. He noticed [the defendant] was nervous and that he watched the officers in the rear view mirror as the car passed beyond. [The defendant] drove to the end of the alleyway, turned right to the street on which the building fronted, turned right again to the front of the building and parked immediately across the sidewalk from the point where the kit had been discovered. From that time on he was under constant surveillance by the officers. He left his automobile and walked along the sidewalk in the direction from which the car had approached. He peered into a window of a barbershop and then returned in the direction of his automobile. At this point the officers detained him and requested his identification."

Was the detention lawful?

"The officers observed only that [defendant] was nervous, appeared to be wary of them, and that he parked his car adjacent to the point where the kit was found and thereafter took a rather aimless walk in the near vicinity. Further observations by the arresting officer to the effect the defendant looked like an untruthful person and as though he did not belong in the Cadillac are not impressive and appear to add little to create any real suspicion, even considering that the officer was an experienced narcotics investigator familiar with the conduct of suspects in like circumstances. There is little, if anything, to distinguish the defendant from any other harried citizen who may have innocently parked his automobile in the same spot as did Reulman."

Suppose we change the facts: At 10 A.M., "an officer observed [the defendant] Moore in a telephone booth [near a refreshment stand at the corner of an intersection]. The officer had made several narcotic arrests in the area and testified that addicts go to this location to make purchases from street peddlers. As the police car drove into an adjacent parking lot, [the defendant] appeared to be talking on the telephone, seemed to observe the police car, moved from a comfortable position in the telephone booth, and turned his back on the police car. [The defendant] appeared nervous. The officer thought that [the defendant] 'was trying to avoid' him and due 'to the area and the surrounding circumstances . . .' thought it was suspicious.

"The officer left his car, went to the telephone booth, and asked [the defendant] his name and several questions. He asked [the defendant] if he had ever used narcotics in the past. The defendant said he had but not since he left jail. The officer then asked defendant if he might inspect the latter's arms."

Was the detention for questioning lawful?

"The only suspicious circumstances relied upon by the officer were that the area was one where narcotic transactions had taken place in the past, and, that [the defendant], upon seeing the officers' car, turned his back on them, moved from a comfortable position, and appeared nervous. [The defendant] was talking on a telephone in a booth at ten in the morning, and, again, there seems little to distinguish him from any other citizen who may have been making a telephone call at that time and place. To hold that police officers should, in the proper discharge of their duties, detain and question all persons in that location, or all those who act nervous at the approach of officers, would, for practical purposes, involve an abrogation of the rule requiring substantial circumstances to justify the detention and questioning of persons on the street." (*People* v. *Moore*.)

Whether or not a reasonable basis exists to detain someone for investigation of criminal activity depends largely on the context of the time, place, and circumstances of the detention. "Probable cause to detain" is shaped largely by the context in which it emerges. Thus, in the first example, the defendant Irwin was detained in a public airport frequented by thousands of people. He stood in the passenger area and did nothing to distinguish himself from other passengers. Although a crime had been reported, another person had already been arrested, and no evidence connected Irwin with that crime. In the second example, a crime had also been reported as having occurred on a public street, but no one had been arrested for its commission. Yet aside from his proximity to the location of the crime, the defendant was walking on a public street like anyone else. The officer could only describe a general nervousness—clearly not enough to meet a standard of detention which requires some observed activity out of the ordinary and related to crime. "Nervousness" is not sufficiently incriminating to justify a detention.

Note: A frequent justification for detention is the officer's testimony that he observed evasive gestures or movements. "Furtive conduct" can be an additional factor that justifies detention, or possibly arrest, since an inference can be drawn that the person detained is attempting to conceal or dispose of seizable evidence. This topic is relevant here, but is discussed in chapter 3, Arrest, under the heading Observational Probable Cause.

In the last of the preceding case examples, the officers added a significant factor to "mere presence": a high incidence of narcotic sales in the area. But that fact alone was not sufficient to warrant the detention of someone who happened to be in the area. Yet this case does mark the transition between unlawful and lawful detention. By adding other circumstances, or other factors, officers approach the required standard of detention: unusual activity relating to crime.

Suppose these facts occur:

At 4:30 P.M., three officers were cruising in an unmarked police car near a public park, an area of known narcotics activity. The officers were in plain clothes. One officer testified that he first observed the defendant walking away from the area of a rest room. He noticed that the defendant held a wadded object that protruded about an inch from his clenched fist. (The officer had admittedly a purely speculative idea that the object might be a narcotics kit.) The car in which the three officers were riding drove past the defendant and ahead of him. It appeared that the defendant was going to cross the street had he continued on his course. However, the defendant looked in the direction of the police car and abruptly changed his direction by traveling away from the car and thus away from the street which he would have crossed had he continued in his prior course. The car containing the officers passed the defendant. At this point, the defendant changed the object from one hand to another. At all times the defendant kept looking at the car containing the police officers. The car passed the defendant again, at which point the officer put the car in reverse, and the defendant walked away from the police car, reversing his direction from westbound to eastbound. The officer put the car in forward gear, pulled alongside the defendant, and stopped. He then called to the defendant, "Come here." When he opened the car door, the defendant started running. The officer testified that he did not identify himself as a peace officer or state his purpose of wanting to talk to the defendant because he did not have a chance to do so. The officer then chased the defendant, who ran out of the park and into the backyard of a nearby house. On the way the defendant bumped into a hedge. He was finally stopped. The officers went back to the hedge (the other officer having seen the defendant throw an object at the time he hit the hedge), and found a wadded piece of magazine paper that contained two rubber balloons and six paper bindles of heroin, plus three five-dollar bills. The officer testified that the packaging of narcotics as described was the way narcotics were normally packed for sale.

The court will bear in mind the officer's specialized knowledge, and consider the specific and articulable facts available to them, together with reasonable inferences to be drawn from those facts, to ascertain whether or not the action of the officer in saying "Come here" was such an intrusion into the life of the defendant as to be constitutionally impermissible. If the officer had the right to say to the defendant, "Come here," then the defendant's actions in running away would be an additional circumstance that would obviously allow the subsequent detention and arrest. (While it might be argued with considerable merit that the mere speaking to an individual by a police officer, as was done in this case, is not a sufficient intrusion into that individual's life to put into effect the rules of detention, assume that the words used in this case were a sufficient show of authority to apply the rules.)

Consider these factors:

First, the area—an area known to the officers to be one of considerable narcotics activity. For the trained officer, the sight of someone passing a transparent bag containing a leafy substance to another and receiving money in exchange is evaluated together with the environment in which the transaction takes place. Seeing that transaction take place in an area of known narcotics activity is a suspicious circumstance. Seeing the same transaction take place on the floor of a Chicago Grain Exchange would probably (and hopefully) be meaningless.

Second, the appearance of the officers. When evaluating the conduct of the officers, the court will keep in mind the concurrent conduct of the defendant and the officers' awareness of that conduct. Those involved in the narcotics trade are a skittish group—literally hunted animals to whom everyone is an enemy until proven to the contrary. Thus, the average law-abiding citizen seeing three grown men sitting in a slow-moving car at 4:30 in the afternoon would probably give them no more than a passing glance. But to the person involved in the narcotics traffic, three men in plain clothes, riding in an unmarked car, cruising at a slow speed in an area of high narcotic activity are about as inconspicuous as three bull elephants in a back-yard swimming pool. Any normal person in the narcotics culture would assume them to be "narcs."

With these first two factors in mind, pass to the third factor—the activity of the defendant in this case. There were others in the park whom the officers studiously avoided. It was the activity of the defendant that brought him to their attention. On seeing the officers' car, the defendant did not give it the passing glance of the upright, law-abiding citizen. His eyes were glued on that car. To him, it represented danger until proven otherwise. When it appeared that the car was going to intercept him had he continued on his path, he changed his course of travel and walked away. When the car again neared him, he again altered his course and proceeded in a different direction. At the same time he was making these changes in his course of travel and watching the police car closely, he changed an object in his hand (which the officer without any articulable reason thought was a narcotic kit) to another hand. By this time there was obviously no question in the defendant's mind as to who the three gentlemen in the car were. When the officer shouted, "Come here," it was, to him, a show of authority. Just as obviously, the defendant knew that they were police officers as reflected by his subsequent and almost instantaneous behavior.

Of course officers can detain on the basis evidence that suggests the commission of other crimes. Consider the following example:

"About noon, during a heavy rainstorm, [a burglary investigator] for the police department saw the defendant without a raincoat walk by his patrol car, heading west on a sidewalk, and carrying what appeared to be a new portable-typewriter case. Because many burglaries in that area involved stolen typewriters, and because the defendant was apparently exposing a new portable typewriter to a heavy downpour (most typewriter cases are not waterproof), [the officer] followed. [The defendant] continued west and then north toward an area of several pawnshops. From time to time he looked back in the officers' direction. After he crossed an intersection, the officers drove past him, and when they did so, he reversed his direction. As the officers made a U-turn, the defendant turned into a local park. At that point, the officers left their car and stopped the defendant.

"The officer, after identifying himself, asked the defendant where he was going. Santa Monica (a city twenty-five miles away), the latter replied. How would he get there? Walk. What was in the case he had set down? Radios. Did he have a receipt for the radios? 'No.' " After the arrest, a search of the case revealed four radios with department-store tags still attached.

That the lawfulness of a detention is shaped by its circumstances is illustrated in this case. "[The defendant] was walking without a raincoat in heavy rain, making no attempt to protect what appeared to be a valuable piece of machinery. The area was one in which many burglaries involving typewriters had occurred. When first observed, [the defendant] appeared headed for a pawnshop area, but on the visible interest of the police in his movements, he reversed his direction and went into a park. A commonplace of law enforcement is that a great amount of stolen property funnels into pawnshop areas. When defendant's activity and conduct are appraised in the light of the area and the circumstances in which they took place, they reasonably suggest the possibility that defendant was about to pawn a stolen typewriter, a suggestion sufficiently tangible to warrant investigation." (People v. Manis.)

Observations alone will often suggest that a person is engaged in some kind of unusual activity. But relating that unusual activity to crime may require that the observation be supplemented by other evidence.

For example: "About 2:30 P.M., two police officers, [using binoculars,] saw the defendants, whom they did not know, seated on the grass in a public park. They appeared to be dividing objects which shone in the sunlight. One officer who observed the defendants testified they appeared to be counting coins and passing them back and forth. He could not actually see coins, but when one of the defendants got up, the officer saw him put what appeared to be a roll of coins in his pocket. The defendants then walked to a parked car and drove off, driving in a normal fashion and observing the traffic laws. The police officers followed in a patrol car, then drove alongside the defendants, identified themselves, and ordered the defendants to stop their vehicle.

At that time, [one of the occupants] leaned forward and appeared to put something under the front seat and the car continued about three hundred feet before stopping." (*People* v. *Henze.*)

This case is close, but if the officers could have testified to additional facts, the case for a lawful detention would have been strengthened. If this incident had taken place during the hours of darkness, its timing alone might have provided a sufficient extra factor to justify temporary detention for investigation. The law in many instances draws a sharp distinction between the controls that may be exercised by peace officers during the nighttime and those to which they are limited during daylight hours. Most of the cases upholding temporary detention for investigation and questioning have arisen out of incidents that occurred at night.

Yet nighttime activity is not essential to the validity of temporary detention. Other factors may provide a sufficient basis for temporary detention:

"Had the officers had a report of a current burglary, that factor might have furnished sufficient added suspicion to justify detention. But here the officers had no knowledge of any burglary, either at the time of their original observations or at the time of the detention.

"Had the park where the police observed the defendants been known as a place where crimes, such as the sale of narcotics, had frequently and currently taken place, this might have provided sufficient justification for the detention.

"Had the police received information that criminal activity was scheduled to take place in the park of a type consistent with what the suspects were seen doing, this might have justified the detention.

"Had these officers known of a rash of recent petty burglaries in the neighborhood, this, too, might have provided the necessary additive to justify temporary detention.

"Had the officers known that one of the defendants had previously been convicted of burglary, this might have provided sufficient reason for the detention.

"Had the defendants been observed driving their car in an erratic or suspicious fashion, this might have provided sufficient justification for stopping them.

"Had the defendants been sitting in a parked car at an unusual time and place, this might have justified their detention.

"Had the defendants given the officers cause to believe that they were violating the motor vehicle laws, this, too, would have justified their detention for investigation."

Almost every case of detention occurs on public streets and is based on conduct observed by the officer. But suppose that the officer is told by someone else that criminal activity is taking place. Must the officer corroborate this statement by his own observation in order to detain a person, or may he act on the informant's statement alone?

For example: "An officer, driving alone early in the morning on patrol duty in a high-crime area, was approached by a person known to him and informed that an individual seated in a nearby vehicle was carrying narcotics and had a gun at his waist.

"After calling for assistance on his car radio, the officer approached the vehicle to investigate the informant's report. He tapped on the car window and asked the occupant, one Williams, to open the door. When the occupant rolled down the window instead, the officer reached into the car and removed a fully loaded revolver from his waistband. The gun had not been visible to the officer from outside the car, but it was in precisely the place indicated by the informant. The occupant was then arrested by the officer for unlawful possession of the pistol. A search incident to that arrest was conducted after other officers arrived."

In *Adams* v. *Williams,* the U.S. Supreme Court held that the officer acted justifiably in responding to his informant's tip. "The informant was known to him personally and had provided him with information in the past. This is a stronger case than in the case of an anonymous telephone tip. The informant here came forward personally to give information that was immediately verifiable at the scene. Thus, while the informant's unverified tip may have been insufficient for an arrest or search, the information carried enough reliability to justify the officer's forcible stop.

"[In reaching its conclusion], the court rejected the defendant's argument that reasonable cause for a stop and frisk can only be based on the officer's personal observation, rather than on information supplied by another person. Informants' tips, like all other clues and evidence coming to a policeman on the scene, may vary greatly in their value on reliability. One simple rule will not cover every situation. Some tips, completely lacking in reliability, would either warrant no police response or require further investigation before a forcible stop of a suspect would be authorized. But in some situations—for example, when the victim of a street crime seeks immediate police aid and gives the description of his assailant, or when a credible informant warns of a specific impending crime—the police may respond appropriately."

Officers, therefore, can use personal observation, information obtained from others, and inferences drawn from the time and place of the confrontation to approach and detain a person for investigation of criminal activity. But whether the official purpose of the involuntary detention is to question or to forcibly detain, the reasons therefor must be articulated.

Extent of Detention

Just as the original circumstances must justify an intrusion of personal security, there must be factors to justify the extent or duration of that intrusion. Generally speaking, the scope of police investigation during a forcible or involuntary detention must be reasonably related to the circumstances that justified the initial stop. Whether stopped for a traffic citation or detained as a pedestrian, a citizen cannot be detained an unreasonable length of time for "further investigation" unless other factors justify investigation of a different crime.

For example, two officers were patrolling at about 7:30 A.M. "They saw a person standing alone next to a road sign. His only observable possession, a green back pack, strapped closed, was 'leaned up against a road sign' and he was 'eighteen inches to two feet away.'

"It is a local police practice to talk to hitchhikers who appear to be under age, ask them for identification, and advise them of the dangers of hitchhiking. [The officers] believed that the defendant 'looked to be a juvenile' and they alighted from their patrol car and approached him. One of the officers asked for identification, and the defendant produced it. His identification established that he was over 18 years of age.

"At this juncture defendant was asked if he had 'any weapons—knives or guns or explosives.' He replied that he had 'three knives.' He was requested to produce them, and he withdrew one pocket knife from his coat pocket and another from his pants pocket. After the officers examined the two knives, they were returned to him. They inquired about the third knife, and the defendant stated that it was in the pack. [One of the officers] asked if he could see it. Defendant answered 'yes' and walked over and started opening his pack:

"Without looking into the pack, [the officer] reached into the small pocket on the underside of the flap and brought out a book and a road map. On reaching into the pocket a second time, he withdrew a 'roach clip.' [The officer] thought he detected a brown residue on the teeth of the clip. The officer then turned his attention to the main part of the pack and pulled out a pair of bluejeans. In the back pocket of the jeans he found a 'Corina Mini' cigar box. He indicated that he was not looking for the third knife in that small box, but he did open it and discovered its contents to be two cigars and nineteen hand-rolled cigarettes. Suspecting that the cigarettes contained marijuana, the officers [placed the defendant under arrest]. . . .

"[One officer] testified that throughout the period of street detention the defendant appeared somewhat nervous and uneasy, but not more so than 50 percent of other persons stopped and questioned by the officers. The defendant did not make any furtive motions while under observation and did not appear to be under the influence of drugs or alcohol. Until the officers discovered the 'roach clip,' they perceived nothing that caused them to believe the pack contained contraband. [The officer] further stated that he was not apprehensive of being attacked by the defendant during the period of time he was in contact with him. . . .

"No hard and fast rule can be formulated for determining the reasonableness of the period of time elapsing during a detention. The dynamics of the detention-for-questioning situation may justify further investigation, search, or arrest. The significance of the events, discoveries, and perceptions that follow an officer's first sighting of a candidate for detention will vary from case to case. Nevertheless, in determining the reasonableness of further detention, favorable answers, observations, or perceptions must be regarded by the detaining officer as suspicion-allaying, rather than suspicion-heightening." (*Pendergraft* v. *Superior Court.*)

In this case, the defendant established he was over eighteen years of age, thus dispelling the officer's suspicion about his age. No other evidence suggests any reason for the officer to continue his detention other than curiosity.

In this chapter, detention has been isolated from all other factors that present themselves when an officer confronts a citizen. And the term has been used to describe detention for investigation of criminal activities. Often, however, the officer's initial contact with the person may arise in a noncriminal context, i.e., when the officer is responding to a request for medical assistance or merely stopping a motorist for a minor traffic violation. The brief period incidental to noncriminal investigation may reveal additional factors that reflect criminal activity. Under these circumstances, the officer may escalate his response from "mere contact" to detention. Although in a fast-moving situation the distinction may blur between mere contact, detention for investigation of criminal activity, traffic infraction, misdemeanor, or felony, all the factors will be sorted out later in the courtroom.

Limited Search—the Frisk

It has become routine to discuss the topic of detention as "stop and frisk." The possible misinterpretation implicit in this joinder of words is that if the "stop" is lawful, a "frisk" is automatically legitimated. The U.S. Supreme Court has clearly held that a stop does not necessarily authorize a frisk. A stop is a *seizure* within the meaning of the Fourth Amendment, and a frisk is a *search* within the meaning of the Fourth Amendment. Each must be based on constitutionally adequate grounds and each must be separately evaluated. Analytically, the frisk should be discussed as a search, albeit a limited search (see chapter 4, Search). For reasons of convenience of discussion, however, and because the two acts have become so closely related, it will be discussed here.

Again the leading case is *Terry* v. *Ohio*. In *Terry* the officer forcibly detained the defendant based upon facts which, objectively viewed, indicated that Terry was about to enter a store and rob it. Simultaneous with the detention, the officer ran his hands over the outer clothing of Terry to determine whether weapons were on his person. The Court had to decide whether such conduct constituted a search within the meaning of the Fourth Amendment. The Court observed that this frisk, which followed the act of forcible detention, was a separate act invading personal security and that it had to be considered apart from the detention. The Court agreed that running the hands over the outer clothing was not a search in the full sense of the word. But such conduct was nevertheless an invasion of personal security that had to be balanced against the governmental interest of preventing crime. Reviewing the history of violence of American criminals, the justices agreed that police protection against guns and knives was an overwhelming social concern. Because detention in itself may elicit an emotional response, the Court ruled that street confrontations must be conducted in an atmosphere conducive to the officer's safety:

> We cannot blind ourselves to the need for law enforcement officers to protect themselves and other prospective victims of violence in situations where they may lack probable cause for arrest. When an officer is justified in believing that the individual whose suspicious behavior he is investigating at close range is armed and presently dangerous to the officer or to others, it would appear to be clearly unreasonable to deny the officer the power to take necessary measures to determine whether the person is in fact carrying a weapon and to neutralize the threat of physical harm.

The Court reasoned, however, that even a limited search of the outer clothing for weapons constitutes "a severe, though brief, intrusion upon cherished personal security, and it must surely be an annoying, frightening, and perhaps humiliating experience." The Court authorized,

> A narrowly drawn authority to permit a reasonable search for weapons for the protection of the police officer, where he has reason to believe that he is dealing with an armed and dangerous individual, regardless of whether he has probable cause to arrest the individual for a crime. The officer need not be absolutely certain that the individual is armed; the issue is whether a reasonably

prudent man in the circumstances would be warranted in the belief
that his safety or that of others was in danger. . . .

The Court said, too, that due weight should be given, not to
inchoate and unparticularized suspicions or hunches, but to the specific
reasonable inferences which the officer is entitled to draw from the
facts in the light of his experience. The Court also warned that the
search must be "confined in scope to an intrusion reasonably designed
to discover guns, knives, clubs, or other hidden instruments for the
assault of the police officer."

To disable a person from potential violence is entirely reasonable,
and the Court has approved a narrowly drawn constitutional authority
for police to conduct a limited search for weapons—only if there is
a reasonable basis for assuming that the person stopped is armed and
dangerous. Of course the officer need not be positive, but he must
be able to articulate the basis for his belief.

If the officer confronts someone whom he reasonably believes
to be armed and dangerous, he may undertake precautionary steps
to determine the validity of the suspicion. Normally this includes a brief
patting down of the outer clothing, or in some cases perhaps a cursory
search into a nearby area accessible to the individual detained, i.e.,
a limited search of the car. If the pat-down reveals to the sense of touch
the possibility of a dangerous weapon inside the clothing, a further
intrusion into the pockets or clothing is authorized for the purpose
of neutralizing the danger. The *Terry* case, and subsequent state court
cases, indicate that the first intrusion on the suspect's outer clothing
does not automatically authorize a second intrusion inside the clothing
unless the first search reasonably reveals the basis for a more intensive
quest. The act of reaching inside the pockets or clothing of a person
is a separate search in the constitutional sense and must be founded
on constitutionally adequate ground. If the pat-down reveals the
possibility of a concealed weapon, this factor is constitutionally adequate to authorize a further limited search and removal of the weapon.
The discovery of the invisible object may dispel the officer's concern
for his safety—in which case a more intensive search is unnecessary.
Or, if the object removed is a weapon, grounds for arrest may emerge.
Generally speaking, the scope and intensity of the frisk must be
reasonably related to the need to remove a source of danger to the
officer. Beyond that, no further invasion of personal security is permissible.

Would the officer be justified in frisking under the following
circumstances?

An officer testified that while he was patrolling his beat in
uniform, he observed the defendant "continually from the hours of

4:00 P.M. to 12:00, midnight . . . in the vicinity of a major intersection. [He stated that] during this period of time he saw the defendant in conversation with six or eight persons whom the officer knew from past experience to be narcotics addicts. The officer testified that he did not overhear any of these conversations, and that he did not see anything pass between the defendant and any of the others. Late in the evening the defendant entered a restaurant. The officer saw the defendant speak with three more known addicts inside the restaurant. Once again, nothing was overheard and nothing was seen to pass between the defendant and the addicts. The defendant sat down and ordered pie and coffee, and, as he was eating, the officer approached him and told him to come outside. Once outside, the officer said, 'You know what I am after.' According to the officer the defendant 'mumbled something and reached into his pocket.' Simultaneously, the officer thrust his hand into the same pocket, discovering several glassine envelopes, which, it turned out, contained heroin."

In this case the officer's observations of unusual activity relating to crime were marginal at best. But assuming they were adequate to detain the defendant, the nature and scope of the officer's search were so clearly unrelated to the detention as to render the heroin inadmissible. "The search for weapons approved in *Terry* consisted solely of a limited patting of the outer clothing of the suspect for concealed objects which might be used as instruments of assault. Only when he discovered such objects did the officer in *Terry* place his hands in the pockets of the men he searched. In this case, with no attempt at an initial limited exploration for arms, the officer thrust his hand into the defendant's pocket and took from him envelopes of heroin. His testimony shows that he was looking for narcotics, and he found them. The search was not reasonably limited in scope to the accomplishment of the only goal which might conceivably have justified its inception—the protection of the officer by disarming a potentially dangerous man." (*Sibron* v. *New York.*)

Suppose the case for detention is stronger: Two veteran narcotic officers, working in plain clothes, assumed a vantage point near a refreshment stand in an area of high narcotic activity. "One of the officers, who was seated facing the street, observed the defendant and a companion walking towards him. His suspicion aroused by 'the manner in which they were walking up the sidewalk and talking to each other and looking around. . . . looking back and to the side as to see if anyone was watching,' one officer told his partner to 'keep an eye' on the suspects as they passed the hot dog stand and proceeded toward a nearby park—the direction in which his partner was facing. 'Having some experience in this type of thing concerning the area,' both officers agreed that by looking around, the suspects were 'acting in a suspicious manner . . . being apprehensive about someone observing them.' The officer observed the defendant and his companion, apparently engaged in conversation, walk 40 to 50 feet east of the refreshment stand and stop.

"Although his view was somewhat obscured by the park chain-link fence, the officer saw the suspects continue to look around; noticed that the defendant laughed and that the companion leaned against a parked car; observed each of the suspects reach into his pants pocket. The companion appeared to extract an object—although the officer could not actually see an object—while the defendant extracted what appeared to be money. The two placed their hands together in an apparent exchange. Having then observed the suspects for a total of three to four minutes, the officer told his partner, 'Okay, the deal has gone down.'

"The officers left the refreshment stand and approached the suspects who were walking toward them. The officers identified themselves and asked 'Were you two dealing?' After receiving a negative reply they ordered the suspects to return to the site of the suspected transaction 'to determine whether or not a narcotic transaction had been made.' One officer reached into the defendant's pocket, pulled it up, observed balloons subsequently determined to contain heroin, shoved the balloons back into petitioner's pocket, and handcuffed him." (*Cunha v. Superior Court.*)

Assuming that the officers' observations were insufficient to justify an arrest for sale of narcotics, the facts were sufficient to warrant detention. Absent probable cause to *arrest* (which would allow an unlimited incidental search of the person), officers can only conduct a limited search for weapons. The purpose of the frisk incidental to a detention is the removal of weapons, not the seizure of evidence. And the frisk is only authorized if there is a reasonable basis to believe the suspect is armed and dangerous. No evidence of the officers' belief that defendants were armed and dangerous appears from their testimony. The pat search, therefore, was unwarranted by the circumstances and evidence seized from their person was excluded.

Because observation of conduct possibly reflecting sale or possession of narcotics may not be significantly different from innocent conduct, officers must use particular care in distinguishing criminal activity from innocent activity. But detention for suspected criminal activity, even in narcotic cases, will not justify a frisk without evidence that the officer believes the defendant to be armed and dangerous. Because narcotics are so easily disposed of or concealed, the officer's task in detaining and simultaneously preventing the loss of possible evidence is difficult.

Assume now that the detention of a suspect is reasonable and that the officer reasonably believes the suspect to be armed and dangerous. The officer is authorized to make a cursory search of the exterior of the suspect's clothing. If the cursory search reveals a lump in the shirt pocket, may the officer remove the object?

In balancing the safety of police officers against the Fourth Amendment's proscription of unreasonable intrusions, *Terry* and *Sibron* concluded that in searching a legally detained individual reasonably suspected of being armed, a police officer must be limited to "a careful exploration of the outer surfaces of [the] person's clothing" until and unless he discovers specific and articulable facts reasonably supporting his suspicion. Only then may an officer exceed the scope of a pat-down and reach into the suspect's clothing for the limited purpose of recovering the object thought to be a weapon.

"Feeling a soft object in a suspect's pocket during a pat-down, absent unusual circumstances, does not warrant an officer's intrusion into a suspect's pocket to retrieve the object. A pat-down must 'be confined in scope to an intrusion reasonably designed to discover guns, knives, clubs, or other hidden instruments for the assault of the police officer.' The obvious purpose of holding that officers cannot go beyond exploration of the surfaces of a suspect's clothing without being 'able to point to specific and articulable facts which, taken together with rational inferences from those facts, reasonably warrant that [additional] intrusion' is to ensure that the scope of such a search cannot be exceeded at the mere discretion of an officer, but only upon discovery of tactile evidence particularly tending to corroborate suspicion that the suspect is armed. To permit officers to exceed the scope of a lawful pat-down whenever they feel a soft object by relying upon mere speculation that the object might be a razor blade concealed in a handkerchief, a 'sap,' or any other atypical weapon would be to hold that possession of any object, including a wallet, invites a full search of an individual's person. Such a holding would render meaningless *Terry's* requirement that pat-downs be limited in scope absent articulable grounds for an additional intrusion.

"Accordingly, an officer who exceeds a pat-down without first discovering an object which feels reasonably like a knife, gun, or club must be able to point to specific and articulable facts which reasonably support a suspicion that the particular suspect is armed with an atypical weapon which would feel like the object felt during the pat-down. Only then can judges satisfy the Fourth Amendment's requirement of a neutral evaluation of the reasonableness of a particular search by comparing the facts with the officer's view of those facts. Thus, for example, an officer who believes a soft object is a 'sap' in the form of a small bag of sand must be able to point to its weight and consistency to justify an intrusion into the suspect's pocket." (*People* v. *Collins*.)

One of the most difficult legal problems, for police and the courts, is the skyrocketing use of contraband narcotics, drugs, and marijuana. The distinctive packaging of heroin in tinfoil or condoms is common to police experience. Officers quickly learn to detect the telltale feel of tinfoil or tightly packed contraceptives containing heroin. If an officer carefully manipulates the outer clothing of someone whom he has detained and detects the presence of these distinctive containers inside the clothing or in pockets, he is instantly alerted to the possible presence of contraband. Can these concealed materials be seized as evidence?

The answer is not easy. On the one hand, an officer is entitled to remove concealed objects from inside the clothing if he believes the object is a potential lethal weapon. Tinfoil and condoms are not in that category. On the other hand, if the officer's sense of touch reveals to him the presence of contraband, an arrest should ensue for possession of an illegal substance. A crime is being committed in his presence. If the Constitution does indeed authorize a set of flexible police responses to varying situations, then the officer may escalate his searching authority according to the circumstances. Thus, if an officer initially entertains a reasonable basis for believing a suspect is armed and dangerous, a pat search for weapons is authorized—but not a search for contraband. If the pat reveals facts that lead the officer to conclude the suspect is carrying contraband instead, the officer must articulate the reasons for his belief. His basis probably could not be supported by the sense of touch alone since he cannot verify his belief until he observes the concealed item. For this reason, many courts are reluctant to approve a search inside a suspect's clothing based on the officer's opinion that his sense of touch revealed the presence of contraband on the suspect's person. Some judicial reticence to accept such testimony stems from an unwillingness to allow the right to pat-search for weapons to be expanded too broadly. The courts will often demand corroborating facts. Aside from the officer's experience in the detection of narcotics—which is relevant, if he observes a person's dilated eyes, needle marks on his arm, slurred speech or other indicia of heroin or narcotic use—these factors are important in corroborating the sense of touch. As these corroborating factors increase, the likelihood of judicial approval of a search for contraband inside the clothing is increased; as these corroborating factors decrease, the opposite result is likely. An officer who can catalog the factors corroborating his sense of touch and articulate them at trial is most likely to convince the court that the search inside the clothing or of the pockets was reasonably based.

Cases and Materials

Tiffany, McIntyre and Ratenburg, *Detection of Crimes,* Little, Brown & Co., Boston (1967).

Wayne R. LaFave, "Street Encounters and the Constitution," 67 *Michigan Law Review* 40 (1968).

Detention

Adams v. *Williams,* 32 L. Ed. 2d 612.

Commonwealth v. *Berrios,* 437 Pa. 338, 263 A. 2d 342.

Commonwealth v. *Meadows,* 293 A. 2d 365 (Pennsylvania).

Cunha v. *Superior Court,* 2 Cal. 3d 352, 466 P. 2d 704.

Ingram v. *State,* 264 So. 2d 109 (Florida).

Irwin v. *Superior Court,* 1 Cal. 3d 423, 462 P. 2d 12.

Pendergraft v. *Superior Court,* 15 Cal. App. 3d 237, 93 Cal. R. 155.

People v. *Collins,* 1 Cal. 3d 658, 463 P. 2d 403.

People v. *Henze,* 253 Cal. App. 2d 986, 61 Cal. R. 545.

People v. *La Grange,* 40 Mich. App. 342, 198 N.W. 2d 736.

People v. *Mack,* 26 N. Y. 2d 311, 258 N.E. 2d 703.

People v. *Manis,* 268 Cal. App. 2d 653, 74 Cal. R. 423.

People v. *Mickelson,* 59 Cal. 2d 448, 380 P. 2d 658.

People v. *Moore,* 69 Cal. 2d 674, 446 P. 2d 800.

People v. *One 1960 Cadillac Coupe,* 62 Cal. 2d 92, 396 P. 2d 706.

People v. *Rivera,* 14 N. Y. 2d 441, 201 N.E. 2d 32.

People v. *Taggart,* 20 N. Y. 2d 335, 229 N.E. 2d 581.

Sibron v. *New York,* 392 U.S. 40, 80 S. Ct. 1889, 20 L. Ed. 2d 917.

State v. *Onishi,* 499 P. 2d 657 (Hawaii).

Terry v. *Ohio,* 392 U.S. 1, 88 S. Ct. 1868, 20 L. Ed. 2d 889.

1. Officers properly stop a vehicle for a minor traffic violation, but observe no conduct by the motorist indicating that he poses any threat to the officers. The officer asks the motorist to alight from the vehicle and enter the patrol car. When the motorist enters the car, the officer notices him drop a bundle of heroin. Would the seizure of the evidence be reasonable? What authority does the officer have to request the motorist to leave his vehicle under these circumstances? If no such authority exists, the motorist has been unlawfully seized and the subsequent observations may be unreasonable. (*People* v. *Robles,* 28 Cal. App. 3d 739, 104 Cal. R. 907.)

2. Defendant, holding an airplane ticket for a domestic flight, passes through a magnetometer prior to entering the airplane. The magnetometer, a device which reflects the presence of metal on the person, reacts positively. The defendant is prevented from boarding the plane and frisked. No weapons are found. His luggage is then opened and officers observe contraband narcotics. May a seizure follow even if no weapons were found?

Suppose a prospective passenger fits the "highjacker profile." May he be stopped and frisked, without more evidence, prior to boarding an airplane? What about a search of his luggage?

("Airport Searches and the Fourth Amendment," 71 *Columbia Law Review* 1039.)

3. "While his car was stopped at a traffic light at 1:45 A.M., a police officer observed the front seat passenger of a following vehicle pick up what appeared to be a beer can, drink from it, and then put the can out of view. A few moments later the police car's red light was activated, causing the other automobile to stop. The purpose was to see if there was an open container, or drinking, of an alcoholic beverage in violation of the Vehicle Code. The driver of each vehicle left his car. Asked by the police officer what his passenger was drinking the driver said that it was an 'orange drink.' The officer testified, 'He said that he would like to show me.' He walked back to the vehicle, opened the left front door and said, 'Officer, come here, look for yourself.' At that point I did approach the left front door that was open. I looked inside and observed the person in the right front seat, which was Padgett, holding a Fanta brand name orange can in his left hand; and also on the seat next to his left leg was what appeared to be a six-inch .38 revolver.

"Obviously considering the probability that the gun was loaded the officer 'backed up, and pulled [his] service revolver [and] advised [his] partner that there was a gun in the car. [They] ordered the occupants to get out.'"

Was the original detention lawful?

(*People* v. *Superior Court* [Acosta], 20 Cal. App. 3d 1085, 98 Cal. R. 161.)

4. At approximately 10:45 A.M., an officer and his partner, wearing sport clothes and driving in an unmarked vehicle, were on patrol duty. When they were approximately thirty to forty yards away, they observed a parked vehicle adjacent to the roadway and saw three males (one of whom was defendant) standing near the rear of the parked car. As the officer approached the vehicle, the young men started to leave. The officer stopped the police vehicle; he and his partner alighted and announced that they were police officers. With guns in hand they walked up to the three persons, directed them to turn toward the parked car, and made a cursory search of their persons for weapons.

The officer testified that in the pat-down he did not feel any weapons. He testified that, as to one of these three (not the defendant), he could "observe . . . numerous half dollars, the silver variety, which aren't in circulation any more." He said he also could see "an extremely large amount of currency in his left front pants pocket which bulged considerably being folded once."

Was this a reasonable detention? Why would the officers approach with drawn guns under these circumstances? Did they fail to articulate their reasons adequately?

5. Two officers were proceeding southbound on a boulevard at approximately 12:30 A.M. in an unmarked police car, when they observed a vehicle parked on a street near the northwest corner of an intersection.

"As they approached the vehicle, the officers noticed that it was occupied by three men who were looking across the street in the direction of a motel. One officer testified that as they passed the vehicle, the occupants 'looked at us and their heads seemed to follow us as our vehicle passed theirs, and after we had passed them, the headlights went on; we then pulled in to the curb across the other side of the street.'

"The officers continued to observe the car and saw the headlights 'go out again'; the three occupants again appeared to direct their attention towards the area of the motel. After approximately five minutes, defendant's vehicle left the scene and made a right turn. The officers turned their car around and saw defendant turn left into another street. The officers turned on their red light and defendant stopped his car. There is no indication that defendant's car had been driven otherwise than in a legal manner during this period.

"As the officer approached the car on foot, defendant got out of the car, but the other occupants remained seated therein. All three were asked to identify themselves. They showed various papers and stated that they had just been driving around for about an hour. Defendant, who had been driving the car, admitted ownership.

"The officers proceeded to search the car, and in addition to two open beer bottles found lying on the floor behind the front seat, they discovered five shotgun shells in the glove compartment and a sawed-off shotgun hidden in the ventilator shaft under the dashboard. This gun was not visible from outside the car, nor from the vantage point of a person seated in a normal fashion on the front seat."

Were the officers' actions reasonable?

(*People* v. *Cowman*, 223 Cal. App. 2d 109, 35 Cal. R. 528.)

Chapter Three

Arrest

Statutory Requirements

Early English common law authorized certain designated persons to arrest subjects for the purpose of securing their presence at trial for an alleged criminal offense. But the English and colonial tradition of maximum freedom from governmental interference reflects concern over the potential abuse of such awesome power. Because of this concern, English and American legal history records a continuing attempt to strike a balance between the need to preserve individual freedom and the need to allow the state to prevent injury to the person and property of its citizenry. It has not always been easy to achieve this balance, yet perhaps the tension between freedom and authority helps maintain it.

No one can forget the legacy of oppression facilitated by indiscriminate arrest power. The extensive statutory definitions of arrest power, i.e., requirements of notice of the reason for arrest, immediate delivery of the arrestee to the magistrate, provisions for bail, the right to be present with counsel at trial, the right to testify and present evidence, and the right to confront accusers—all flow directly from the initial arrest. Legislatures have attempted not only to define carefully the arrest itself, but also to assure that any subsequent conviction be obtained in open court before an impartial tribunal. "Fair trial" is only the final stage that originated with the arrest.

Of course, countless arrests never result in any subsequent trial, but the forcible jailing of anybody nevertheless triggers a series of judicial responses. Incarceration of a person is subject to judicial review by writ of habeas corpus, in which law enforcement agencies must justify custody of the arrestee to the court. Or a magistrate will review the circumstances of the custody, even if no crime is charged as yet, to determine whether bail is authorized. And, in some cases, the arrest may be the subject of a federal suit alleging violation of civil rights. Lastly, the arrest record impairs the academic and employment application of an arrestee so that he may seek to expunge the record by judicial relief.

The power of a peace officer, or in some cases of a private person, to arrest and thereby involuntarily deprive a citizen of his liberty is universally defined by statute. Generally speaking, peace officers are authorized to arrest for the commission of at least two classes of crimes: misdemeanors and felonies. The states differ widely as to the kinds of crimes that constitute misdemeanor or felony, but the former includes minor offenses subject to fine, or brief imprisonment, or both; the latter involves more serious offenses, often warranting imprisonment for longer periods of time.

The power to arrest for either class of offense is related to the nature of the offense. Officers may arrest for misdemeanors only when these misdemeanors are committed in their presence. The usual misdemeanor offense is not a sufficiently grave risk to person or property to justify an arrest based on statements by another person, or even if the officer himself believes the offense was committed at an earlier time. Under such circumstances, when a misdemeanor offense is not committed in the officer's presence, his remedy is to obtain a warrant from the court authorizing the arrest.

Incidentally, with the extensive growth of vehicular traffic, a new classification of crimes has emerged: the infraction. Because most traffic violations are classified as misdemeanors, i.e., crimes, the entire array of procedural and substantive criminal law is invoked. Yet most traffic violations are negligent acts, not intentional violations of the law, and motorists are dismayed to be enmeshed in a procedure that was never designed to apply to them. The increasing use of traffic citations, easy bail forfeiture, and a traffic court is a response to the absurd ritual of criminal trials for traffic offenders. The use of the term *infraction* has evolved to avoid burdening the courts with vehicular trivia.

Whatever the merits of the new classification of infraction, the term only becomes important here in the context of search and seizure. As discussed earlier in chapter 2, Detention and Arrest, the officer's initial contact with the citizen often is the result of a traffic violation.

If the traffic violation is a misdemeanor, the offense is committed in the officer's presence, therefore authorizing him to arrest. Many state statutes, however, specifically describe the procedure to be followed when an officer detains for the purpose of issuing a citation. Normally the motorist must be released on his promise to appear unless the statute authorizes arrest on some other ground, such as the motorist's demand to be taken before a magistrate immediately or his inability to provide satisfactory evidence of a driver's license, vehicle registration, or identification.

Many courts have been reluctant to classify this brief detention as an arrest, although functionally speaking the motorist has been involuntarily deprived of his personal liberty. Yet the routine traffic offense has created a significant legal issue that highlights the distinction between *statutorily* authorized arrest and *constitutionally* authorized arrest, or seizure. The right to search incident to detention for a traffic violation flows from constitutional origin, i.e., the Fourth Amendment, and not from statutory authority (see chapter 4, Search). For our purposes, it should be noted that an arrest for a traffic violation authorized by statute must still be examined constitutionally to determine whether the detention was a seizure within the meaning of the Fourth Amendment.

Felonies constitute the other major category of crimes. Arrests may be effected even if these more serious crimes are not committed in the officer's presence. If the officer has probable cause to believe that a felony has been committed, he may arrest. In this instance, the officer relies not solely on his observation of the crime, but on information provided by others, or on his own strong suspicion that a felony has been committed. Or, in many cases, he acts on a combination of these factors. Because the Fourth Amendment also requires that arrests, or seizures, must be based on reasonable cause, the following section of this chapter is especially relevant.

Constitutional Requirements

The lawfulness of an arrest does not depend merely on compliance with a statute defining or authorizing an arrest. It is the court's responsibility to determine whether the arrest was lawful constitutionally, not statutorily. Just as a detention is a seizure within the meaning of the Fourth Amendment, so also an arrest is a seizure in the constitutional sense.[1] An arrest, which is an act invading a citizen's

---

1. On the constitutional significance of a traffic violation as an arrest, see chapter 2, Detention and Arrest.

personal security, may be effected only in conformity with the constitutional command that citizens are to be secure against unreasonable searches and seizures.

In order for an arrest to be reasonable within the meaning of the Fourth Amendment, the seizure must be based on *probable cause*. In the absence of sufficient evidence of probable cause, the arrest will be held unlawful, and any evidence seized as a consequence thereof will be excluded. Requiring all arrests to be founded on probable cause prevents officers from using the arrest as a pretext to conduct a search. The court must implement the constitutional requirement of probable cause by reviewing any invasion of personal security that resulted in the seizure of evidence subsequently offered at trial.

Probable Cause Defined

We have noted that peace officers are usually authorized by statute to arrest misdemeanants only if the offense is committed in the officer's presence. Because misdemeanors normally involve no injury or damage to person or property, officers must either see the offense committed or obtain a warrant. For more serious crimes, officers are usually statutorily authorized to arrest based on probable cause to believe that a crime has been committed. The Fourth Amendment also requires all arrests to be based on probable cause, however, and therefore a state statute cannot authorize an arrest on a standard less strict than that required by the Constitution. The standard of probable cause must be consistent with the Fourth Amendment as interpreted by the courts and particularly by the U.S. Supreme Court.

Probable cause has been defined as follows: facts and circumstances within the knowledge of the officer, and of which he had reasonably trustworthy information, which were sufficient to warrant a prudent man in believing that an offense had been committed or was being committed.

Another court has said: "There is no exact formula for the determination of reasonableness. Each case must be decided on its own facts and circumstances and on the total atmosphere of the case. Reasonable cause has been generally defined to be such a state of facts as would lead a man of ordinary care and prudence to believe and conscientiously entertain an honest and strong suspicion that the person is guilty of a crime. Probable cause has also been defined as having more evidence for than against; supported by evidence which inclines the mind to believe, but leaves some room for doubt." (*People* v. *Ingle*).

It is important to note that the standards for evidence that proves the guilt of an offense differ from those for evidence that establishes probable cause to arrest. Guilt must be proved beyond a reasonable doubt under established rules of evidence. The law of evidence—which is defined either by statute or by cases decided by courts of each state—has developed through attempts to filter the truth by excluding certain kinds of evidence that could prejudice or mislead the jury. On the other hand, probable cause deals with probabilities, i.e., factual and practical considerations of everyday life on which reasonable and prudent men act. Probable cause is a practical, nontechnical conception that affords a compromise between the citizen's privacy and the officer's execution of the law.

Probable or reasonable cause is a legal test measuring the quality of evidence. When the issue is presented to him, the judge must determine whether there are sufficient facts and circumstances that would warrant a reasonable man in believing that an offense has been committed. The court bears the responsibility for determining whether the officer has testified to facts sufficient to support a finding of probable cause. In the majority of cases, the validity of the arrest is critical at trial when the prosecution offers evidence seized by the officers at the time of arrest. If the court finds that the arrest was not supported by probable cause, the search incidental to arrest will not be reasonable within the meaning of the Fourth Amendment, and the seized evidence will be excluded.

As in detention for investigation of criminal activity, probable cause is shaped by the context in which it emerges. Yet some patterns can be outlined. But first, let us consider some general observations about the doctrine of probable cause itself.

An officer testified that he was at home in his apartment at about 1 P.M. "He had just finished taking a shower when he heard a noise at his door. He looked through the peephole into the hall, and saw 'two men tip-toeing out of the alcove toward the stairway.' He immediately called the police, put on some civilian clothes and armed himself with his service revolver. Returning to the peephole, he saw 'a tall man tip-toeing away from the alcove and followed by this shorter man, toward the stairway.' The officer testified that he had lived in the 120-unit building for 12 years and that he did not recognize either of the men as tenants. Believing that he had happened upon the two men in the course of an attempted burglary, the officer opened his door, entered the hallway and slammed the door loudly behind him. This precipitated a flight down the stairs on the part of the two men, and the officer gave chase. His apartment was located on the sixth floor, and he apprehended the defendant between the fourth and fifth floors. The defendant explained his presence in the building to the officer by saying that he was visiting a girl friend. However, he declined to reveal the girl friend's name, on the ground that she was a married woman. The officer patted the defendant down for weapons, and discovered a screwdriver in his pocket.

"By the time the officer caught up with the defendant on the stairway between the fourth and fifth floors of the apartment building, he had probable cause to arrest him for attempted burglary. The officer heard strange noises at his door which apparently led him to believe that someone sought to force entry. When he investigated these noises he saw two men, whom he had never seen before in his 12 years in the building, tiptoeing furtively about the hallway. They were still engaged in these maneuvers after he had called the police and dressed hurriedly. And when the officer entered the hallway, the man fled down the stairs. It is difficult to conceive of stronger grounds for an arrest, short of actual eyewitness observation of criminal activity." (*Peters* v. *New York*).

In this example the officer's observation of unusual conduct led to a strong suspicion that a burglary was being attempted in his presence. But in other cases, probable cause must necessarily rest on inference and deduction from known facts. Consider the following example.

"On three prior occasions, purchases of marijuana cigarettes had been made by an undercover agent from one Garcia. On the night of the arrest, the agent again purchased marijuana cigarettes from Garcia. On each of these occasions the same general plan of operation was followed. The agent would obtain money with which to make the purchases, he would then drive to Garcia's house, Garcia would come to his car, the latter would give Garcia this money for the purpose of purchasing marijuana, Garcia would take the money and leave, returning in 15 or 20 minutes. On his return he would hand marijuana cigarettes to the agent. Garcia's car was a 1948 maroon-colored Chevrolet. The automobile in which the defendant was seated at the time of arrest was that used by Garcia in these transactions. On each occasion another officer, while keeping the defendant under observation, saw Garcia's car pull into the driveway in front of his house, observed someone leave the house and approach the car on the driver's side, and observed that shortly thereafter the car would leave. On one occasion there were two separate trips made by Garcia to purchase cigarettes for the agent, and Garcia's Chevrolet was twice observed in the defendant's driveway at those approximate times. The time during which the agent waited for Garcia to return coincided with the time required for him to make the trip to the defendant's house and return. The cigarettes contained marijuana.

"On the night of the arrest the agent again met Garcia at the latter's premises and stated he wanted to buy marijuana, giving him an envelope containing $20 in currency. This money, consisting of two $5.00 and ten $1.00 bills, had been placed in the agent's envelope after the serial numbers thereon had been listed. At approximately 7 P.M. Garcia received this envelope and departed. He returned about 8:10 P.M. About 7:15 Garcia's car was seen pulling in the defendant's driveway, someone approached the car and after a short delay the car left. When Garcia returned to the agent's car, he handed him 36 marijuana cigarettes. At that moment the agent signaled waiting police officers that the marijuana had been delivered. Garcia was immediately arrested. He had returned on foot, his car was not in the driveway, and the officers set out at once to look for it. A few minutes later they found it half a block away occupied by the defendant and a known addict whom they immediately arrested.

"At that moment the officers knew that the defendant was a peddler and user of marijuana. He was definitely implicated in the purchases, and the presence of himself and a companion in the car at that particular time and place, under all of these circumstances, motivated the officers in making the arrest and search of both men, although they had no previous knowledge as to the defendant.

"Was the sole ground for the defendant's arrest the fact that he was sitting in an automobile with a known dope user and peddler? No. Officers arrested the defendant not merely because he was sitting in an automobile at night with a known addict, or because the automobile was parked in a neighborhood where the narcotics trade was known to flourish. These arresting officers had just participated in the arrest of Garcia. They knew that a narcotics transaction had just taken place in which Garcia, Garcia's car and the defendant's house were directly implicated. They knew that contraband had just been transported in that car. They knew that the defendant's companion was not only a peddler but a user. They had reasonable grounds for inferring that the narcotics sold to the agent had been purchased from the defendant or from someone with whom he was then working." (*People* v. *Ingle.*)

Probable cause must be based on facts that directly, or circumstantially, lead to a strong suspicion that a crime has been committed. Suppose officers attempt to combine observation and inference in the following case:

An officer testified that "he observed one Edwards step out of an automobile containing two women and some small children and hold a conversation in the street with one Gould, whom the officer knew to be a burglar. He afterwards examined police records and ascertained that Edwards also had a burglary record. By tracing the license number of the car, the officer obtained the address of defendant's home. Later that day officers commenced a surveillance of defendant's home and saw Edwards and some small children entering and leaving the house at various times over a period of three days. Three days later, about 9 P.M., the officer with six or seven other officers gathered in the street opposite defendant's home. None of the officers was in uniform and they were all dressed in 'rough clothing.' They saw Edwards and the defendant at the window of a front bedroom looking in their direction. The officers proceeded across the lawn, knocked on the front door, and 'almost instantly . . . the lights went out.' They called out that they were police officers and receiving no response, they kicked in the front door. The officers arrested Edwards. . . . At the time of Edwards' arrest, none of the officers knew of any specific burglary or had reason to believe that Edwards had committed a burglary or any other felony.

"The question of probable cause to justify the arrest of Edwards and the search of the premises incident thereto must be tested upon the facts which the record shows were known to the officers at the time the arrest was made. Those facts were: 1. Some days before the arrest Edwards was seen talking to a known burglar; 2. police records showed that Edwards had a previous record for burglary; 3. Edwards, the defendant and their children over a period of three days were seen in and about defendant's home; 4. when seven or eight men wearing rough clothing walked across the lawn, after seeing Edwards and defendant looking out of a bedroom window, and knocked at the door the lights went out, and when they identified themselves as police officers there was no immediate response. Taken separately or all together, these facts could not constitute reasonable cause to believe that Edwards had committed a felony so as to justify his arrest without a warrant. The facts that Edwards had a burglary record and was seen talking to a known burglar, while relevant, are not sufficient to constitute reasonable cause to believe that Edwards had committed a burglary or any other felony. The conduct of Edwards in entering and leaving the defendant's home is not shown to have been accompanied by any suspicious conduct of any sort. There is nothing to support a reasonable belief that any man, no matter how bad his past record, has committed a felony simply because he is seen going in and out of a private home in a normal manner. This leaves only the turning out of lights and the failure briefly to respond to the call of 'police officers' after seven or eight roughly dressed men crossed the lawn in a body and knocked at the door in the darkness of night. While evasive conduct upon the approach of police officers may under proper circumstances justify an arrest and search, the observed approach to a private home in the nighttime of a party of seven or eight roughly dressed men and their knocking on the door might reasonably lead the most innocent of persons to extinguish the lights hoping that they would depart. And their subsequent announcement that they were police officers might reasonably arouse a degree of skepticism that would lead the occupants to make no immediate response or indeed any response at all, except possibly to telephone for the aid of those whom they knew with certainty to be police.

"Whether or not Edwards and Gould are characterized as 'professional burglars' because they both had a past burglary record, whether or not their street conversation is characterized as 'making a meet' (thus by a semantic slant putting an aura of criminality about what so far as the police officers knew was an entirely innocent conversation), and whether or not the additional fact is that a large number of burglaries were committed in the area, the evidence is insufficient to connect either of them or the defendant with the commission of any one or more burglaries." (*People* v. *Privett.*)

In this case, the inferences drawn from what the officers observed and what they knew did not constitute a strong suspicion that a felony had been committed. And if they had found incriminating evidence inside the house, such evidence could not have been used to support probable cause. Probable cause must be based on facts known to the officers *prior* to an arrest. Facts that are discovered subsequent to the arrest are not admissible.

For example: An officer testified that he had received information that a "shooting gallery" (the smoking of marijuana) was to take place at a particular address. Two officers drove to the address and parked nearby at about 1:20 A.M. The building appeared to consist of an upper and lower flat. No lights shone in it. Four men entered the building. The officers called for two more policemen, and the four officers approached the steps leading to the building entrance. Two of the men who had recently entered came through the front door. An officer called to them, identifying himself as a policeman. One of the men called out "cops." Both reentered and slammed the door against the police, who promptly broke it in, pursued the two men upstairs, and arrested all four men in the apartment.

In this case, even assuming there was some basis for detention, no evidence of probable cause to arrest existed prior to the officers' observation of the men (the information, as discussed later in this chapter, was wholly inadequate to justify arrest). The furtive conduct of the suspects, therefore, cannot be substituted for the lack of probable cause. The conduct was in response to an unlawful display of authority and is inadmissible on the issue of probable cause.

Similarly, if officers went to an apartment, lacking probable cause, they could not demand to be admitted. If the occupants opened the door and then learned the identity of the officers, their response by slamming the door cannot be construed as anything more than an indirect demand for a search warrant. The act, although uncivil, was in response to an unlawful show of authority.

Probable cause is composed of bits and pieces of evidence, the sum total of which yields a strong suspicion that a crime is being or has been committed. Probable cause cannot be based on a hunch or intuition; rather, the officer must articulate those facts and circumstances, known to him prior to the arrest, which equaled a "strong suspicion." These facts and circumstances can arise from several sources and may be classified as *factors of probable cause.*

Observational Probable Cause

This category includes all kinds of evidence that are presented directly to the officer's senses: what the officer sees, hears, smells, or touches. In the case of such evidence, the officer is a witness to the events and can testify to facts directly perceived. Most often the officer will testify to what he saw. His observations will be measured at trial against the standard of probable cause to determine whether he saw enough to warrant a strong suspicion that a crime was being committed.

The same facts that justify an arrest may also reliably justify a detention. Since the standard for the quality of evidence necessary to detain is less strict than that for probable cause to arrest, officers can often detain a person and utilize the detention to establish additional evidence to arrest. Or officers can use the detention to dispel their original suspicions and effect a release of the suspect immediately instead of making an arrest. If the circumstances allow, a detention should always precede an arrest so that officers can develop additional evidence during this investigative stage without risking a premature arrest.

Furtive Movements

Perhaps the most frequent observation used to establish probable cause is the officer's testimony that he observed an arrestee's "furtive movements." This phrase is verbal shorthand to describe the conduct of an arrestee when confronted by an officer. If the arrestee attempts to dispose of, conceal, or destroy evidence when confronted by the officer, the prosecutor can logically argue that such conduct was sufficiently incriminating to warrant the officer's "strong suspicion" that a crime had been committed. Attempting to prevent the officer's discovery of contraband or other seizable evidence certainly suggests guilty knowledge that qualifies as probable cause, even if the officer could not point to the specific crime involved. And the courts have tended to agree that furtive gestures do imply guilt at least sufficient to justify arrest, although not necessarily sufficient to convict.

Difficulty arises in determining what constitutes "furtive conduct." At the outset, the courts have said that the officer himself cannot intentionally induce such conduct by another. For example, if an officer confronts someone on the street for no reason and threatens to search him, any furtive conduct by the person in response is unlawfully induced. Any evidence seized as a consequence would be inadmissible as a product of an unlawful arrest.

In the vast majority of cases, the officer testifies that he observed a motorist, or his passenger, make a furtive movement when the officer signaled the vehicle to stop. Note at this point the legal analysis: the officer observes a traffic violation—usually a misdemeanor—committed in his presence. The statute authorizes an arrest, or at least the temporary immobility of the vehicle for the purpose of issuing a citation. In the constitutional sense, this detention constitutes at least as much a seizure as the temporary detention of a pedestrian in *Terry*. (See chapter 2, Detention and Arrest.) If the momentary detention reveals additional evidence of possible criminal activity, a different misdemeanor offense, or a felony, may emerge. The significance of a furtive gesture during or after the traffic stop escalates a traffic offense into a possible felony, i.e., possession of contraband. The distinction between arrest authority and search authority, to be considered in more detail later, is clear in this example: the misdemeanor was committed in the officer's presence and justified an arrest on that basis. The felony—possession of contraband—is implied from the conduct of the occupant of the vehicle even if the officer did not see the object of suspicion. The "furtive conduct" establishes the strong suspicion necessary to prove probable cause to arrest for a felony.

"The difficulty is that from the viewpoint of the *observer*, an innocent gesture can often be mistaken for a guilty movement. He must not only perceive the gesture accurately, he must also interpret it in accordance with the actor's true intent. But if words are not infrequently ambiguous, gestures are even more so. Many are wholly nonspecific, and can be assigned a meaning only in their context. Yet the observer may view that context quite otherwise from the actor: not only is his vantage point different, he may even have approached the scene with a preconceived notion—consciously or subconsciously—of what gestures he expected to see and what he expected them to mean. The potential for misunderstanding in such a situation is obvious.

"It is because of this danger that the law requires more than a mere 'furtive gesture' to constitute probable cause to search or to arrest. The United States Supreme Court recently reaffirmed this rule in the case of *Sibron* v. *New York*: 'deliberately furtive actions and flight at the approach of strangers or law officers are strong indicia of guilt, and when coupled with specific knowledge on the part of the officer relating the suspect to the evidence of crime, they are proper factors to be considered in the decision to make an arrest.' That knowledge, of course, may be derived from the usual twin sources of information and observation; it is the information known to the police officers or the suspicious circumstances which turn an ordinary gesture into a furtive one, but in the absence of information or other suspicious circumstances, a furtive gesture alone is not sufficient.

"A few distinguishable examples will serve to set the scene. A furtive gesture coupled with prior reliable information may constitute probable cause, i.e., the downward motion of a juvenile sitting with others in a car parked in an area where officers had been told to expect a gang fight. Detention, or possibly arrest, may also be predicated on a furtive gesture coupled with an actual observation of contraband in the portion of the vehicle to which the gesture was directed, i.e., the downward motion of an occupant of a parked car, followed by the officer's observation of a marijuana cigarette under the seat. And the officer need not even see recognizable contraband so long as he observed the suspect in the act of deliberately hiding a package or box which, in the circumstances, it is reasonable to believe contains contraband, i.e., a motorist and his companions refused to leave a service station at 3 A.M.; when officers arrived and asked for identification, he was seen to take a small white package from his pocket and drop it into the open motor of a parked car.

"In each of the foregoing cases the gesture of the suspect could reasonably be given a guilty connotation from prior reliable information, or from the officer's personal observation of contraband, or a deliberate act of concealment under otherwise suspicious circumstances. It is true that to reach a conclusion of probable cause in each instance the officer was required to draw certain inferences from the known facts; but the inferences were eminently reasonable, and the chain of his deductions was correspondingly strong and compelling.

"In the typical case, an officer on patrol observes a motorist commit a routine traffic violation, and turns on his siren or red light to stop the violator's car and issue a citation; upon giving such a signal, the officer sees the driver or other occupant of the car suddenly 'lean forward' or 'bend down' or otherwise reach toward the dashboard or floor. Assuming these are the only 'facts known to the officer' at that moment, do they give him probable cause to believe that the person he observed moving in the car is in possession of contraband? Careful analysis reveals there are too many weak links in the officer's chain of deductions to support that conclusion. The flaws may be conveniently grouped around two assumptions.

"First, the argument assumes that the movements in question were purposeful responses to the officer's appearance on the scene. But the person observed might not in fact have seen the police car, in which event any movements he made would be irrelevant. If he did see a vehicle following, he might not have recognized it to be a police car; many of the 'furtive gesture' cases have arisen in the dark of night, with the officer's car some distance behind. If he recognized it as such, he might not have understood that the police were attempting to bring his own car to a halt. If he correctly inferred the intent of the police, his movements might not have been made in *response* to that awareness; they might simply have been movements he was on the point of making in any event. And if his movements were responsive to the situation, they still might not have been *purposeful:* i.e., when suddenly facing an imminent confrontation with the police for some unknown misdeed, many citizens with nothing to hide will nevertheless manifest an understandable nervousness by means of random, undirected gestures or movements.

"Secondly, the argument assumes that only the guilty will react in the described manner to a policeman's signal to stop their car. To begin with, every motorist knows that the approaching police officer will in all likelihood ask to see his driver's license, and probably also the registration card of the car. The observed movement, therefore, might well be nothing more than the driver's act of reaching for his wallet so as to have his license ready for inspection, or reaching for the steering post or glove compartment to obtain the registration card. And as many women drivers keep their handbag—containing their license and other identification—next to them on the floor or between the seats, a reaching motion in that direction would be no less natural for them.

"Furthermore, every motorist knows that the officer will wish to speak with him, however briefly; simple preparations for that conversation are therefore to be expected. It may be necessary, for example, for the driver to roll down his window. If the radio is playing at the time, the driver or a passenger might lean forward to reduce the volume or turn off the set. If the driver was smoking, he might well reach down to extinguish or store his cigarette in the car's ashtray. And if an occupant of the vehicle was consuming food or beverages, similar movements would probably follow.

"Additionally, many motorists expect to alight from their car, whether voluntarily or upon request, when they are stopped by the police. Again, certain preparations are usually in order: seat belts may have to be unbuckled; passengers may have to remove road maps, packages, folded coats, or infants from their laps; and clothing may have to be adjusted, shoes or hats put on, belts tightened, and outer garments buttoned.

"Finally, when a driver stops his car in a situation in which he knows he may alight from the vehicle, it is both customary and prudent for him to apply his parking brake. Yet in many automobiles the parking brake handle or lever is on or below the dashboard, and the driver is therefore compelled to lean forward or downward in order to apply it.

"Each of the foregoing gestures in some degree resembles—and could reasonably be mistaken for—the movements of a person engaged in secreting contraband inside a car. Yet each is wholly innocent, and has been made at one time or another by virtually every driver or passenger on the roads today.

"Of the various circumstances, perhaps the most persuasive is a driver's failure to stop his car promptly when a police officer signals him to do so. Even this fact, however, is subject to interpretation. Little difficulty is experienced when the motorist in this situation continues to drive for a substantial distance and makes sharp turns or other unusual maneuvers; such conduct can fairly be deemed evasive action, implying consciousness of guilt. Yet in other instances a delay in stopping may well be reasonable. It is a motorist's duty to use due care at all time, and when requested to pull over by a police officer he should do so at the first *safe* opportunity. But road conditions, speed, or other traffic may sometimes compel him to proceed a short way before bringing his car to a halt. The line may be a fine one in certain cases, but it must be drawn realistically and in light of all the facts.

"A second circumstance is that the confrontation took place in the nighttime. Here, however, the possibility of mistake is greater. As distinguished from a deliberate delay in stopping his car, the fact that it is night when the police appear is not 'conduct' of the motorist 'in response to' the officer's signal. The significance of this fact should therefore be appraised with caution; it does not, without more, transform an innocent gesture into a culpable one furnishing probable cause to search."

Other circumstances bearing on the question of whether the furtive gesture has a criminal connotation include the remoteness of the area where the confrontation takes place; a report of a recent crime of violence in the neighborhood, with a description of the suspect; the damaged condition of a car giving ground for belief that it might be stolen; the motorist's lack of a driver's license and other identification; erratic or dangerous driving by the operator of the suspected car; and "nervousness" of the motorist while under police investigation.

By requiring a more patient investigation subsequent to an observed furtive movement, the courts prevent an arrest predicated on a tenuous interpretation of criminal misconduct. Normally the traffic stop allows the officer sufficient time to develop additional facts to corroborate or dispel his original impression. Undeniably an experienced officer can intuitively detect the presence of contraband or suspect the recent commission of a crime. But these suspicions must be rational, and they must be articulated. Otherwise the constitutional requirement of probable cause would evaporate under subjective evaluation. What is necessary is the officer's verbalization of the arrestee's criminally significant conduct. That testimony need not be confined only to the conduct he observed; the officer may combine other factors of probable cause to corroborate his suspicions. Thus, the suspect's statement which he heard; the conduct and behavior which he observed; the odor of contraband he smelled; his experience in detecting narcotic violations; all such factors of probable cause may be invoked.

Arrest for Grand Theft Auto

Closely related to the arrest of motorists in the context of furtive movements, although not necessarily so, are arrests for grand theft auto. Often these arrests begin also with the temporary detention of the motorist to issue a citation. If the license plate of the vehicle is not listed on a "hot sheet," the officer must determine whether the vehicle has been stolen based on a record check or on his own field investigation. Given the widespread use of computers to determine vehicle theft, most officers resort to these resources instantly. Absent any affirmative information, the officer must proceed solely upon his field investigation.

Officers tend to conclude that the inability of a motorist to produce a driver's license or satisfactory evidence of vehicle registration indicates theft. Obviously both these factors suggest that judgment. Yet officers often fail to take any additional steps to fortify their conclusions. The danger exists that a court may conclude that absence of a license or registration is easily explained by many innocent drivers. In fact, failure to produce a valid driver's license or registration certificate is an extremely trivial offense, and often the motorist can purge himself of the citation merely by presenting the correct papers later in court. At most, a small fine is levied. Aside from turning up the revoked or canceled license, however, little significance is attached to these offenses. Thus, officers who rely solely on these two factors may find courts disapproving arrests, and subsequent searches, based on such a slim thread. To prevent such a result, officers can often use their detention time to develop additional evidence that will substantiate evidence of theft. Usually the driver's conflicting statements, his demonstrable falsehoods, or his inability to identify the owner of the car, coupled with an attempt by the officer to verify lawful possession of the vehicle, will be sufficient corroborating evidence of grand theft.

Street Sales of Narcotics

The following case closely parallels a situation described in chapter 2 on Detention. Compare this apparent narcotic transaction to that on pages 29–30.

During the daytime, a police sergeant was parked in an unmarked police vehicle at a street intersection adjacent to a high school and near a location designated by the school as a smoking spot for students. "The defendant, age 20, was leaning against a chain-link fence about 40 feet from the police officer's vehicle. A young man wearing a red and white shirt and carrying a notebook folder walked up to the defendant, and the two appeared to converse. The defendant then handed Red and White Shirt 'some type of paper currency . . . green in color.' Red and White Shirt reached into his notebook folder and pulled out a package 'five inches long, about an inch and a half

to two inches wide. It appeared to be flat and wrapped in wax paper.'
He gave it to the defendant who put it in his right rear pocket. After
further brief conversation, Red and White Shirt entered the school
campus. . . .

"The sergeant, commander of the vice and narcotic bureau, had
participated in approximately 500 narcotic arrests. In his experience,
marijuana is normally packaged in waxed paper bags when sold to
young people in $5 and $10 quantities. The sergeant waited a few
minutes for the arrival of an assistant and then arrested the defendant
for possession of marijuana. In the latter's right rear pocket he found
a folded waxed paper bag containing marijuana.

"In this case, an experienced police officer saw the defendant and
another engage in conversation and then saw the defendant hand the
other person paper currency and receive back a flat waxed paper
package of the size and appearance used for the sale of marijuana in
small quantities. The sergeant's observations differed in degree of
specificity from those, for example, where a suspicious package is
observed, but neither money nor merchandise is seen to change hands.
In contrast, the sergeant observed all the elements of a completed
sale—preliminary negotiation, a delivery of paper currency, and a recip-
rocal delivery of a suspicious package, specifically, a waxed paper
package of a type known by him to be commonly used for marijuana
sales.

"It is difficult to imagine what further visual evidence of a street
sale of narcotics could be required to establish reasonable cause for an
arrest, for here the officer observed each element in the sale carried
out before his eyes. Of course, it is possible that on close examination
the subject matter of the sale might turn out to be something other than
contraband—as for example alfalfa grass, catnip, pipe tobacco, balsam
needles, or aromatic herbs. But reasonable cause for arrest requires
probabilities only, not certainties, and the circumstances make it highly
unlikely that the waxed paper package contained anything other than
contraband, for non-contraband items in waxed paper bags are not
normally exchanged for paper currency on street corners." (*People* v.
Garrett.)

Use of Other Senses

A more difficult problem occurs when the officer relies on his
sense of smell to justify an arrest. For example: officers lawfully
entered a temporarily unoccupied house and observed a closed container lying on the table. The strong odor of marijuana alerted the
officers to the presence of contraband inside the bag although they
could not verify their belief until they opened the bag. One court has

said that officers cannot rely solely on their sense of smell to *search*. Since no one was present in the house, there was no arrest. Consequently, the court held that the sense of smell was not sufficient by itself to justify a warrantless search. Had an occupant been present, however, the significant odor emanating from the bag might well have been probable cause to arrest.

This doctrine, therefore, would not apply to an arrest of the occupants of a car. If after lawfully stopping a motor vehicle, officers detect the odor of marijuana emerging from inside the car, the sense of smell would constitute a strong suspicion that the occupants were committing, or had committed, a crime, thereby establishing probable cause for their arrest and an incidental search for the contraband.

The odor of marijuana can also be detected from outside an apartment or dwelling house when officers approach the door. May entry and arrest follow? If there is a reasonable basis for believing that the dwelling house is occupied, the odor of marijuana constitutes probable cause to arrest the occupants. If the dwelling house is unoccupied, the odor is only evidence that contraband is present, but no occupant is subject to arrest. The odor may provide probable cause to search—in which case a search warrant will be necessary—but it does not authorize entry in the absence of someone to arrest.

Most courts are reluctant to approve arrests based on probable cause supported by the use of the sense of smell. Their reluctance is partly attributable to a concern that such testimony is not susceptible to effective cross-examination and is thus open to abuse. This same judicial reluctance to allow an arrest appears when probable cause is supported by evidence of the officer's sense of touch. An officer cannot verify completely what he smells or touches until he sees it. As noted earlier (see Limited Search—the Frisk in chapter 2), the sense of touch is often unreliable without some corroboration. Therefore, in developing probable cause to arrest from the sense of touch or smell, officers should proceed cautiously. They are well advised to employ temporary detention, rather than arrest, to obtain corroboration of the sense of smell or touch, even if they are positive in their own minds. An officer must remember that his opinion alone is not sufficient; he must convince the court of the validity of his strong suspicion. This responsibility can be best accomplished by presenting as many corroborating factors of probable cause as possible.

Informational Probable Cause

Note: Although this section discusses "informational probable cause" in the context of *arrest*, officers also may develop probable cause to *search* from the same sources. In the latter case, the use of probable cause serves as a basis for the affidavit in obtaining a search warrant. Because the sources of probable cause may justify either an arrest or search, the subject is treated more fully in the section entitled The Affidavit in chapter 5, Search Warrants.

Although most arrests are based on conduct personally observed by officers, other kinds of evidence are also admissible to establish probable cause. Information received from other officers, victims, witnesses, and informants is relevant and admissible to establish the strong suspicion necessary for probable cause.

Information received from others, however, is a classic example of hearsay, and several judicial rules have been created to require at least a minimum reliability for this kind of evidence. Statements made by others to peace officers would not normally be admitted in evidence at trial on the issue of guilt. Such statements, i.e., hearsay, would not be admitted because the hearsay rules generally require the witness himself to testify to what he saw, or did, or heard. By requiring a witness or victim to testify to events he observed, or to statements he heard, the court is able to observe his demeanor and assess his credibility in person. Defense attorneys can cross-examine the witness in an attempt to contradict or modify their statements. If statements from absent witnesses or informants are to be admitted at all, the courts must maintain some control so that the fact-finding process is not subverted.

Hearsay, i.e., statements by parties who are not witnesses at trial, may be received and are admissible to establish probable cause to arrest. But such statements are inadmissible to establish guilt of the charge. Largely for this reason, the court determines the lawfulness of an arrest in the absence of the jury. The task of separating statements into admissible and inadmissible forms is probably too difficult a one to demand of a lay jury. In addition, probable cause is a question of law for the court, not an issue for the jury. Thus, hearsay statements can be offered in evidence to establish the lawfulness of the arrest without seriously impairing the defendant's right to a fair trial on the issue of guilt.

Officers receive information from a variety of sources. For purposes of analysis, it is useful to classify informants according to the source. Informants may be categorized as criminal informants and citizen informants.

Criminal Informants

Although the characterization of someone as a criminal informant is not entirely accurate, the term generally connotes a person who supplies information to law enforcement agencies in exchange for pay, immunity from arrest, or a promise of lenient treatment. Because this kind of informant is himself often heavily involved in illicit activities, his information must be subjected to careful scrutiny. History testifies to careless or sinister use of informants, and courts will not allow reports from such sources to be received without some verification. And that verification cannot be supported by a subsequent arrest and search that confirms the informant's statement. Probable cause must be established prior to an arrest—not after.

Most courts admit hearsay statements related to an officer by an informant if there is a reasonable basis for relying on the informant's credibility. In other words, an arrest may be based on such information if the informant is "reliable." The reliability of an informant is usually established by the officer's previous experience with him. If an informant has reported criminal activities that have proved accurate on prior occasions, it is reasonable to rely on his present statement of criminal activity. The accuracy of the previous information can be established by testimony from the officer that a specific number of arrests and/or convictions were obtained based on the informant's statement. It is not critical that criminal *convictions* result from the informant's reports, but that arrests and subsequent trials were held based on the informant's reports. The quantity of arrests or trials that resulted from the informant's information is not decisive, but rather the quality of his evidence. That quality can be improved by supplementing the informant's statements with the officer's own investigation, observation, experience, and other information.

If an officer testifies to facts that lead the judge to conclude there is a reasonable basis for the informant's reliability, the first step in establishing probable cause to arrest is completed. The courts require, however, that the reliable informant must not be repeating hearsay from others. The informant must speak from personal knowledge of the events that he relates to the officer. When the officer-witness testifies in court that his informant reported to him certain incriminating facts about the defendant, the court must determine whether the informant himself saw, or heard, the facts. In other words, the informant must have said that "he saw," or that "he heard the defendant say," whatever was done or said; or, the informant's statement must be sufficiently detailed to infer personal knowledge. Moreover, the facts that the informant relates to the officer cannot simply be innocent or meaningless facts, such as a description of the car, or of the suspect, or of his companions. The informant must inform the officer about his personal knowledge of incriminating facts, i.e., those facts that strongly indicate the commission of a criminal act.

The second category of criminal informant may be characterized as the untested informant. Probable cause to arrest cannot be supported by information from an anonymous or untested informant unless the information is corroborated. The corroboration required here is not that which is often required to corroborate an accomplice's testimony at trial. The rule of corroboration of an untested informant requires officers to validate and confirm information furnished by a source whose reliability is unknown or untested.

Corroboration can be obtained from a variety of sources: information from other untested informants; observation of the defendant; prior record of the defendant; information from other officers who have known the defendant; information from official records. Again the decisive factor is not so much the quantity of information as its quality. An unverified tip is not equivalent to a strong suspicion that a crime has been committed. The "strong suspicion" must emerge from several factors, none of which may be significant in itself, but which in conjunction with each other indicate probable cause. Corroborating an untested informant converts him into a status equivalent to that of a reliable informant—and then an arrest may be made.

For example: "An officer received information from two untested informants that one 'Al' was selling narcotics, 'mainly dangerous drugs.' The informants gave the officer Al's physical description, indicated that he drove a dark blue Mustang convertible, and gave the address of the apartment where he allegedly carried on his unlawful activity. The officer and his partner went to the address given by the informants and observed on the mailbox for apartment 207 the names 'Sutherland' and 'A. Fein.' A blue Mustang convertible was parked in the carport to the rear of the apartment.

"The officer went to the door of apartment 207, knocked and a female voice from inside asked 'Who's there?' The officer stated, 'Police officers. Narcotics Investigation.' The reply from the same female voice was 'Just a minute.' The officer then heard noises from within the apartment which sounded like people moving about and running, together with a noise described as 'like a plastic type vial landing or falling to a hard floor surface.' After a lapse of about 30 seconds, the door was opened about 1½ feet by a codefendant. When the officer asked if 'Al' was there, she opened the door completely, stepped backwards and said, 'Yes, he's the one on the couch.' The officer observed defendant seated on the couch in the apartment, stepped in the apartment about three feet and stated that he, the officer, had a complaint concerning the use and selling of narcotics at the location. The officer could observe lying on an end table what appeared to him to be two burnt marijuana seeds. The officer retrieved these two seeds from the end table, placed them in an envelope and then in his pocket. Thereupon, he arrested defendant. A search revealed contraband.

"If the officers had reasonable cause to arrest defendant, the search would have been justified as incident to a lawful arrest. Although the information which the officers received from their untested informants justified further investigation, that information standing alone was not sufficient to constitute reasonable cause for an arrest or search. Information given by an untested informant may be sufficient if corroborated in essential respects by other facts, sources or circumstances. It could be argued that the informants' reliability was corroborated by the fact that certain information furnished by them proved to be correct, such as defendant's first name, his presence at the apartment, and the presence of the blue Mustang. However, in order for corroboration to be adequate, it must pertain to defendant's alleged *criminal* activity; accuracy of information regarding the suspect in general is insufficient.

"Even if there are two informers the statements of one do not necessarily corroborate the statements of the other. The quantification of the information does not necessarily improve its quality; the information does not rise above its doubtful source because there is more of it. Although there may be circumstances where corroborative information from separate, unrelated sources will thereby establish its credibility, nevertheless in the instant case there is no showing of what information each informer furnished the officers, or whether the information was furnished independently by each informer. Accordingly, there is no basis for holding that their statements were truly corroborative.

"Cases have held that suspicious conduct observed by officers may furnish the necessary corroboration for an untested informer. Without attempting to set forth a rule of general application, the sounds heard here by the arresting officer do not sufficiently corroborate the informers' statements that defendant was selling narcotics. The apartment door was opened shortly after the officers announced their presence, no plastic vial was discovered by them, and the sounds described by the officer were wholly consistent with innocent activity.

"Does the officer's observation of what he thought were two burnt marijuana seeds sufficiently corroborate the information furnished by the informants and afford reasonable cause for defendant's arrest? It is apparent that evidence of prior marijuana *use* is not strongly corroborative of information regarding alleged *sales* of narcotics, 'mainly dangerous drugs.' Secondly, it seems clear that the mere presence of two burnt marijuana seeds would not give rise to a reasonable inference or strong suspicion that the occupants of the apartment in which the seeds were found were presently guilty of a crime. Evidence of useless traces or residue of narcotic substances do not constitute sufficient evidence to sustain a conviction for possession of narcotics. Although the presence of two burnt marijuana seeds might reasonably suggest that defendant or another occupant of the apartment formerly possessed and used marijuana, that inference would not justify their arrest for present use, possession or sale.

"Apart from searches of automobiles, and other movable property, it is the general rule that probable cause to believe that a search will reveal contraband does *not* justify a warrantless search. Therefore, even if the presence of two burnt marijuana seeds could, under the circumstances in the instant case, have supported an inference that a search would uncover larger, usable quantities of drugs, that inference should have been drawn by a neutral and detached magistrate and not solely by the officer. However strongly convinced officers may be that a search will reveal contraband, their belief does not justify a search without a warrant.

"It follows that ordinarily an arrest may not be based solely upon suspicion that a subsequent search will reveal contraband. It is settled that an arrest may not be used as a pretext to search for evidence, and that an arrest cannot be justified by the fruits of a subsequent search." (*People* v. *Fein.*)

With regard to the requirement that an informant speak from personal knowledge, the officer-witness faces a dilemma. He often desires to conceal the identity of his informant from the defendant because disclosure would end the informant's usefulness or possibly subject him to retaliation from the defendant or others. By careful cross-examination, the defendant can readily determine the time, place, and persons present when the informant obtained his personal knowledge. By a process of elimination, the defendant may be able to ascertain indirectly the informant's identity. This dilemma is unavoidable in many cases, but the officer must be aware of the possibility of indirect disclosure and tailor his investigation accordingly. The more knowledge he can acquire independently of the informant, the stronger his case and the less he will need to rely on the informant.

The U.S. Supreme Court has indicated that an informant need not be disclosed on the issue of probable cause. But many courts have held that disclosure will be required if the informant is a material witness on the issue of guilt. In most cases the informant's information will be admissible on both issues. Because the informant must have personal knowledge of incriminating facts, he becomes, in effect, a witness to the crime. The defendant can easily argue that due process requires disclosure of material witnesses on the issue of guilt. Thus, even though disclosure could be withheld on the issue of probable cause, concealing the informant's identity on the issue of guilt may not be possible. In California, a statute authorizes the judge to hold a special hearing on the issue of disclosure in the absence of the defendant and his counsel. After hearing prosecution evidence, including the possibility of naming the informant, the court may deny disclosure to the defendant and order the transcript of the hearing sealed. The sealed transcript may be opened only by a reviewing court.

Just as the officer must inform the magistrate about his source of information that amounted to probable cause to *arrest,* he must supply similar information in his affidavit for a warrant to *search.* Whatever object the officer intends to seize under the authority of a warrant, he must inform the magistrate about his source of information. If the source of information for the warrant is an informant, the officer must also recite sufficient evidence of the informant's reliability and his personal knowledge of the facts he relates.

If this information does not inevitably tend to disclose the identity of an informant whom the officer wishes to conceal, the defendant can still attempt to challenge the factual accuracy of the affidavit. Some state courts allow the defendant to offer evidence of the officer's misunderstanding of the facts related to him by the informant, or even evidence that the informant's statements are false. This type of inquiry further removes the cloak of secrecy from the informant. And even disclosure of the informant's identity does not end the inquiry. For in many cases disclosure of identity does not improve the defendant's legal position. The informant's identity, without the ability to locate him, is an empty gesture. What the defendant will demand is the production of the informant in court as a potential witness. In reality, the defendant realizes that a demand for disclosure and production forces the prosecuting attorney into another dilemma. If the prosecutor refuses to disclose the name of an informant who is a material witness, the defendant is denied his right to due process, and the officer's statement or testimony of probable cause will be stricken. If he does disclose, at the very least the informant's further usefulness disappears.

One state has held that if the officer uses an informant as an active agent, arrangements must be maintained that will enable officials to locate the informant and subject him to the process of the court if he is a material witness. Failure to do so deprives the defendant of due process of law because testimony cannot be obtained from a material witness.

Whether a court will order disclosure, and perhaps production, of informants depends on judicial policy more than state legislatures. The "fair trial" concept reposes considerable discretion in the courts to determine these issues. The competing choices are difficult: crimes often can be investigated and solved only by drawing on those people who know the most about their perpetration. The average citizen is ignorant about crime and criminal offenders. The person possessed of

such knowledge is frequently closely associated with crime. His credibility, however, is often weak. In order to solve crimes, particularly
so-called "victimless" crimes, informants are indispensable. But once
disclosed, their utility—and perhaps their lives—are gone.

Ultimately the judiciary must decide the issue of disclosure and
production of informants. Statutes are too rigid, and only in a discre-
tionary setting can the issue be resolved. The closed hearing at which
the judge hears evidence only from the prosecutor is an attempt to
allow judicial discretion. Inevitably the case will arise where the defendant must be allowed to cross-examine on the issue of disclosure
just as he would on the issues of probable cause or guilt. Perhaps on
balance the closed hearing offers the best compromises. Much confi-
dence is thereby reposed in judicial discretion, but who else is suited
for impartial judgment?

There are those who claim that the use of informants to enforce
victimless crimes further compromises the police and the courts; that
such crimes are not violent and pose no threat to person or property;
that disproportionate police resources—and use of informants—could
be redirected. Whether society is prepared to adopt such a policy is
immaterial here except insofar as a reduction in the quantity of informants is concerned. Yet the criminal law will continue to require the
use of informants for crimes of violence and for those victimless crimes
that clearly cannot be approved as a way of life.

Citizen Informants

The courts have recognized a distinction between those who
regularly supply information to the authorities and others who provide
information openly and without expectation of any reward or immunity. The latter informant has been characterized as a "citizen
informant." Most often a citizen informant is a victim or witness of a
crime involving injury to person or damage to property. His report,
often easily verifiable from the circumstances, may properly constitute
the sole source of probable cause to arrest. Because a citizen
informant's statement can be easily corroborated, and because his
report is openly submitted, the courts have approved arrests solely
upon this source of information. A single citizen informant can provide
sufficient evidence of probable cause as long as he has personal knowledge of the facts that he relates. All the officer needs to establish is
the informant's status as a "citizen."

In most cases the status of an informant is obvious from the
circumstances. The injured liquor store operator who shouts for help
after a robbery is a clear example of a citizen informant. But, on
occasion, a citizen informant may provide information about clandes-

tine crimes not involving violence or damage. The prevalence of marijuana, drugs, and narcotics is such that few people are unaware of this illicit traffic. But familiarity with indicia of drug use is not automatically converted to expertise. Officers need to exercise caution when receiving reports from citizen informants about narcotic use. Careful questioning is essential in order to evaluate the informant's ability to identify contraband. Often a supplemental investigation will be necessary to corroborate the informant's report. This is probably routine police practice in any event, but the courts will scrutinize the informant's report in order to determine whether the source is an informed citizen or merely an uncorroborated, untested informant.

Official Channels

An arrest, or detention, is not always made on the officer's personal knowledge or on what an informant told him. Modern law enforcement requires radio communication, in which the authority to arrest is directed from a central transmitting facility. Or, in some cases, one officer delegates his arrest authority to another. In either case, the arresting officer himself cannot testify to any facts that qualify as probable cause. To allow arrests without the original information would open the door to abuse. Consequently, the courts hold that although an arrest is lawful even if the arresting officer himself lacks probable cause, the defendant may demand to cross-examine whoever possessed the probable cause initially. The source may be a victim, a witness, an informant or another peace officer. Consider the following.

"At 8 o'clock in the morning an officer, while sitting in his radio car, saw two men, the defendant and another person, standing and talking with one another in the alley bordering a service station. The two men walked over to the service station attendant, then walked away from the attendant in opposite directions from each other. The officer approached the attendant and asked him if he knew the two men and what they were doing there. The attendant replied that he did not know them, and 'I was just going to call the station because they had been hanging around acting suspicious.' This colloquy constitutes the entire conversation between the officer and the attendant. The attendant did not testify at the trial. Another employee of the service station arrived on the scene in time to see the defendant and his companion parting from each other and walking away from the station. The officer called out to the defendant asking him to come back because he wanted to talk to him. Defendant kept on walking. This officer radioed another officer who was driving a different patrol car, and told him "to stop a male Negro that was walking northbound in the alley, that he was a suspicious person." The officer drove his radio car down the alley to stop the defendant. The officer patted the defendant down for weapons and felt what appeared to be a pistol inside his waistband on the right side.

"The direction by one officer to another to pick up the defendant was not, standing alone, justification for the detention. An order by one officer to another insulates the complying officer from assuming personal responsibility for the acts done in obedience to the order, but the order did not itself supply legal cause for the detention any more than the fact of detention supplies its own cause. If the first officer had adequate cause to detain the defendant, he could properly delegate the detention to the other officer, but if he did not have cause to detain the defendant, he could not create such cause simply by relaying an order to a fellow officer." (*People* v. *Hunt.*)

Circumstantial Factors

Whether relying on informants, or on personal observation, officers should attempt to detail specific circumstances that are significant to them even if not to the average person. The officer can testify to his experience, training, or education that enabled him to attribute criminal significance to otherwise seemingly innocent conduct. His expertise can be valuable in giving meaning and direction to facts observed and heard.

In addition, the officer can articulate other factors—circumstantial factors—that again may not be significant in themselves, but together form an incriminating pattern. In some cases, the combination of otherwise unrelated factors may be significant. Thus, some of the following circumstances should be considered as possible factors: location; time of day; number of people; previous knowledge of the suspect; knowledge of his associates; knowledge of the area; conduct at the time of observation (sometimes called "furtive conduct." Certain gestures or movements of a suspect may be significant, particularly in narcotic arrests. As we have noted earlier, however, the officer cannot induce the furtive conduct by his own threatening actions and then rely on the suspect's response). In summary, the officer must paint the picture of probable cause with as many factors as he can and should not overlook neutral circumstances that may be significant.

Examine the facts in the following case in which the officers combine their observation, information, and other factors known to them in an attempt to develop probable cause to arrest.

At night, two undercover officers were standing in front of a restaurant on a main city street. "One officer observed defendant standing outside talking with a 'hippie-type' male; she looked around 'over either shoulder,' removed a tinfoil package from her purse, and then 'nodded in a motion that they both go inside.' The officers could not tell what was inside the tinfoil package. Both officers followed the couple inside. The officers approached the defendant who was standing next to a table and said, 'Why don't we go outside and have a talk.' At about the same time, his partner reached into the defendant's purse and removed the package from it.

"The other officer had not seen the defendant holding the tinfoil package outside. As they approached the defendant he noticed a tinfoil package in her purse; he could see only the large tinfoil wrapping, and not the individually wrapped packets contained inside the larger wrapping. He reached into her purse and removed the tinfoil package. The package contained Seconal tablets individually wrapped in tinfoil. . . .

"One officer further testified that he had been working with a special platoon in the department for about two months prior to and including the date of the arrest, and that he had made 'numerous arrests' for narcotic violations during that period. He also testified that he had been informed by other officers that defendant was selling dangerous drugs, but that he did not know of any officers who ever purchased narcotics from defendant and that he did not know whether the basis of this information was an informer or some officer who observed defendant make a sale; he did not see a 'rap sheet' or any other official department records that dealt with defendant. The officer described the area of arrest as having 'a reputation with the Police Department as being an area where there is a great deal of drug traffic. . . .' Finally, he testified that in his experience dangerous drugs were packaged either in plastic baggies or in tinfoil.

"The other officer testified that a few weeks prior to the arrest he had briefly discussed with the other officer a previous arrest of defendant for assault and possession of dangerous drugs, and that the officer—who 'handled' the previous case—had indicated that defendant was not actually involved in the assault but that large quantities of pills were found in the apartment where the assault occurred and in defendant's possession. The officer testified that he had seen the 'rap sheet' which reflected the above arrest, and that he recalled no other arrests of defendant; however, he had made no attempt to determine whether the above charges against defendant had been dropped, and, in fact, at the time of the hearing was unaware that the charges against the defendant had been dismissed at [an earlier hearing]. . . ." Finally, the officer testified that his experience was that Seconal tablets are usually packaged in tinfoil.

"The evidence indicated that there was only one prior arrest of defendant; that there was no evidence offered at the earlier hearing as to any drugs found in the apartment where the defendant was arrested, other than those found in another person's pockets; that the charges against defendant were dismissed at the earlier hearing; and that the dismissal was prior to defendant's arrest in the instant case. In addition, the prosecutor conceded that during the prior arrest no dangerous drugs were found on the person of the defendant.

"In the abstract, no implication of guilt can be drawn from the fact that a suspect indicates an apparent concern with privacy by looking around to see whether anyone is observing him, and that a showing that an area is known to be the site of frequent narcotics traffic cannot convert into sufficient cause to arrest circumstances that are as consistent with innocence as with criminality, although specialized knowledge may render suspicious what would appear innocent to a layman, the test remains whether the circumstances would warrant a man of reasonable caution—who possessed such knowledge—in the belief that the action taken was appropriate.

"The act of showing a tinfoil package to a companion is even less suspicious than that of engaging in a sidewalk sale. Neither officer was able to see the contents of the package or any impressions on the tinfoil wrapping, and both admitted that for all he knew at the time he approached defendant, the tinfoil package could have contained cookies. Defendant exhibited little concern with her surroundings; and her apparent concern was consistent with innocent activity —such as keeping an eye out for acquaintances.

"The fact that the area is known to be the site of frequent narcotics traffic cannot convert circumstances as innocent as those involved in this case—an individual being generally concerned with her surroundings while displaying a tinfoil package to a companion—into sufficient cause to arrest."

What about the special knowledge and experience of the arresting officers that dangerous drugs are often packaged in tinfoil? "Even if dangerous drugs are often packaged in tinfoil, so many other legitimate items—such as foods or tobacco—are packaged in tinfoil that a tinfoil package is not a suspicious circumstance, and a man of reasonable caution who possesses the knowledge that dangerous drugs are often packaged in tinfoil would not be justified in assuming, upon seeing a tinfoil package, that it is likely to contain drugs.

"It is thus clear that in itself a tinfoil package is so commonly used for legitimate purposes that it is not a suspicious circumstance. And the officers heard nothing of the conversation between defendant and [her] companion, and the record evidences nothing which would distinguish a layman's estimate of the suspiciousness of defendant's behavior from the officers' estimate. . . .

"[As to the defendant's criminal record:] It is well settled that while it may be perfectly reasonable for officers in the field to make arrests on the basis of information furnished to them by other officers, when it comes to justifying the total police activity in a court, the People must prove that the source of the information is something other than the imagination of an officer who does not become a witness. To hold otherwise would permit the manufacture of reasonable grounds for arrest within a police department by one officer trans-mitting information purportedly known by him to another officer who did not know such information, without establishing under oath how the information had in fact been obtained by the former officer. If this were so, every utterance of a police officer would instantly and automatically acquire the dignity of official information; 'reasonable cause' or 'reasonable grounds,' . . . could be conveniently fashioned out of a two-step communication; and all Fourth Amendment safe-guards would dissolve as a consequence.

"In sum, when an officer furnishes to another officer information which leads to an arrest, the People must show the basis for the former officer's information. More specifically in relation to the instant case, when an officer furnishes to another officer information as to alleged prior criminal activity of an individual relied upon for an arrest relating to subsequent activities of that individual, then the People must show the basis for the former officer's information. The absence of such a requirement would allow a police officer to manu-facture reasonable grounds to arrest while circumventing the necessity of pointing to 'specific and articulable facts' justifying his suspicions.

"The officer had known nothing about defendant's 'criminal record'—i.e., her arrest for assault and possession of dangerous drugs, the charges having been dismissed for lack of evidence. He testified that he had known nothing of defendant's prior activities other than what other officers had told him—that defendant sold dangerous drugs. He did not see a 'rap sheet' or any other department records that dealt with defendant, nor did he know of any officers who had ever purchased drugs from defendant. Indeed, he did not know whether the basis of the information given him was an informer or some officer who observed defendant make a sale. The prosecution did not produce any of the officers who allegedly had informed the officer about defendant's narcotics sales.

"In such a situation, the officer's testimony as to his knowledge of defendant's activities cannot be utilized as an ingredient in the probable cause equation. To do so would permit the manufacture of a known criminal background—in this case, sales of dangerous drugs by defendant—within a police department by one officer transmitting information to another officer without establishing the basis for his information.

"One officer testified that he had been informed by his partner that during the prior arrest large quantities of pills (dangerous drugs) had been found in the apartment where defendant had been arrested and in defendant's possession. This testimony can be given no weight, since it was conceded by the prosecutor at the hearing that no dan-gerous drugs had been found on defendant and that no evidence had been produced at the ensuing preliminary hearing as to any drugs found in the apartment, other than those found in another person's pockets.

"The officer also testified that he had seen the 'rap sheet' reflecting defendant's prior arrest, but that he had made no attempt to determine whether the charges against defendant had been dropped and did not even know at the time of the hearing that the charges against defendant had been dismissed.

"A prior related *conviction,* when known by the arresting officers, has at best only a slight tendency to establish a present violation of the law; obviously, a prior related *arrest* where there is no conviction must have even less than a 'slight tendency' to establish a present violation of the law. Where, as in this case, the charges upon which the prior arrest had been based were dismissed, not because of any legal technicality unrelated to the merits of the charges against defendant, but because the charges had been held to be unfounded—because, in other words, defendant had been found innocent of the charges—the officer's knowledge of that arrest should be given no weight. As defendant states, to allow an arresting officer's knowledge of a suspect's prior arrest to convert into probable cause circumstances that otherwise would not constitute probable cause when the prior charges were dismissed because of insufficient evidence is to hold that persons arrested on unfounded charges would thereafter become second-class citizens, with lesser rights than other citizens." (*Remers* v. *Superior Court.*)

This case illustrates that a combination of observation, information and other factors will not always justify an arrest unless care is taken to develop all the facts in the officer's possession that add up to a strong suspicion that a felony has been committed. Sometimes, of course, the evidence is simply insufficient—as in the case just reviewed.

Delay in Arrest

Not all arrests are made immediately after the crime has been committed—even if committed in the officer's presence. Serious problems of fairness arise.

For example: " 'Charles H.' was hired by a local police department to work as an undercover agent in a narcotic 'buy' program. [In June] he went to defendant's apartment to attempt to purchase marijuana. Later that evening, H. purchased a quantity of marijuana from defendant. No arrest was made at the time but this sale was the basis for a complaint which was subsequently issued for the arrest of the defendant.

"The complaint against defendant was filed in mid-November

of the same year and defendant was arrested shortly thereafter. Another officer testified at the preliminary hearing that defendant was not arrested sooner because H. was working on a number of other cases as an undercover agent, and the police department did not want H.'s identity disclosed until they were ready to make all the arrests connected with the 'buy' program."

The preliminary hearing was held in December. The defendant moved to dismiss on the ground that there was an unreasonable delay between the time of the alleged offense and the time of arrest.

"In cases involving narcotic 'buy' programs, there is no hard and fast rule establishing how much of a delay in defendant's arrest constitutes a denial of due process to him. Each case must be resolved by balancing public interest and the rights of the defendant. The necessity of using undercover agents to detect violations of the narcotic laws is obvious. It is within the realm of common knowledge and common sense that uniformed or otherwise known policemen are unable to penetrate the *sub rosa* world of the narcotics peddler. Extensive, time-consuming investigations by undercover operatives, who daily risk their lives, are required to get to the retail and wholesale sources of illicit narcotics. It is equally obvious that the effectiveness of such an agent does not survive the time it becomes known that he is a policeman. The public thus has a substantial interest in keeping the officer's identity secret for a reasonable period of time while he continues his investigations. This public interest is a legitimate reason for delaying the arrest of an individual wrongdoer. The courts have recognized this fact, and the cases are legion which have upheld the use of narcotic 'buy' programs as acceptable police practice.

"This does not mean, however, that the public interest must always prevail. The accused has substantial rights which must be protected, and the delay between the alleged offense and the time of arrest must not result in a deprivation of due process. Delaying the arrest of the accused may hinder his ability to recall or reconstruct his whereabouts at the time the alleged offense occurred. The accused has no way of knowing, to say nothing of proving, where he was at the time and on the day the policeman says his diary shows he made a sale of narcotics to the policeman. An additional problem resulting from such delays is misidentification, where an undercover officer saw the accused only occasionally and then for brief periods of time. There is no doubt that under certain circumstances the delay in filing the accusation makes it difficult or impossible for an accused to adequately prepare his defense.

"But the fact that the question in this type of case must be resolved by balancing interests does not mean that there are no guidelines for a court to follow. An accused must show two things to establish "unfairness" resulting from claimed delay in his arrest: that there was no legitimate reason for the delay, and that he was prejudiced by the delay." (*People* v. *Wright.*)

Arrest with Warrant

An arrest warrant is a process, issued in the name of a legal authority and directed to a law enforcement officer, commanding him to take the named individual into custody. In most jurisdictions the procedure for an application to obtain a warrant, the form of the warrant, and the service of the warrant are set forth by statute. Yet the Fourth Amendment, which states that "no warrant shall issue but upon probable cause, supported by oath or affirmation, and particularly describing the . . . person . . . to be seized," supersedes any statute. An arrest is a seizure within the meaning of the Fourth Amendment, and any arrest pursuant to an arrest warrant must be effected pursuant to the constitutional provision.

Until recently, most state, as well as federal, courts routinely issued arrest warrants without seriously considering the necessity of establishing probable cause to support the warrant. But, in 1957, in *Giordenello* v. *United States,* the U.S. Supreme Court examined a federal warrant that had been issued ordering the defendant's arrest for possession of contraband. The warrant provided as follows: "The undersigned complainant being duly sworn states: that on or about January 26, 1956, at Houston, Texas in the Southern District of Texas, Veto Giordenello did receive, conceal, etc., narcotic drugs, to-wit: heroin with knowledge of unlawful importation; in violation of Section 174, Title 21, United States Code.

The officer executed the warrant and, incidental to the defendant's arrest, seized contraband on his person.

Federal Rules of Criminal Procedure provide that an arrest warrant may be issued only upon a written and sworn complaint (1) setting forth "the essential facts constituting the offense charged," and (2) showing "that there is probable cause to believe that [such] an offense has been committed and that the defendant has committed it. . . ." In *Giordenello,* the Court said the provisions of "these Rules must be read in light of the constitutional requirements they implement. The language of the Fourth Amendment, that '. . . no Warrants shall issue, but upon probable cause, supported by Oath or affirmation, and particularly describing . . . the persons or things to be seized,' applies to arrest as well as search warrants. The protection afforded by these Rules, when viewed against their constitutional background, is that the inferences from the facts which lead to the complaint '. . . be drawn by a neutral and detached magistrate instead of being judged by the officer engaged in the often competitive enterprise of ferreting out crime.' The purpose of the complaint is to enable the appropriate magistrate, here a Commissioner, to determine whether the 'probable cause' required to support a warrant exists. The Commissioner must judge for himself the persuasiveness of the facts relied on by a complaining officer to show probable cause. He should not accept without question the complainant's mere conclusion that the person whose arrest is sought has committed a crime.

"When the complaint in this case is judged with these considerations in mind, it is clear that it does not provide any basis for the Commissioner's determination that probable cause existed. The complaint contains no affirmative allegation that the affiant spoke with personal knowledge of the matters contained therein; it does not indicate any sources for the complainant's belief; and it does not set forth any other sufficient basis upon which a finding of probable cause could be made. These deficiencies could not be cured by the Commissioner's reliance upon a presumption that the complaint was made on the personal knowledge of the complaining officer. This is illustrated by the facts of this case, for the agent's testimony later showed that he had no personal knowledge of the matters on which his charge was based. In these circumstances, the Commissioner could not be expected to assess independently the probability that the defendant committed the crime charged. If the complaint in this case were upheld, the substantive requirements would be completely read out of the rules, and the complaint would be of only formal significance entitled to perfunctory approval by the Commissioner. This would not comport with the protective purposes which a complaint is designed to achieve."

In *Giordenello,* the U.S. Supreme Court interpreted the Federal Rules of Criminal Procedure and, arguably, were not applying Fourth Amendment standards. If such were the case, the decision would only apply to federal arrests and not to arrests by state officers. But the issue was apparently resolved a short time later when the Court summarily disposed of a similar question involving an arrest warrant under a state statute. In any event, the clearly safer practice is to issue a warrant of arrest in harmony with the requirements of the Fourth Amendment. How can this be done?

In California, the magistrate issues arrest warrants only if accompanied by a "constitutionally adequate" complaint or declaration. The declaration must recite sufficient facts that will enable the magistrate to determine the existence of probable cause. Establishing probable cause to support an arrest warrant parallels establishing probable cause necessary to arrest. Or, more specifically, probable cause to support an arrest warrant must be shown just as probable cause to issue a search warrant must be presented. A mere recital of a violation of a statute in the language of the statute is insufficient.

If an arrest is made pursuant to a constitutionally defective complaint, any evidence seized incidental to the arrest will be excluded. Yet the prosecution can still validate the arrest on alternative grounds, because the legality of an arrest cannot depend exclusively on the validity of the warrant since an arrest without a warrant may stand if based on probable cause. In *Giordenello* v. *United States,* the government had argued to the Supreme Court that "the arrest was justified *apart* from the warrant." The Court held that in the event of a new trial the government could seek to justify the defendant's arrest without relying on the warrant. In other words, if the prosecution can establish probable cause to arrest without a warrant, the invalid warrant will not void a lawful search incident to the arrest.

A search undertaken pursuant to an invalid search warrant, which could otherwise be upheld as incident to an arrest based on probable cause, presents an analogous problem. In *Marron* v. *United States,* police officers conducted a search of the defendant's business premises pursuant to a *valid* search warrant but seized items which were not specified by the warrant. After stating that: "The requirements that warrants shall particularly describe the things to be seized makes general searches under them impossible and prevents the seizure of one thing under a warrant describing another," the Supreme Court held the seizure valid on the ground that the search by means of which the officers found the seized items was incident to the arrest of the defendant's agent, who was committing a crime on the premises in the presence of the officers.

Policy considerations for the rationale allowing the prosecution to validate an arrest independent of an invalid arrest warrant are: First: "Although certain nonwarrant arrests and searches are permissible, the policy of the law is to encourage officers to use search warrants. . . . Second: The rule which excludes evidence obtained by illegal searches was adopted [partially] for the purpose of eliminating the incentive for police officers to use illegal methods. That principle does not call for a rejection of the evidence. . . . Given a choice between a nonwarrant arrest and a search based upon a magistrate's warrant, officers will be impelled to forego the latter if a defect in the warrant procedure will invalidate an arrest and search which would have been legal without a warrant." (*People* v. *Chimel.*)

In addition to setting forth the probable cause that justifies the issuance of a warrant of arrest, the officers must provide a description of the arrestee. Officers do not always know the name, or even alias, of the person suspected of committing the crime involved. "The weight of authority holds that to meet the constitutional requirements, a 'John

Doe' warrant must describe the person to be seized with reasonable particularity. The warrant should contain sufficient information to permit his identification with reasonable certainty. This may be done by stating his occupation, his personal appearance, peculiarities, place of residence or other means of identification. Where a name that would reasonably identify the subject to be arrested cannot be provided, then some other means reasonable to the circumstances must be used to assist in the identification of the subject of the warrant. If a fictitious name is used the warrant should also contain sufficient descriptive material to indicate with reasonable particularity the identification of the person whose arrest is ordered." (*People* v. *Montoya.*)

Cases and Materials

Brinegar v. *United States*, 338 U.S. 160, 69 S. Ct. 1302, 93 L. Ed. 1879.

Carroll v. *United States*, 267 U.S. 132, 45 S. Ct. 280, L. Ed. 543.

Draper v. *United States*, 358 U.S. 307, 79 S. Ct. 329, 3 L. Ed. 2d 327.

Dyke v. *Taylor Implement Co.*, 391 U.S. 216, 88 S. Ct. 1472, 20 L. Ed. 2d 538.

Freeman v. *DMV*, 70 Cal. 2d 235, 449 P. 2d 195 ("presence").

Giordenello v. *United States*, 357 U.S. 480, 78 S. Ct. 1245, 2 L. Ed. 2d 1503.

Henry v. *United States*, 361 U.S. 98, 80 S. Ct. 168, 41 L. Ed. 2d 134.

Honore v. *Superior Court*, 70 Cal. 2d 162, 449 P. 2d 169.

Marron v. *United States*, 275 U.S. 192, 48 S. Ct. 74, 72 L. Ed. 231.

McCray v. *Illinois*, 386 U.S. 300, 87 S. Ct. 1056, 18 L. Ed. 2d 62.

People v. *Chimel*, 68 C 2d 436, 439 P. 2d 333.

People v. *Fein*, 4 Cal. 3d 747, 484 P. 2d 583.

People v. *Garrett*, 29 Cal. App. 3d 535, 104 Cal. R. 829.

People v. *Hunt*, 250 Cal. App. 2d 311, 58 Cal. R. 385.

People v. *Ingle*, 53 Cal. 2d 407, 348 P. 2d 577.

People v. *Miller*, 7 Cal. 3d 219, 496 P. 2d 1228.

People v. *Montoya*, 255 Cal. App. 2d 137, 63 Cal. R. 73.

People v. *Privett*, 52 Cal. 2d 330, 341 P. 2d 1.

People v. *Sesslin*, 68 Cal. 2d 418, 439 P. 2d 321.

People v. *Superior Court* (Kiefer), 3 Cal. 3d 807, 478 P. 2d 449 (furtive conduct).

People v. *Superior Court* (Simon), 7 Cal. 3d 186, 496 P. 2d 1205 (car theft; traffic searches).

People v. *Wright,* 2 Cal. App. 3d 732, 82 Cal. R. 859.

Peters v. *New York*, 392 U.S. 40, 80 S. Ct. 1889, 20 L. Ed. 2d 917.

Remers v. *Superior Court*, 2 Cal. 3d 659, 470 P. 2d 11.

Rios v. *United States*, 364 U.S. 253, 80 S. Ct. 1431, 4 L. Ed. 2d 1688.

Roviaro v. *United States,* 353 U.S. 53, 77 S. Ct. 623, 1 L. Ed. 2d 639 (disclosure of informant).

Whitley v. *Warden*, 401 U.S. 560, 83 S. Ct. 407, 9 L. Ed. 2d 441.

Wong Sun v. *United States*, 371 U.S. 471, 83 S. Ct. 407, 9 L. Ed. 2d 441.

1. Officers arrest the defendant for vagrancy. At trial, officers testify that based upon the conduct they observed, no probable cause existed to arrest defendant for robbery. The court finds that the arrest for vagrancy was illegal but, despite the officers' opinion, probable cause did exist to arrest for robbery. How is probable cause measured? Must the officers *subjectively* believe the defendant is guilty of the crime they arrest him for, or is probable cause measured by an objective evaluation of the facts? If an officer himself does not believe he has probable cause to arrest for a particular crime, why should the court validate an arrest that is objectively lawful?

2. While conducting an investigation of a burglary, officers remove unidentified palm prints from a windowsill. Several days later, a large number of juveniles are arrested, fingerprinted, and released. Subsequent investigation reveals that prints of one of the juveniles matches those found on the windowsill. The juvenile is rearrested. At trial he objects to the introduction of his fingerprints on the ground that they are the product of an unlawful search.

Are fingerprints, which are not physical evidence like personal property, subject to the exclusionary rule?

Does detention for the purpose of obtaining fingerprints require probable cause?

"Detention for fingerprinting may constitute a much less serious intrusion upon personal security than other types of police searches and detentions. Fingerprinting involves none of the probing into an individual's private life and thoughts that marks an interrogation or search. Nor can fingerprint detention be employed repeatedly to harass any individual, since the police need only one set of each person's prints. Furthermore, fingerprinting is an inherently more reliable and effective crime-solving tool than eyewitness identifications or confessions and is not subject to such abuses as the improper line-up and the 'third degree.' Finally, because there is no danger of destruction of fingerprints, the limited detention need not come unexpectedly or at an inconvenient time." Do you agree?

(See *Davis* v. *Mississippi,* 394 U.S. 721, 89 S. Ct. 1394, 22 L. Ed. 676.)

3. Officers receive information from a reliable informant that a specifically described individual will transport baggage containing marijuana on a particular flight. Later, officers observe a man resembling the description as he checks his baggage on the reported flight. When the luggage arrives in the baggage check room, the officer unleashes a dog specifically trained to detect marijuana. The dog instantly runs to the described luggage and barks furiously, scratching at the luggage. This reaction is in response to his training in the detection of marijuana. Is such evidence admissible on the issue of probable cause to search?

4. Four armed men robbed a residence. One of them was arrested. At the time of arrest, he was driving the defendant's car, and a search of the car produced property stolen in the robbery the day before. He admitted taking part in the robbery and implicated defendant. He told the police that he was sharing an apartment with the defendant. He also stated that the guns used in the robbery and other stolen property were in the apartment.

One of the investigating officers then checked official records on the defendant, verifying his prior association with the arrestee, his age and physical description, his address, and the make of his car. The information the officer uncovered corresponded with the general descriptions by the robbery victims and the statements made by the arrestee.

Four officers went to the apartment, verified the address, and knocked. One of the officers testified: "The door was opened and a person who fit the description exactly of the defendant, as I had received it from both the cards and from the arrestee, answered the door. . . . We placed him under arrest for robbery."

After arresting the man who answered the door, they asked him whether he was the defendant and where the guns and stolen goods were. The arrestee replied that he was not the defendant, that his name was Miller, that it was the defendant's apartment, and that he was waiting for the defendant. The arrestee then produced identification indicating that he was in fact Miller, but the police were unimpressed, proceeded to search the apartment, and discovered incriminating evidence in plain sight.

Subsequent investigation confirmed that indeed the man was Miller and not the defendant.

The defendant was arrested later, and at his trial he contended the search of his apartment was unlawful since the mistaken arrest of Miller was not supported by probable cause to arrest Miller. Therefore, the defendant argued, the incidental search was unlawful. What should be the result?

5. Officers execute a federal arrest warrant and arrest the named arrestee after forcing entry into his apartment. While inside they observe contraband and seize it. At his trial in the state court for possession of the contraband, the defendant attacks the validity of the federal warrant on which his arrest was originally authorized.

 a) Can a state court declare a federal warrant invalid?

 b) If so, does the unlawful warrant taint the entry and arrest?

c) Assuming the warrant is invalid, would the odor of burning marijuana smelled from outside the apartment by the officer make any difference? *People* v. *Rice*, 10 Cal. App. 3d 730, 89 Cal. R. 280.

6. A statute provides that anyone arrested pursuant to an arrest warrant must be arraigned in court within forty-eight hours after the arrest. The defendant is arrested on the authority of a warrant and sixty-two hours after his arrest tells officers that stolen property is in his house. He consents to their entry. He is then arraigned on the warrant. At trial, he objects to the introduction of evidence seized from his house on the ground that his statement was made after he should have been arraigned; if he had been arraigned within the forty-eight-hour period he would not have made such a statement. Or, in the alternative, the late arraignment was unduly coercive, contributed to an involuntary consent, and was not a free act of his will. What should be the result?

Chapter Four

Search

The Fourth Amendment prohibits unreasonable searches. Before it can be determined whether the officer's action was unreasonable, the court must first ascertain whether or not there was a "search." A search, at least in the constitutional sense, is an act that a law enforcement officer undertakes with the intent to discover objects concealed from view.

The "Plain View" Doctrine

Because of this definition, the courts developed the "plain view" doctrine. Under this rule, an officer may seize any evidence that is open to view because the property is not concealed. Seizing property in plain view does not constitute a search, and it is therefore immaterial whether the officer's action was reasonable or unreasonable. Only if the officer's act disclosed items previously concealed, i.e., if it were a search, would the issue of "reasonableness" arise.

The Right to View

Whether or not an object is open to view is not the only issue in determining whether a search was conducted. Officers must also have the right to be in a position to obtain the view. This rule requires the officer to justify his plain view of seizable evidence by establishing that he violated no other constitutionally protected rights of the suspect in obtaining his view. Thus, an officer could not forcibly enter a dwelling house on no basis whatsoever and then observe seizable evidence in plain view. Nor could he needlessly stop a motorist and obtain a view of the interior of the car to determine whether seizable evidence was in plain view. In other words, each investigative step prior to the officer's plain view will be scrutinized to determine whether the view was obtained in violation of any constitutional rights.

Overcoming the Trespass Objection

Often in narcotic investigations, officers will maintain close surveillance of premises in an attempt to observe conduct inside the house. Necessarily this involves entering the occupant's land, walking on the property, or perhaps standing on a porch step of the house in order to facilitate visual entry—as distinct from actual physical entry. Although some courts have said that the Fourth Amendment prohibits unreasonable searches—not trespasses—nevertheless a police officer's entry on private property without the consent of the owner is a factor in evaluating the officer's right to have his view. If the property is unfenced and no gate or other barrier prevents one from entering the property, the degree of trespass is significantly less than if the officer must open a locked gate or climb over a fence or shrubbery. Officers who intend to obtain visual entry to premises must overcome the trespass objection—preferably by establishing a reasonable basis for investigation that requires entry. That basis may rest on a neighbor's report, a report from a victim of or a witness to a crime, or a report from an informant. Establishing the basis for limited entry on the land reduces the trespass objection.

Assuming that the officers are reasonably on the land and thereby establish their right to be present, the usual technique is to peer into windows in an attempt to verify information or to obtain corroborating facts. The act of looking through a window and observing something in plain view would not constitute a search within the meaning of the definition. Nor would a view of the interior obtained by looking through an open door be a search. But officers cannot improve their view by removing any obstruction to their line of sight. To push aside a drape, or open a closed but unlocked screen door would be impermissible.

Nor can officers employ a ruse or trick to facilitate visual entry. Thus, if officers lacked probable cause to arrest prior to their visual or physical entry, any evidence they seized inside would be the product of a search because they obtained its disclosure by subterfuge. But there is nothing unlawful in tricking an occupant into opening the door if officers have previously developed probable cause to arrest. If probable cause to arrest exists, officers can forcibly enter in any event; subterfuge merely avoids the potential violence of a forcible entry.

The Right of Privacy

The courts, including the U.S. Supreme Court, have expressed some dissatisfaction with the classic definition of a search. Recent decisions hold that the "plain view" rule, and the rule that requires the officer to establish his "right to have the view," are not always a sufficient justification for visual searches conducted from the exterior of the house. The U.S. Supreme Court has held that the Fourth Amendment embodies a right of *privacy* that cannot be unreasonably invaded. In order to understand the relevance of this doctrine in the context of search, some background is necessary.

In *Hester* v. *United States,* the U.S. Supreme Court enunciated the "open fields" doctrine. In this case, officers had concealed themselves from fifty to one hundred yards from the house of Hester's father; they saw Hester leave the house and hand a bottle to one Henderson. When an alarm sounded, Hester and Henderson ran. Hester dropped a jug, which broke, and Henderson threw away the bottle. The officers retrieved the jug and bottle, as well as a broken jar that was thrown from the house, and recognized their contents as moonshine. The opinion states: "It is obvious that even if there had been a trespass, the [officers'] testimony was not obtained by an illegal search or seizure. The defendant's own acts, and those of his associates, disclosed the jug, the jar and the bottle—and there was no seizure in the sense of the law when the officers examined the contents of each after it had been abandoned. . . . The only shadow of a ground for bringing up the case is drawn from the hypothesis that the examination of the vessels took place upon Hester's father's land. As to that, it is enough to say that, apart from the justification, *the special protection accorded by the Fourth Amendment to the people in their 'persons, houses, papers, and effects,' is not extended to the open fields."* (Italics added.)

Although many lower federal court decisions have applied the "open fields" doctrine of *Hester* v. *United States* in upholding the legality of a search or seizure, they contain conflicting statements as to whether the *ground* area of the curtilage[1] is protected by the Fourth Amendment. Some, relying on *Hester,* have declared that the "grounds"

---

1. It has been stated that "Whether the place searched is within the curtilage is to be determined from the facts, including its proximity or annexation to the dwelling, its inclusion within the general enclosure surrounding the dwelling, and its use and enjoyment as an adjunct to the domestic economy of the family. The word originally signified the land with the castles and outhouses, enclosed often with high stone walls, and where the old barons sometimes held their court in the open air. The presence of a fence or other boundary has been said to be an important, but not controlling, factor in determining the extent of the curtilage." (*McDowell* v. *United States.*)

or "enclosed or unenclosed . . . grounds or open fields around . . . houses are not included in the prohibition of the Fourth Amendment." Under the foregoing rule, it was held that the Fourth Amendment was not violated by the examination of a jug left on the ground under a car apparently parked by the porch of a shack belonging to one of the defendants or by the detection of an odor by the porch of the defendant's premises.

Several California decisions, in rejecting claims of unlawful searches and seizures, have stated that "the premises around a house" or " 'enclosed or unenclosed grounds or open fields' around a house" are not protected by the Fourth Amendment. Other California cases have emphasized the degree of privacy the defendant enjoyed in the place in question.

In one case, an officer entered the side yard of a duplex through an open gate. A sidewalk went from the gate to a side porch that was unroofed; there were no bushes or hedges nearby. The officer stood on the first step of the side porch and looked through a window into the interior of the house where he observed certain matters. The court concluded that under the circumstances the officer's acts did not constitute an unconstitutional invasion of the defendant's privacy. The court said that looking through a window does not become an unreasonable search merely because a police officer may be on the defendant's premises when he makes the observation, and that the degree of privacy which defendant enjoyed in the place involved is an important factor in determining the reasonableness of the search.

The U.S. Supreme Court recognized in *Katz* v. *United States* that "the security of one's privacy against arbitrary intrusion by the police [is] at the core of the Fourth Amendment. The Fourth Amendment protects people, not places, and wherever an individual may harbor a reasonable 'expectation of privacy,' he is entitled to be free from unreasonable governmental intrusion . . . ." In *Katz,* federal agents, by means of an electronic device, listened to, and recorded, the defendant's end of a conversation made from a public telephone booth, the door to which apparently had been closed by the defendant. The court held that "The Government's activities in electronically listening to and recording the petitioner's words violated the privacy upon which he justifiably relied while using the telephone booth and thus constituted a 'search and seizure' within the meaning of the Fourth Amendment," and that, in the absence of prior judicial authorization, the search and seizure were unreasonable. The Court also noted that, although it had occasionally described its conclusions in terms of "constitutionally protected area," it had "never suggested that this concept can serve as a talismanic solution to every Fourth Amendment problem."

Thus, the analysis of cases involving searches of open fields or grounds adjacent to a house no longer will be resolved on a trespass–plain-view theory. In answering the question: Did the officer have the right to have his view? the answer may well depend on whether there was a violation of the arrestee's reasonable expectation of privacy. The answer will vary, depending, in part, on whether there was a trespass. And of course, the location of the officers when they observed either seizable evidence or unlawful conduct will be relevant, as well as the location of the observed evidence itself. Thus, although "trespass," "plain view," and "right to have the view" are no longer quick answers, they are still relevant in evaluating privacy.

For example: A police officer was contacted by a neighbor, who lived next door to defendants, and who reported that about a week before he had seen on defendants' back porch a large plastic bag containing described packages, one of which was torn and contained a dark green vegetable substance that appeared similar to alfalfa, but did not smell like alfalfa, and had a "small funny type seed." Officers walked down the railroad tracks behind the defendants' residence and entered into "the open back yard area" of that residence. There the officers observed three trash cans two or three feet from the back porch door. The officers did not have a search warrant. Inside one of the trash cans they found, among other things, a bag that contained marijuana.

Here the officers established a basis for being on the land because of the neighbor's report. They did not violate any rights of the defendant prior to observing the marijuana, and they committed only a minor trespass. They observed evidence in plain view. Despite this, the court said that the occupants reasonably expected privacy of the contents of their trash can. "The trash can was within a few feet of the back door of defendants' home and was an adjunct to the domestic economy. Placing the marijuana in the trash can, so situated and used, was not an abandonment unless as to persons authorized to remove the receptacle's contents, such as trashmen. So far as appears defendants alone resided at the house. In the light of the combined facts and circumstances it appears the defendants exhibited an expectation of privacy, and that expectation was reasonable under the circumstances of the case. There are many reasons why residents would not want their castaway clothing, letters, medicine bottles or other telltale refuse and trash to be examined by neighbors or others, at least not until the trash had lost its identity and meaning by becoming part of a large conglomeration of trash elsewhere. Half-truths leading to rumor and gossip may readily flow from an attempt to read the contents of another's trash." (*People* v. *Edwards*.)

This case could have been decided differently if one assumes that no one reasonably expects privacy in their discarded papers. Yet in a different context, where there is no evidence that the property observed was abandoned, any right of privacy could not reasonably be expected. Consider the following example:

"Two police officers testified that they were on duty when they responded to a call to investigate a complaint by two youths, aged 17 and 18. The youths told them that they had met defendant and that he had invited them to his apartment. Accepting the invitation, the boys had accompanied defendant to his car, where they had seen a marijuana cigarette in a clip on the dashboard. At the apartment, defendant had offered them some marijuana. They became frightened and fled the apartment.

"The officers further testified that they returned to the apartment house around midnight with the two boys and two plainclothes officers. Upon arrival, the police officers and one of the boys went to the subterranean garage, where the boy pointed out defendant's automobile. Through the window of the locked car the police officers observed an object lying across the top of an open ashtray that appeared to be a partially smoked marijuana cigarette."

Apparently the apartment garage was a common area; the officers did not commit a trespass by entering it. Nor did the officers conduct an unreasonable search by looking in the window of the car. "Defendant on cross-examination of the apartment house manager elicited testimony that the garage 'was not a common area open to the public' but 'rather a private area not open to the public,' that '[i]n other words, the . . . garage . . . was not an enclosed piece of land that had been set aside for public or municipal use,' and that there were no spaces in the garage for parking by guests. The manager also testified that the garage was a 'common parking area for tenants of the apartment building.' One of the officers who entered the garage testified that there was no indication that the garage was a common area or public parking. His partner stated that the garage was big, that it would definitely hold 5 cars, but that he could not recall whether it would accommodate 105 cars.

"The garage, used in common by the tenants of the apartment building, is similar in nature to a common hallway of an apartment building. The officers apparently entered the garage without force. Defendant's car was parked in the garage and the marijuana was in plain sight on an open ashtray inside the car. Any expectation by the defendant of privacy as to objects in plain sight in the car would have been unreasonable, and no constitutionally protected right of privacy was violated when the officers looked through the window of the car." (*People* v. *Terry.*)

In this case, the entry into a common garage did not invade the defendant's right of privacy because he could not reasonably expect a significant degree of privacy in a facility shared in common with other tenants, most of whom he probably did not even know. Similarly, if visual entry of an apartment is made from a common hall or corridor, a defendant could not argue that he reasonably expected privacy unless special circumstances could be established.

Thus, the evolution of trespass, which is a law of real property, into "privacy" serves the Fourth Amendment better in assessing the officer's actions. What began as an "open fields" doctrine led to a doctrine that attempts to come to grips with visual entries of dwelling houses. But the doctrine of privacy is not confined to dwelling houses. For example, the leading case expanding the right of privacy emerged from electronic surveillance of the occupant of a telephone booth.

Although the most frequent application of the right of privacy results from entry and/or search of a dwelling house, the question also is important in clandestine observation of public rest rooms. It is generally conceded that when a person leaves his home, he sheds a substantial amount of privacy and must tolerate conduct from others that he would forbid in his own home. Yet a person does not surrender all of his right of privacy when he enters public property or places. Most courts that have considered the question have held that a person retains a minimum amount of privacy when he enters a public rest room and closes the toilet door. Despite the well-known pattern of homosexuals in entering adjoining toilet stalls to engage in mutual masturbation, sodomy, and similar acts which violate penal laws, the courts have held that absent some basis to arrest the occupants prior to entering the toilet stalls, the act of spying and waiting to observe illegal conduct constitutes a "search" without probable cause in the constitutional sense and one that is consequently unreasonable. These rules necessarily reduce the use of spy holes, two-way mirrors, and similar police practices. Of course, if the conduct was open to the view of anyone inside the rest room, officers could arrest for a public offense committed in their presence. Because of these rulings, many public places have removed toilet stalls or restructured the premises to allow open surveillance. As a consequence, no one can enjoy privacy in the elimination of bodily waste. Curiously, this result occurred because the courts attempted to preserve privacy.

Cases and Materials

Bielicki v. *Superior Court*, 57 Cal. 2d 602, 371 P. 2d 388.

Britt v. *Superior Court*, 58 Cal. 2d 469, 374 P. 2d 817.

Coolidge v. *New Hampshire*, 403 U.S. 443, 91 S. Ct. 2022, 29 L. Ed. 2d 564.

Harris v. *United States*, 390 U.S. 234, 88 S. Ct. 992, 19 L. Ed. 2d 1067.

Hester v. *United States*, 265 U.S. 57, 44 S. Ct. 445, 68 L. Ed. 895.

Katz v. *United States*, 389 U.S. 347, 88 S. Ct. 507, 19 L. Ed. 2d 576.

McDowell v. *United States*, 383 F. 2d 599.

People v. *Edwards*, 71 Cal. 2d 1096, 458 P. 2d 713.

People v. *Sirhan*, 7 Cal. 3d 710, 102 Cal. R. 385.

People v. *Terry*, 70 Cal. 2d 410, 454 P. 2d 36.

1. Officers lawfully enter a home based on information that the defendant had just sold marijuana to an informant. Discovering no one inside, they observe a closed paper bag lying on the floor. This bag, and its contents, emit a strong odor of marijuana. On opening the bag, officers observe marijuana. Several hours later the defendant returns home and is arrested.

Was there a search?

2. Officers received untested information that the defendant possesses stolen property in his home. After securing approval of the adjoining landowner, they maintain a constant surveillance of the defendant's home from a vantage point in the second story of the neighbor's house. Unable to see clearly, they use binoculars to improve their view.

Is such conduct an unreasonable violation of the defendant's privacy? Suppose that the officers observe the defendant commit a homicide while they are seeking evidence of possession of stolen property? Would the legal analysis differ if they see only the stolen property?

3. "An officer testified that he received an anonymous telephone call. He was advised that a female Caucasian, about 20 years old with long blond hair, was engaged in prostitution at a specific apartment. Officers went to the above address to investigate the informer's tip. Upon arrival, the officers walked to the fourth floor of the building. No activity was observed in the hallway. A fire escape was located at the south end of the hallway next to defendant's apartment, and was attached to the outside of the building. To gain access to the fire escape it was necessary to pass through a doorway marked "Exit." Photographs of the fire escape, introduced into the record, indicated that the escape ladder could be reached by going directly through the exit door to the head of the descent ladder. The officer stepped out onto the fire escape and stepped to his left two or three feet, which placed him in front of a window of the apartment, through which he could observe the inside of that apartment. Looking through the window the officer observed defendant seated at a kitchen table. In front of her on the table was a clear plastic bag containing marijuana." While one officer was on the outside fire escape, the other officer went to the door of the apartment and knocked on the door. The door was opened, at which time the officer entered and placed the defendant under arrest for possession of marijuana. (*Cohen* v. *Superior Court*, 5 Cal. App. 3d 429, 85 Cal. R. 354.)

Was there a search?

4. An envelope was found by a police officer assigned to security at the rear of a certain residence to keep unauthorized persons away. The officer said that he made a "search" of the residence rear yard, at the back of which is a fence. Several boxes of trash were in the rear, and the officer stated that he found an envelope lying in a box of trash containing garbage and papers. The envelope was partly wadded up, lying in the trash. When subsequently asked by the prosecutor when he made the "search," he said that he had a paper cup and had walked over to drop it in the trash; it was at this time that he noticed the envelope. It had writing on it, and he picked it up out of curiosity, looked at it, and later delivered it to another officer.

Was this act an unreasonable invasion of privacy?

5. An officer received a call from the assistant superintendent of schools who stated that he had reason to believe that there had been marijuana parties at a certain location. He and other officers went to the residence. One officer parked his car and walked along an alley behind the house. Music and voices were coming from inside, which indicated to him that a party was in progress. The officer walked around the side of the house through an orange grove to the front of the house where three windows opened into the dining room. He was aware that he and the other officers were on private property at the time.

"There were bushes along the house in front of the windows. The bushes were so close to the house that their branches touched the windows and house. To get a clear view through the windows, the officers stood between the bushes and the house. Heavy drapes at the sides of the windows did not substantially obstruct the officer's view, and he could see what was going on inside through the thin curtains that covered the windows.

"[The officers] observed the activities in the dining room for about 15 minutes from this position. Two young women were seated at the dining room table and three or four men were standing towards the back of the room. . . . He observed two men smoking a cigarette in a manner that suggested it was a marijuana cigarette. The cigarette itself did not appear to be an ordinary cigarette. Finally, the officer recognized one of the men in the room as a person he had previously investigated in connection with a narcotics case. The officers then saw someone stagger, as though drunk, out the front door to a car. The officer left his position by the window and walked up to the front door." (*Mann* v. *Superior Court,* 3 Cal. 3d 1, 472 P. 2d 468.)

Will a search be lawful?

6. Early one morning police officers observed in a vacant lot a stripped, engineless Ford automobile that had not been there the day before. An immediate investigation disclosed that it had recently been stolen. The defendant, who was known to the officers, lived nearby, from which area the car could have "been pushed." He had, according to officers, "changed parts, put new car parts or newer car parts on old cars, old Fords."

Considering him a suspect, the officers went to his home. Alongside the house was a driveway about thirty feet in length, running from the sidewalk to the backyard. The officers walked up the driveway to the rear edge of the house, where, in the backyard, they saw bucket seats, an automobile transmission lying on the ground and "a homemade wooden A-frame type of hoist with a chain hoist, and a Ford engine hanging from it." They also observed lying on the ground gas receipts and an automobile registration certificate on which could be seen the name of the owner. All of the things seen were in plain sight of the officers. There was no gate or fence between the sidewalk and the property seen in the backyard. From the sidewalk the subject property could not have been seen.

Was this a violation of the defendant's right of privacy in his back-yard?

7. "A deputy sheriff, an experienced narcotics officer, was told by an informer of unknown reliability that defendant had marijuana in his house, was engaged in selling it, and was on parole for its possession. The informer also gave information concerning defendant's car. The next evening the same informer told the deputy that defendant was growing marijuana by a fig tree at the rear of his residence.

"After receiving this second report, he went to the defendant's address. The premises included a house that faced the street; a driveway that ran along the east of the house and terminated in a garage at the rear and east of the house; [the] defendant's residence which was attached to the rear of the garage; and a large 'fenced in yard' to the west of defendant's residence. . . .

"The deputy, noticing that defendant's car was gone, believed he was away and went into the 'rear yard area' to investigate. There he saw a marijuana plant in a keg two or three feet from the base of a fig tree that was about 20 feet from defendant's door. The officer did not know if the tree was in the backyard of the owner (who presumably lived in the front house) or of defendant. It was necessary for the officer to be within almost a foot of the tree to distinguish the marijuana plant. According to the officer, the keg was 'partially covered by the leaves and the limbs of the fig tree.' When later asked if the 'marijuana plant was hidden under the fig tree,' the officer replied, 'I don't believe you could say exactly hidden, however, it was covered by foliage.' He did not have a search warrant."

The appropriate test is whether the person has exhibited a reasonable expectation of privacy, and, if so, whether that expectation has been violated by unreasonable governmental intrusion. "Measured by that test, the officer's discovery and seizure of the marijuana plants in the yard adjacent to defendant's residence did not violate the constitutional prohibitions against unreasonable searches and seizures. From the recited evidence it may be inferred that the marijuana plants were partially but not totally covered by foliage. It does not appear that the plants were covered by nontransparent material, and it may be inferred that at least part of the plants were in plain sight of anyone within a foot of the tree.

Although they were in a rear yard that was fenced to an undisclosed extent, they were located a scant 20 feet from defendant's door to which presumably delivery men and others came, and the front house, as well as defendant's house, apparently had access to the yard. Under the circumstances it does not appear that defendant exhibited a subjective expectation of privacy as to the plants. Furthermore, any such expectation would have been unreasonable." (*People* v. *Bradley,* 1 Cal. 80, 460 P. 2d 129.)

Chapter Five

Search Warrants

The vast majority of cases clearly involve a "search" in the constitutional sense, and the issue now becomes whether the search was "reasonable." Because reasonable searches are not defined in the Fourth Amendment, the courts have fleshed out the concept of reasonableness. By constitutional definition, a search executed pursuant to the authority of a lawful warrant is reasonable. Search warrants are clothed with a presumption of legality, and the burden rests on the defendant to rebut the presumption. For this reason, searches conducted pursuant to warrants are more easily sustainable in court.

Although search-warrant procedure varies from state to state, the U.S. Supreme Court has held that the authority of the Fourth Amendment is paramount over state statutes. A search warrant that is drafted and executed in harmony with the Fourth Amendment will be a lawful search despite state statutes that may not specifically authorize seizure of a particular form of evidence under the authority of a warrant. For example, a state statute may not specifically authorize seizure of "mere evidence," as distinct from seizure of contraband or stolen property. Yet the U.S. Supreme Court has interpreted the Fourth Amendment to include the seizure of mere evidence as the substantial equivalent of a seizure of contraband. Mere evidence, therefore, could be seized pursuant to a search warrant, even if not specifically authorized by a state statute. A state could specifically *prohibit* the seizure of mere evidence, however, since the U.S. Supreme Court has always held that state courts or state constitutions may be more restrictive than the Fourth Amendment.

A search warrant is a judicial order commanding a peace officer to search for specific property, seize it, and return it to court. The U.S. Supreme Court has held that "property" includes not only tangible physical evidence, but also telephone conversations (see chapter 12, Wiretapping and Eavesdropping). But most warrants issue for the search of contraband, stolen property, weapons, instrumentalities of a crime, or for evidence of a crime. An officer seeking to search for any of these items must obtain a judicial order, i.e., the warrant, based on a showing that there is probable cause to believe that the designated property is present on the premises or in the vehicle to be searched. The process of obtaining a written search warrant generally requires three stages: application for the warrant, declaration of probable cause, and filing an inventory of property seized.

The Warrant

In some states, the warrant is preprinted to conform to statutory requirements. The warrant alleges that a specific peace officer applied for the warrant and, based on a showing of probable cause, the magistrate issued the warrant. The warrant authorizes a search of specific premises, or of a specific motor vehicle, to seize specific property. If necessary, a search warrant can authorize the seizure of property located elsewhere, i.e., in a safe-deposit box, first-class mail, airport locker, luggage, or other containers. These two requirements—where to search and what to search for—are all that the officer needs in preparing the warrant itself.

The requirement of specificity of place to be searched and things to be seized is in conformity with the warrant clause of the Fourth Amendment. That clause states: ". . . and no warrants shall issue . . . but upon probable cause . . . particularly describing the place to be searched and the things or persons to be seized." This clause was included in the Fourth Amendment to prevent the then familiar colonial practice of issuing general warrants. Royal magistrates issued warrants sufficiently vague to justify the search of any house, boat, or wagon that seemed appropriate to the executing officer. Nor was there any limit to the extent or scope of the search once begun. To prevent these practices, the framers of the Constitution required all warrants to specify the particular place to be searched, and restricted the scope of that search to particularly described property.[1]

---

1. The requirement that the . . . . "person to be seized" must also be particularly identified applies to warrants of arrest as well.

For these reasons, an applicant for a search warrant must describe the place to be searched as specifically as the facts allow. Normally, a specific residential address is sufficient, but additional identifying details strengthen the warrant, i.e., nearest intersecting streets; a description of the exterior of the house; the location of adjoining property or buildings. Officers can also expand the place to be searched by listing garages, sheds, or storage areas. In the case of a search warrant for an apartment, the individual living unit should be isolated and identified. In the case of motor vehicles, the most precise available description of the vehicle should be inserted.

In describing "things to be seized," officers should include as many details of the property to be seized as possible. The more specific the description, the stronger the warrant. In applying for a search warrant to seize narcotics, officers frequently include an order to seize all paraphernalia that frequently accompanies the use of heroin, cocaine, and similar contraband. To strengthen the connection of the defendant to the ownership of the seized property, officers may request a judicial order to seize rent receipts or utility bills that establish occupancy and, presumptively, possession of the seized property. Ordinarily a preprinted form can accomplish these objectives.

The Affidavit

The Fourth Amendment commands that "no warrants shall issue but upon probable cause . . ." The affidavit is a statement of probable cause reciting the officer's basis for believing specifically described property will be located at a specific location. The affidavit contains all the personal observations of the officer, reports of informants, circumstantial factors, or the results of an investigation that would lead the magistrate to conclude the warrant should issue. The affidavit must recite facts, not conclusions, from which inferences can be drawn. But the quantity of facts is not necessarily persuasive—it is the quality of those facts which, when combined together, add up to probable cause.

In most cases, the officer's affidavit will be based on the hearsay statements of an informant. The sufficiency of this information to establish probable cause is measured under a "two-prong" test enunciated by the U.S. Supreme Court in *Aguilar* v. *Texas*: "Although an affidavit may be based on hearsay information and need not reflect the direct personal observations of the affiant . . . the magistrate must be informed of some of the underlying circumstances from which the informant concluded that the narcotics were where he claimed they were, and some of the underlying circumstances from which the officer concluded the informant . . . was 'credible' or his information 'reliable.' "

This test can be restated thus: first, the statement of the informer recited in the affidavit must be factual in nature rather than conclusional and must indicate that the informer had personal knowledge of the facts related; second, the affidavit must contain some underlying factual information from which the issuing judge can reasonably conclude that the informant was credible or his information reliable. In other words, the magistrate's finding of probable cause can be sustained only if the affidavit presents a substantial basis for crediting the hearsay.

As discussed earlier (see the section Informational Probable Cause in chapter 3, Arrest), the requirement of an informant's personal knowledge, i.e., the "first prong," is essential to enable a magistrate to rely on something more substantial than a casual rumor circulating in the underworld or on accusations based merely on an individual's reputation. It is not entirely clear in all jurisdictions whether the affidavit must reflect a direct statement of the informant's personal knowledge. Arguably, to permit a conclusional allegation of "personal knowledge" to satisfy the requirements of *Aguilar* would defeat the policy in favor of specificity reflected by that case, as well as the requirement of a showing before a magistrate sufficient to provide a reasonable basis for intrusion on Fourth Amendment rights. "In common usage, 'personal knowledge' is not always the equivalent of 'I saw,' but often refers merely to matters which the informer heard or read from a source which he credits, and the test is not whether the informer had doubts about his information, but whether an independent magistrate should credit the informer's information." (*Price* v. *Superior Court.*) For example:

"A detective engaged in the investigation of illicit narcotics traffic, testified that he had been informed by a certain named juvenile that one 'Dewey' had furnished marijuana and restricted dangerous drugs to said juvenile within the immediately preceding three weeks; that 'Dewey' was presently dealing in narcotics at a certain address; and that 'Dewey' had previously dealt in narcotics at other premises described by the juvenile; that lists of telephone numbers and names contained in the juvenile's wallet contain the name of 'Dewey,' among others, and contained a telephone number (which was verified to be a number listed at the premises alleged to be 'Dewey's' present address); and that he removed notes from [the juvenile's] wallet which the juvenile identified as being a price list for 'stuff,' which was identified by the juvenile as marijuana and a price list for 'spoons' for meth-amphetamine. The juvenile stated the price list was furnished to him by 'Dewey.' Finally, the landlady at the premises alleged by the juvenile to be 'Dewey's' present address had told the officer that the premises were occupied by a man matching the physical description of 'Dewey' provided by the juvenile." (*People* v. *Scoma.*)

In this case, the hearsay statements reporting illegal activity are factual in nature and clearly indicate that the informant had personal knowledge of such illegal activity.

In *Spinelli* v. *United States*, the affidavit stated that the FBI, one of whose agents had prepared the affidavit, " 'has been informed by a confidential reliable informant that William Spinelli is operating a handbook and accepting wagers and disseminating wagering information by means of the telephones which have been assigned the numbers WYdown 4-0029 and WYdown 4-0136.' The affidavit also stated that independent investigation had confirmed that the telephones in question were located in a certain apartment at which Spinelli was a frequent visitor." The court, holding that the affidavit fell short of constitutional sufficiency because it did not reveal the basis of the informant's conclusion, stated: "The tip [of the informant as reflected in the affidavit] does not contain a sufficient statement of the underlying circumstances from which the informer concluded that Spinelli was running a book-making operation. We are not told how the FBI's source received his information—it is not alleged that the informant personally observed Spinelli at work or that he ever placed a bet with him. Moreover, if the informant came by the information indirectly, he did not explain why his sources were reliable."

Compare this officer's affidavit: "That said affiant was informed . . . by a confidential reliable informant that Nora Mae Hamilton and John Doe Tony have in their possession at a white single story, one-family dwelling located on a [certain street] . . . approximately three hundred (300) rolls of dangerous drugs wrapped in tin foil in groups of ten pills per roll. That further your affiant reviewed the County Sheriff Office report which indicated Nora Mae Hamilton and Raymond David Padilla were arrested in that house within the last two months for possession of marijuana and possession of dangerous drugs found there. The pills found in that arrest were amphetamine, wrapped in tin foil in groups of 10. That said confidential reliable informant has furnished information in the past which has led to eight (8) arrest[s] and convictions for narcotic and dangerous drug offense."

The court said: "While the courts do not reject the possibility that an informant who fails to provide factual allegations of his own experience might nevertheless provide a description of the contraband itself, or its particular location, so detailed as to warrant the inference of personal observation, the description here in question is insufficient for that purpose. Thus, in the *Spinelli* case, it was urged that the facts provided by the informant, and especially the specific telephone numbers given by him, were sufficient to show 'that the informer had gained his information in a reliable way.' The court rejected this argument: 'This meager report could easily have been obtained from an offhand remark heard at a neighborhood bar.' Similarly, in the instant case, the informant could have obtained his information as to the amount of dangerous drugs involved, and the way in which it was packaged, from an unreliable source. In order to infer, in the absence of direct factual allegations, that the informant had personal knowledge of the incriminating facts related by him, more significant detail must be recited than is present in the instant affidavit." (*People* v. *Hamilton*)

Although an express declaration of personal knowledge is legally stronger, the court might approve an implied personal knowledge inferred from recited facts.

For example, an officer testified that at about 10 P.M. on Saturday, he listened to a telephone call to his partner from an informer, whose voice the officer recognized from a prior telephone conversation about eight months previous, and whose tips had resulted in arrest and conviction on at least six prior occasions. He testified as follows:

"The information was that a person known as Benny Aguirre— and the [informant] also gave us a license number of his car—had crossed the border on Saturday night and was bringing a large shipment of dangerous drugs into the United States and that he would have these drugs in his apartment. And he gave the address."

On cross-examination, the officer testified that he had a second conversation with the same informant on Sunday. With respect to this conversation, the officer testified that the informant told him Mr. Aguirre was in Los Angeles, that he had brought a very large shipment of dangerous drugs to Los Angeles, that he brought it in sometime Saturday night, and that it was now in his apartment.

It is clear that had the informer alleged that he had been inside the house and had seen the contraband, this would have satisfied the personal knowledge requirement. The informer here could not make his allegation based on personal observation, which if his vision were satisfactory would prove a highly reliable report. He instead relied on what he was told by defendant.

"The officer did not testify that the informant had said that the personal word from defendant was his source of knowledge for the balance of the information—that on Saturday he had crossed the border with the drugs and that now (Sunday) defendant was at his apartment and that the contraband was there. However, information from an informant that the defendant told him what he would do in the near future and then that he had done it (although the latter is not attributable to direct word from defendant) appears to meet the *Aguilar-Spinelli* standard. The source aspect of the first segment of information carries over to the second." (*People* v. *Aguirre*.)

In analyzing the second prong of the *Aguilar* test—facts indicating the credibility or reliability of the informant—the magistrate must conclude from the recited facts that the informant is a source he can credit in determining whether to issue the warrant (or, to assess probable cause to arrest). The basis for that decision lies with the officer's recital of the identity of the informant and his past experience with him or of evidence of corroborating facts.

For example: An arresting officer testified that he and two fellow officers had had a conversation with an informant in their unmarked police car. The officer said that the "informant had told them that the defendant, with whom the officer was acquainted, 'was selling narcotics and had narcotics on his person and that he could be found in the vicinity of a nearby intersection at this particular time.' The officer said that he and his fellow officers drove to that vicinity in the police car and that when they spotted the defendant, the informant pointed him out and then departed on foot. The officer stated that they observed the defendant walking with a woman, then separating from her and meeting briefly with a man, then proceeding alone, and finally, after seeing the police car, 'hurriedly walk[ing] between two buildings.' 'At this point,' the officer testified, 'my partner and myself got out of the car and informed him we had information he had narcotics on his person, placed him in the police vehicle at this point.' The officer stated that the officers then searched the defendant and found the heroin in a cigarette package. . . .

"The officer testified that he had been acquainted with the informant for approximately a year, that during this period the informant had supplied him with information about narcotics activities 'fifteen, sixteen times at least,' that the information had proved to be accurate and had resulted in numerous arrests and convictions. On cross-examination the officer was even more specific as to the informant's previous reliability, giving the names of people who had been convicted of narcotics violations as the result of information the informant had supplied.

"The other officer testified the informant 'said he had observed [the defendant] selling narcotics to various people, meaning various addicts, in the same vicinity.' He testified that he had known the informant 'roughly two years,' that the informant had given him information concerning narcotics '20 or 25 times,' and that the information had resulted in convictions.

"Each of the officers in this case described with specificity 'what the informer actually said, and why the officer thought the information was credible.' The testimony of each of the officers informed the court of the underlying circumstances from which the informant concluded that the narcotics were where he claimed they were, and some of the underlying circumstances from which the officer concluded that the informant . . . was 'credible' or his information 'reliable.' " On the basis of those circumstances, along with the officers' personal observations of the defendant, the court was fully justified in holding that at the time the officers made the arrest "the facts and circumstances within their knowledge and of which they had reasonably trustworthy information were sufficient to warrant a prudent man in believing that the defendant had committed or was commiting an offense." (*McCray* v. *Illinois.*) Although in this case the information led to arrest, rather than an affidavit for a search warrant, the principles are similar.

In the foregoing case, the officer testified to his own previous experience with the informant and the results of that experience. Now reexamine the testimony of the officer in *Scoma*, whose informant was Dewey (page 90).

It is clear that no facts were stated relative to informant Dewey's identity that indicate the reliability of information given by him. Further, there are no facts indicating past police experience with the informant. Thus, the only significant facts suggesting that the informant's report of illegal activity was reliable are "(1) [from other testimony] that certain substances found in the informant's possession were identified by laboratory analysis as narcotics; (2) that the landlady at 'Dewey's' alleged residence confirmed that a man matching 'Dewey's' description lived at that address; (3) that certain lists of names and telephone numbers obtained from the informant's wallet contained the name and telephone number of 'Dewey' among others; and (4) that certain notes found in the informant's wallet were identified by him as narcotics price lists which had been furnished to him by 'Dewey.'

"The foregoing facts provide no basis upon which the magistrate could reasonably conclude that the informant's report of illegal activity on the part of 'Dewey' was reliable information. The fact that the informant was found to possess narcotics gives no credence to his assertion that he obtained such narcotics from a named person; he obviously obtained them from someone, but mere possession cannot constitute support for his claim that he obtained them from one person rather than another. Of no greater assistance is the fact that 'Dewey's' past and present addresses were those provided by the informant; again, no inference of criminal activity on 'Dewey's' part may be drawn from that 'fact.'

"Despite the detailed information recited by the officer, he could not establish the reliability, or credibility, of his source. Absent a reliable source, the officer could create a substantial basis for crediting the hearsay only if he could corroborate the informant. Did the notes and list obtained from the informant provide corroboration of the information? Granting that the lists and notes might have been written before the informant was apprehended or knew that he was going to be interviewed by police, this would show at most only that the informant possessed a narcotics price list and that the name and telephone number of the person he accused of illegal activity appeared 'among others' on a list in his wallet. It cannot reasonably be maintained that the list of names and telephone numbers supported the informant's accusation of 'Dewey' any more than it would have supported his accusation of any other person on that list.

"Thus it appears that none of the facts provide corroborative support for the informant's accusation of illegal activity on the part of 'Dewey.' This is so because they amount to merely a reiteration of the accusation by the informant; there is nothing to indicate that additional facts independently known or discovered by the police supported the accusation to thereby impart credit to the informant." (*People* v. *Scoma.*)

In cases where no investigation is conducted to corroborate the informant, or where the investigation is insufficient to corroborate the informant's statement, the officer may be able to establish the informant's reliability from the statement alone if the statement is internally reliable and is corroborated by other significant evidence.

For example: A federal tax investigator testified that the defendant "has had a reputation with me for over 4 years as being a trafficker of nontaxpaid distilled spirits, and over this period I have received numerous reports from all types of persons as to his activities. A constable located a sizable stash of illicit whiskey in an abandoned house under [his] control during this period of time. I received information personally from a person whom I have found prudent, and gained the following information: This person has personal knowledge of and has purchased illicit whiskey from within the residence described, for a period of more than 2 years, and most recently within the past 2 weeks, has knowledge of a person who purchased illicit whiskey within the past two days from the house, has personal knowledge that the illicit whiskey is consumed by purchasers in the outbuilding known as and utilized as the 'dance hall,' and has seen [the defendant] go to the other outbuilding, located about 50 yards from the residence, on numerous occasions, to obtain the whiskey for this person and other persons.

"The substance of the tip recounts personal and recent observations by a known informant of criminal activity. The facts show that the information had been gained in a reliable manner, as distinguished from information which fails to explain how the informant came by his information. The affidavit in the present case contained a substantial basis for crediting the hearsay. The informant purported to relate his personal observations—a factor that clearly distinguishes cases where the informant failed to explain how he came by his information. The affidavit recites prior events within the affiant's own knowledge—the prior seizure of alcohol—indicating that the defendant had previously trafficked in contraband."

The Court said that a policeman's knowledge of a suspect's. reputation—something that policemen frequently know—is a factor on which an officer (or a magistrate) may properly rely in assessing the reliability of an informant's tip.

Moreover, the informant stated that over the past two years he had many times and recently purchased "illicit whiskey." These statements "were against the informant's penal interest, for he thereby admitted major elements of an offense under the Internal Revenue Code. Common sense in the important daily affairs of life would induce a prudent and disinterested observer to credit these statements. People do not lightly admit a crime and place critical evidence in the hands of the police in the form of their own admissions. Admissions of crime, like admissions against proprietary interests, carry their own indicia of credibility— sufficient at least to support a finding of probable cause. That the informant may be paid or promised a 'break' does not eliminate the residual risk and opprobrium of having admitted criminal conduct. Concededly, admissions of crime do not always lend credibility to contemporaneous or later accusations of another. But here the informant's admission that over a long period and currently he had been buying illicit liquor on certain premises itself, implicated that property and furnished probable cause."

In this case, *United States* v. *Harris*, the U.S. Supreme Court concluded that the following facts were relevant in evaluating the reliability of the source: a statement reflecting the informant's personal observation of the seizable evidence on the suspect's person or in his possession; a statement against the informant's penal interest by admitting complicity in the crime; the reputation of the suspect as known to the officers.

Corroboration of the informant can also be supplied by the officers' independent verification of the tip. Consider the following case:

"A federal narcotic agent with 29 years' experience was stationed at Denver; one Hereford had been engaged as a 'special employee' of the Bureau of Narcotics at Denver for about six months, and from time to time gave information to the agent regarding violations of the narcotic laws, for which Hereford was paid small sums of money, and the agent had always found the information given by Hereford to be accurate and reliable. On September 3, Hereford told the agent that Draper (defendant) recently had taken up abode at a stated address in Denver and 'was peddling narcotics to several addicts' in that city.

Four days later, on September 7, Hereford told the agent 'that Draper had gone to Chicago the day before [September 6] by train [and] that he was going to bring back three ounces of heroin [and] that he would return to Denver either on the morning of the 8th of September or the morning of the 9th of September also by train.' Hereford also gave the agent a detailed physical description of Draper and of the clothing he was wearing, and said that he would be carrying 'a tan zipper bag,' and that he habitually 'walked real fast.'

"On the morning of September 8, the agent and a Denver police officer went to the Denver Union Station and kept watch over all incoming trains from Chicago, but they did not see anyone fitting the description that Hereford had given. Repeating the process on the morning of September 9, they saw a person, having the exact physical attributes and wearing the precise clothing described by Hereford, alight from an incoming Chicago train and start walking 'fast' toward the exit. He was carrying a tan zipper bag in his right hand and the left was thrust in his raincoat pocket. The agent, accompanied by the police officer, overtook, stopped and arrested him. They then searched him and found the two 'envelopes containing heroin' clutched in his left hand in his raincoat pocket.

"The information given to the narcotic agent by 'special employee' Hereford may have been hearsay to the agent, but coming from one employed for that purpose and whose information had always been found accurate and reliable, it is clear that the agent would have been derelict in his duties had he not pursued it. And when, in pursuing that information, he saw a man, having the exact physical attributes and wearing the precise clothing and carrying the tan zipper bag that Hereford had described, alight from one of the very trains from the very place stated by Hereford and start to walk at a 'fast' pace toward the station exit, the agent had personally verified every facet of the information given him by Hereford except whether defendant had accomplished his mission and had the three ounces of heroin on his person or in his bag. With every other bit of Hereford's information being thus personally verified, the agent had 'reasonable grounds' to believe that the remaining unverified bit of Hereford's information—that Draper would have the heroin with him—was likewise true." (*Draper* v. *United States.*)

Nor is the determination of a magistrate to issue a warrant confined to the informant's hearsay statements, which may be defective under one of *Aguilar's* two-prong requirements. If the detailed results of the officer's independent investigation of the case are presented, together with the hearsay statement of the informant (inadequate by itself), the affidavit will stand, provided that when taken as a whole, sufficient facts are set forth as would lead a man of ordinary caution or prudence to believe, and conscientiously entertain, a strong suspicion of the guilt of the accused.

For example: The affidavit in support of the warrant was subscribed and sworn to by an officer. "It was quite extensive and reflected an investigation of defendant's activities which had taken place over a period of more than two months. In summary, the affidavit alleged: (a) that pursuant to an informant's tip that the defendant was bookmaking, officers undertook surveillance of a shoe repair shop; (b) that in the course of such surveillance officers saw defendant meeting with known bettors and immediately thereafter placing calls at a public telephone; (c) that in the course of such events officers overheard defendant's conversation indicating he was involved in bookmaking and wished to conduct his activities from a 'phone spot'; (d) that pursuant to a further tip from the informant officers undertook surveillance of a certain apartment wherein defendant was, according to the informant, accepting bets by telephone; (e) that in the course of such surveillance officers observed that defendant occupied the apartment during daytime hours on days when racing took place; and (f) that the officers saw defendant in the company of a person known to head a bookmaking organization and also saw defendant meet with this person at a time when the latter was known to conduct the business of the organization.

"A printed form contained three statements purporting to bear on the question of personal knowledge. The first, which had been stricken out by the affiant, provided: 'Your affiant states that the said confidential reliable informant did speak with personal knowledge when imparting the information hereinafter set forth, unless and except where specifically stated to be otherwise.' The second statement provided: 'The said informant stated that he, the said informant, did speak with personal knowledge, unless and except where specifically stated to be otherwise.' The third statement provided: 'The context and details related by the informant revealed that he, the said informant, did obtain the information through the informant's personal knowledge, unless and except where specifically stated to be otherwise.'

"The hearsay statements of the informant were not sufficient *in themselves* to justify issuance of the warrant. It is clear that the statements appearing on the printed form are not of the factual and specific nature necessary to permit the magistrate to conclude that the incriminating facts related by the informant were gleaned through personal observation rather than rumor or gossip.

"However, consideration of the affidavit is not limited to an assessment of the hearsay statements contained therein. The affiant and his fellow officers here undertook a diligent and careful investigation in order to amass incriminating facts, and the results of that examination are reflected in the affidavit by means of detailed and precise allegations grounded in personal observation. Taking together the allegations based upon the officers' observations and the hearsay statements of the informant, the affidavit as a whole sets forth facts 'such as would lead a man of ordinary caution or prudence to believe, and conscientiously entertain, a strong suspicion of the guilt of the accused.' " (*People* v. *Benjamin.*)

Although drafting the warrant and developing evidence of supporting probable cause may seem complex, the U.S. Supreme Court has eased some of the seemingly strict requirements. In *United States* v. *Ventresca*, a case which established a judicial policy for evaluating search warrants and affidavits, the court said: "If the teachings of the Court's cases are to be followed and the constitutional policy served, affidavits for search warrants, such as the one involved here, *must be tested and interpreted by magistrates and courts in a commonsense and realistic fashion*. They are normally drafted by nonlawyers in the midst and haste of a criminal investigation. Technical requirements of elaborate specificity once exacted under common law pleadings have no proper place in this area. A grudging or negative attitude by reviewing courts toward warrants will tend to discourage police officers from submitting their evidence to a judicial officer before acting. . . . Where . . . circumstances are detailed, where reason for crediting the source of the information is given, and when a magistrate has found probable cause, the courts should not invalidate the warrant by interpreting the affidavit in a hypertechnical, rather than a *commonsense, manner*." [Emphasis added.]

Because issuance of a search warrant is essentially a judicial act, the U.S. Supreme Court has denied authority for nonjudicial officials to issue search warrants. To resolve issues of probable cause, the court requires the judgment of a disinterested magistrate over that of law enforcement officials engaged in the competitive business of ferreting out crime. Despite statutory authorization of various state officials to issue warrants, the Fourth Amendment allows only judicial officers to issue warrants—at least for serious crimes.[2]

In some jurisdictions attempts have been made to avoid the time-consuming procedures involved in written search warrants by experimenting with oral search warrants. Under this system, the officer contacts the District Attorney or magistrate and recites his probable cause over the telephone. If satisfied, the magistrate orally authorizes the officer's search. The officer signs the magistrate's name to a copy of the warrant on the strength of the magistrate's authorization. The

---

2. In *Shadwick* v. *City of Tampa*, 92 S. Ct. 2119, the Supreme Court approved issuance of traffic warrants by city clerks.

magistrate retains a duplicate original warrant for court files. Provision is often made to record and later transcribe the phone conversation for use in court.

Another method is personal examination of the informant by the magistrate. A magistrate places the informant under oath and takes his testimony. This recorded statement of probable cause replaces the affidavit. The personal appearance of the informant improves the magistrate's ability to assess his credibility and enables him to ask questions that would otherwise be impossible if the magistrate were reading a written affidavit.

Although not yet tried, television offers an opportunity to expedite the warrant process. The officer, or even the informant himself, could be questioned over television without the necessity of a court appearance. Television also minimizes security considerations in bringing an informant-arrestee to court. A two-way audio link between the court and officers would enable communication to take place, even if only one-way video were possible.

Execution and Return

The Fourth Amendment contains no provision concerning the service of a warrant, although most state statutes provide for execution of the warrant on the occupants of a house. Often the officers must vocally alert the occupants to their presence and announce their authority to enter pursuant to warrant. An announcement of identity and purpose enables the occupants to permit a peaceful entry and avoid the possible violence incidental to the unannounced forcible entry of officers who are usually in plain clothes.

Yet the notice requirement provides an opportunity for the possessor of contraband or stolen property to dispose of such materials before officers can enter. Modern plumbing has greatly facilitated the disposal of contraband. Even without the toilet, the small size of contraband drugs and narcotics facilitates their disposal or concealment. Confronted with such a dilemma, officers must either obtain advance judicial approval in the warrant to enter unannounced or testify that they had information that the defendant had planned the disposal or concealment of narcotics if confronted by officers. The source may be an informant, or the circumstances at the time of the service of the warrant prior to entry may authorize dispensing with the requirement of notice. (See chapter 11, Entry.)

The affidavit, as a statement of probable cause, normally recites information that reflects past criminal conduct, i.e., activity done prior to the filing of the affidavit. Necessarily, days or hours elapse between the time the informant learned of the criminal activity and the time such activity is presented to the magistrate in the affidavit. Yet search warrants will only issue for the search and seizure of property currently possessed in a car or building. Thus, the affidavit must reflect an inference from past possession of seizable evidence that such evidence is presently possessed in the car or on the premises. "Present possession" must be established, or, put another way, the information must not be stale.

For example: "Jones was an inhabitant of a town, married, gainfully employed, and a nephew of an investigator of the county district attorney's office. He had been a user of marijuana, as a result of which he had knowledge of 'the basic characteristics' of that material and was able 'to tentatively identify' it. On or after May 2, Jones related to an investigator that on May 2, at a residence known as 1184 White Lane, he had observed (1) a quantity of green vegetable matter in a transparent glass jar which he believed to be marijuana; (2) a large transparent glass bottle containing a quantity of what he believed to be marijuana seeds; and (3) a 'male subject exit a vehicle at the address on White Lane and hand a package of unknown substance to another male subject also at this location in exchange for which he received an undetermined amount of currency.' On May 13 another informant advised officers that within the previous 30 days he had observed occupants of that address in possession of marijuana. On May 22 a warrant was issued."

Quoting from *Sgro* v. *United States*, the Court said: "While most statutes do not fix the time within which proof of probable cause must be taken to the judge or commissioner, it is manifest that the proof must be of facts so closely related to the time of the issue of the warrant as to justify a finding of probable cause at that time. Jones' information related to matters occurring on May 2 while the subject of the other informant's report occurred May 13. Thus nine days elapsed between the date marijuana was last seen on the premises and the issuance of the search warrant. While the authorities are not in accord as to how current the facts relied upon should be, an interval of not more than 20 days is probably not so unreasonable as to vitiate the search warrant."

Scope of Search

Under the general rule, when a search is made pursuant to a warrant, the search and seizure are limited by the terms of the warrant. Thus only the premises described in the warrant may be searched and only the property described in the warrant may be seized. The U.S. Supreme Court explained the reasons for the rule in *Marron* v. *United States*: "The requirement that the warrant shall particularly describe the things to be seized makes general searches under them impossible and prevents the seizure of one thing under a warrant describing another. . . . nothing is left to the discretion of the officer executing the warrant." However, the rule is not without exceptions and there are two well-established distinctions which validate the seizure of property not named in the warrant.

"First, under prevailing constitutional doctrine, if a valid arrest is made, a search may be conducted incident to the arrest, and might extend beyond the scope of the warrant's authorization.

"The seizure may also fall within the 'plain sight rule,' [or 'plain view' doctrine] the second exception to the principle that only those articles denominated in the warrant may be seized. Briefly reviewed, that rule provides that if officers are legally on the premises and observe what they recognize as contraband 'in plain sight' they may seize it whether or not they possess a warrant and whether or not the warrant includes the contraband observed. The doctrinal rationale, to the extent that one is necessary, has been that no 'search' has taken place since the articles were in plain view. When officers, in the course of a bona fide effort to execute a valid search warrant, discover articles which, although not included in the warrant, are reasonably identifiable as contraband, they may seize them whether they are initially in plain sight or come into plain sight subsequently, as a result of the officers' efforts. . . .

"If a warrant has been properly issued directing that a search be made of the entire premises occupied by a defendant, and the warrant mandated a search for and seizure of several small and easily secreted items, the officers have the authority to conduct an intensive search of the entire house, looking into any places where they might reasonably expect such items to be hidden. With the issuance of this warrant, the judgment has already been made by a judicial officer to permit a serious invasion of defendant's privacy. No legitimate interest is enhanced by imposing artificial restrictions on the reasonable conduct of officers executing the warrant. No purpose is subserved, other than that of an exquisite formalism, by requiring that when the officers discover contraband in the course of this search they return to the issuing magistrate and obtain a second warrant directing the seizure of the additional contraband." (*Skelton* v. *Superior Court*.)

An early U.S. Supreme Court had held that "mere evidence" could not be seized as though it were in the same category as contraband or stolen property, which were unlawful to possess in themselves. Recently, the Supreme Court eliminated any such distinction and held that "mere evidence" should be treated in the same category as contraband or stolen property. Thus, if an officer is searching for contraband and uncovers "mere evidence" of a crime, he may seize it without applying for an additional search warrant. But the officer must confine his original search to areas where the subject property would reasonably be located. As long as the officer is searching in an area where it would be reasonable to discover the object of his search, he may seize other seizable evidence that he discovers.

After entering the premises, officers must consider the following: security of the premises during the course of the search to prevent entry by others; security of the occupants to prevent anyone from leaving the premises carrying evidence on his person or intending to alert others to the officers' presence; identifying areas to be searched. These considerations are practical as well as legal, but only the legal implications are considered here.

Although no U.S. Supreme Court decision has specifically considered the question, there is little doubt that officers can bar entry into the premises during the course of the search. Frequently, an addict or a potential purchaser of narcotics will seek entry into the premises while unaware of the officers' presence. Mere presence by the visitor on the property, or in the hallway or entryway of a dwelling, does not provide probable cause for his arrest. Officers may admit the visitor and question him briefly concerning his presence.[3] From the visitor's conduct, demeanor, or appearance, the officer may conclude that he is under the influence of a drug or narcotic and therefore arrest him for a public offense committed in his presence.

Although preventing entry into the house seems relatively easy, prohibiting an occupant from leaving, or even moving from room to room, is a more difficult question. As a practical matter, the presence of several occupants poses a problem of tactics. From a legal standpoint, prohibiting people from moving about in their own house requires even more scrutiny. Undoubtedly officers can take steps to assure no interference with their search for at least a reasonable time. But searches for narcotics or drugs often extend over several hours. How long can the occupants be required to remain relatively immobile?

---

3. At this point the interrogating officer must consider the case of *Miranda* v. *Arizona* (384 U.S. 436, 86 S. Ct. 1602, 16 L. Ed. 2d 694), also decided by the U.S. Supreme Court. *Miranda* holds that before a person in custody may be questioned, he must be informed of his Fifth Amendment rights to counsel and silence. *Custody* in this sense does not necessarily mean jail custody. If the facts indicate that the officer has placed the suspect under arrest, the warning must be given. Arrest is the substantial equivalent of custody. And the mere formality of pronouncing the arrestee "under arrest" is not conclusive. The issue is whether the suspect believed he was deprived of his freedom of action in any significant way. Whether he was so deprived depends on an objective appraisal of the officer's words and conduct. When the questioning, or the circumstances in general, shift from brief investigatory questions to those of an accusatory or incriminating nature, *custody*—in the constitutional sense—may attach, and the warnings must be given.

There are few cases on this subject, but officers should be able to provide some basis to a reviewing court that the length of the search was reasonable. Obviously such a test is difficult to define, and a "reasonable time" depends on numerous circumstances, all of which should be brought to the attention of the court. If the house was unoccupied when the officers entered, it is arguable that a longer period of search would be approved since interference with personal liberty is not a factor.

Another issue: What authority do officers have to search the occupant of a house prior to, or during, the search of the premises? Under the terms of the warrant, the magistrate has authorized a search of the premises, but he has not necessarily authorized an arrest. If, during the course of a search, the officer discovers seizable evidence, this factor may establish probable cause to arrest. But whom? Would the presence of contraband in one room of a jointly occupied apartment justify the arrest of a co-occupant if he were present? Suppose the co-occupant was absent at the time of the search. Could he be arrested when he returned, or if he did not return, could a warrant of arrest issue? Or, in another case, could the wife be arrested when contraband was discovered in a house jointly occupied by an arrested husband?

These questions are not easily answered. Frequently one occupant of a house will confess ownership of seized property in order to protect another. At trial, however, the confessor may testify that he/she was motivated to lie out of love or fear. If the prosecution is unable to establish the confessing suspect's knowing possession of the seized property, the state may not be able to establish the corpus delicti.[4] Absent proof of the corpus delicti, the confession would not be received in evidence.

Although at this point the searching officers must initially determine whether they have probable cause to arrest one or more of the occupants, they cannot ignore evidence to establish guilt of the crime itself. It is therefore important to consider whether they can seize evidence that will provide proof of guilt beyond a reasonable doubt in addition to probable cause.

The location of the seized property will be significant in determining whether there is evidence of joint ownership. Contraband discovered in a concealed container inside a closed dresser drawer would be weak evidence of knowing possession by a co-occupant living in another room.

---

4. *Corpus delicti*: often referred to erroneously only in reference to homicide. The correct legal definition of *corpus delicti* refers to the elements of the crime. Every crime, including possession of contraband or stolen property, must be proved by establishing certain elements. To convict a person of possession of contraband, the prosecution must establish that the alleged possessor maintained dominion or control over the material with knowledge that the contents were contraband drugs or narcotics.

Seizure of contraband from a location easily accessible to both occupants is stronger evidence of probable cause, but not necessarily
sufficient to convict. Seizure of evidence accessible to both occupants
in conjunction with corroborating evidence, either physical or verbal,
would strengthen the case.

The relationship of the co-occupant—whether tenant or visitor; the
kind of property seized; the physical condition of the occupants; and
similar facts are all relevant on the issue of probable cause as well as
guilt. If probable cause exists, but evidence of guilt is weak, an arrest
is nevertheless justified, and an incidental search of the person may
yield additional corroborating evidence.

Some courts have held that mere presence on the premises prior
to, or during, a search does not convert itself into a reason for arrest.
Yet it is clear that the search must be conducted in reasonable security
since even the entry of the dwelling house alone, prior to search, will
stimulate emotion. Few cases have considered the question, but undoubtedly officers can undertake reasonable measures for their security.
One such step is detention of the occupants to prevent any interference
with the search. Under stop-and-frisk doctrine, officers are authorized
to detain people on the street if there is a reasonable basis for such
action (see Limited Search—the Frisk in chapter 2, Detention and
Arrest). But a "frisk" on the street requires evidence that the officers
believed that the person confronted was armed and dangerous. Must
there be a similar showing in order to frisk the occupants of a house
prior to searching it?

It could be argued that the occupant of a dwelling house enjoys
maximum privacy in his quarters, and that a stronger showing than a
belief that he was armed and dangerous should be required. Perhaps
the standard should be: probable cause to believe the occupant was
armed. Moreover, the defendant could allege that while it is frequently
unlawful to possess any concealable firearms on the street, firearms can
be lawfully possessed in the dwelling house. In rebuttal, the prosecution
would argue that a stop and frisk in the street is undertaken solely on
the officer's judgment. A search warrant, on the other hand, judicially
authorizes entry and search of a dwelling house for specifically described
property, either unlawfully possessed or connected with the commission
of a crime. Under these circumstances, the occupant's guilty knowledge
of possession could conceivably invite violence. For these reasons, a
limited search of the person would be arguably authorized.

In the absence of any clear expression from the U.S. Supreme
Court, officers should attempt to establish their justification for a limited
search of the person. Evidence of the occupant's history of violence or
previous arrest and conviction record, his mental condition, the nature
of the crime itself are all factors to be considered. Under most circumstances, the court would quickly approve a limited search of the

occupant's person if there was at least minimum evidence of justification.

Another aspect of security of the premises and person arises when officers develop probable cause to arrest an occupant in his house, but cannot await the delay incidental to obtaining a search warrant. Or, perhaps probable cause to arrest an occupant of a dwelling house exists, but probable cause to search the house does not emerge until after the entry and arrest.[5] If the officers must withdraw from the house to await the arrival of a warrant, someone could conceivably enter and conceal or dispose of the seizable evidence. Can the officers remain inside to foreclose such an event?

One California case, *People* v. *Edgar,* has suggested that it is reasonable for the officers to post a guard and prevent entry by unauthorized persons until a warrant can be obtained. Although this course seems reasonable, officers might find themselves in a legal trap under some circumstances. For example, under old constitutional theory, a search was unreasonable under the Fourth Amendment if conducted without a warrant when time allowed to obtain a warrant. Later, this "time allowed" rule was modified and all searches were assessed under the rule of reasonableness, i.e., whether the search was "reasonable" under all the circumstances. If officers developed probable cause to arrest prior to entry and arrest, and only after entry sought a search warrant, the courts might conclude that if time allowed to get a search warrant prior to entry, the officers should have done so. Failure to do so should not permit posting a guard and thereby inconveniencing other occupants until a warrant has been obtained. The occupants might prevail if they convinced the court that their freedom of action was unreasonably curtailed while they awaited the arrival of the officers with the warrant, and then were further immobilized during the course of the search.

Partial remedies to avoid such an argument can be employed when officers seek arrest warrants. Often the statement of probable cause to arrest contained in the crime report can be duplicated and restated as probable cause to search. The report may need some supplementation to establish probable cause to believe seizable property is on the premises.

Return

Most states require the officer to inventory seized property and account to the court. The warrant authorizes the officer to search and seize property and return it to the court. Frequently, however, the law

---

5. The arrest of an occupant of a dwelling house does not automatically authorize search of the premises as an incident of the arrest. In order to search for evidence beyond that which is on the arrestee's person or in plain view at the time of arrest, a search warrant must be obtained. (See chapter 6, Search Incidental to Arrest.)

enforcement agency that seizes property retains custody as a matter of administrative expedience. By filing the "return" of seized property, the officers provide the court with a summary of seized property. Ordinarily, a copy of the property report is sufficient.

The Role of Search Warrants

Despite English and colonial traditions cloaking the home with maximum protection from official invasion, the extensive use of search warrants has only recently been demanded of law enforcement. When the U.S. Supreme Court imposed the Fourth Amendment's exclusionary rule on state officers, the need for warrants became a serious issue. Despite that, the use of search warrants plays a relatively insignificant role in law enforcement. In the face of repeated judicial demand for the use of warrants, most law enforcement agencies infrequently invoke their use.

A number of reasons prevail: the time consumed in obtaining a warrant; the difficulties in drafting it; officers' unfamiliarity with legal requirements; and the unavailability of a magistrate for review and signature. All these objections are valid, but the underlying resistance to the search warrant process probably reflects a distaste for the concept of warrants themselves. Law enforcement officers generally believe that they should be allowed to act on inferences reasonably drawn from known facts just like anyone else. If probable cause objectively exists to believe that contraband or stolen property is concealed at a specific location, why not enter and seize it? What reason is there to await the frustrating delay of a warrant?

The crux of the matter is: Who will decide whether probable cause exists, and who has the right to authorize invasion of a home? The policeman's quarrel is not so much with the courts, but with the Fourth Amendment. The men who drafted the Fourth Amendment expressed a concept: the "right of the people to be secure against unreasonable searches and seizures." But who will implement the concept? Not the police, because the law enforcement role is essentially adversary.

Arguably, the state legislature should have implemented the Fourth Amendment once its provisions were applied to the states. Perhaps the determination of "reasonableness" should be determined by these elected representatives of the citizenry rather than a judiciary insulated from public opinion. After all, the U.S. Supreme Court itself has often ignored its previous decisions and reinterpreted constitutional protections to accommodate changing social conditions. Is not the legislature better suited to the task of revising statutes? This brief review of the issue suggests formulating a debate question: Resolved, "the elected representatives of the people shall draft and enact all rules affecting the search and seizure of person and property." No doubt a case could be made for both sides. Meanwhile, the realities of life are that the rules of search and seizure are vested in the judiciary.

The chief exponent of these rules, the U.S. Supreme Court, has stated repeatedly that warrants are the rule and judicially preferred. The warrant process does not deny the officer the power to enter a dwelling house and search it; only a demonstration of the justification for the entry and search is required. And that demonstration must be entrusted to a referee, not one of the players. Magistrates are not expected routinely to approve police decisions, but rather, to protect the citizenry from unjustifiable forcible invasion of their homes. Courts, and magistrates, exist to protect individual freedoms as much as to pronounce judgments of guilt on those convicted of crime. A trial is not a mere formality ratifying an arrest; a warrant is not a routine concurrence of an officer's judgment of probable cause. A magistrate is empowered to judge, to determine where the balance lies between preserving freedom and maintaining order. The search warrant is the ultimate expression of that role outside the courtroom.

Cases and Materials

Aguilar v. *Texas*, 378 U.S. 108, 84 S. Ct. 1509, 12 L. Ed. 2d 723.

Beck v. *Ohio*, 379 U.S. 89, 85 S. Ct. 223, 13 L. Ed. 2d 142.

Coolidge v. *New Hampshire*, 403 U.S. 443, 91 S. Ct. 2022, 29 L. Ed. 2d 564.

Draper v. *United States*, 358 U.S. 307, 79 S. Ct. 329, 3 L. Ed. 2d 327.

Jones v. *United States*, 362 U.S. 257, 80 S. Ct. 725, 4 L. Ed. 2d 697.

Marron v. *United States,* 275 U.S. 192, 48 S. Ct. 74, 72 L. Ed. 231.

McCray v. *Illinois*, 386 U.S. 300, 89 S. Ct. 1056, 18 L. Ed. 2d 62.

People v. *Aguirre*, 10 Cal. App. 3d 884, 89 Cal. R. 384.

People v. *Benjamin*, 71 Cal. 2d 296, 455 P. 2d 438.

People v. *Edgar*, 60 Cal. 2d 171, 383 P. 2d 449.

People v. *Hamilton*, 71 Cal. 2d 176, 454 P. 2d 681.

People v. *Scoma*, 71 Cal. 2d 332, 455 P. 2d 419.

People v. *Sheridan*, 2 Cal. App. 3d 483, 82 Cal. R. 695.

Price v. *Superior Court*, 1 Cal. 3d 836, 463 P. 2d 721.

Sgro v. *United States*, 287 U.S. 206, 53 S. Ct. 138, 77 L. Ed. 260.

Skelton v. *Superior Court*, 1 Cal. 3d 144, 460 P. 2d 485.

Spinelli v. *United States,* 393 U.S. 410, 89 S. Ct. 584, 21 L. Ed. 2d 637.

Trupiano v. *United States,* 334 U.S. 699, 68 S. Ct. 1229, 92 L. Ed. 1663.

United States v. *DePugh,* 452 F. 2d 915.

United States v. *Harris,* 403 U.S. 573, 91 S. Ct. 275, 29 L. Ed. 2d 723.

United States v. *Ventrusca,* 380 U.S. 102, 85 S. Ct. 741, 13 L. Ed. 2d 684.

1. Officers obtain a valid search warrant for 100 South Almond Street. On arrival, they discover that the correct address of the house to be searched is 110 South Almond. The officers scratch out the incorrect address on the warrant and ink in the correct address. Will this procedure be correct or should the officers have obtained the issuing magistrate's approval for the change?

2. What kind of judicial officer must approve search warrants? See *Coolidge* v. *New Hampshire,* 403 U.S. 443.

3. Officers serve a warrant authorizing them to search the premises at 1860 Laurel Avenue. After the search, officers discover that the correct address of the premises was 1830 Laurel Avenue, but it was the only house on the street. Does this error void the warrant?

4. Most states require that a magistrate must specifically authorize a search at night ("the warrant shall be served in the daytime unless . . . by appropriate provisions in the warrant, and for reasonable cause shown, a magistrate may authorize its execution at times other than daytime; Rule 42(c), Federal Rules of Criminal Procedure"). Suppose officers *know* that the room to be searched is unoccupied, but fail to obtain a specific authorization for a nighttime search. Will the search at night without such authorization be valid? See *U.S.* v. *Ravich,* 421 F. 2d 1196. When does nighttime begin?

5. "An unquestionably reliable informant, previously known to the officers, talked to them around 1:35 A.M. He told them that a narcotic user residing in an apartment on Colden Street, was selling heroin; that another person by the name of Little Joe (defendant) was staying there; that Little Joe was a heroin user and seller and carried the 'stash' either on himself or in his car; that defendant 'carried a gun at all times with him'— while in his Buick Riviera he kept the gun and 'stash' (heroin) underneath the glove compartment in a console between the bucket seats but while away from his car 'he would carry the gun and the heroin on him'; that when outside of his vehicle Little Joe carried the gun in his waistband, at all times it was loaded and 'he [informer] had seen the actual gun'; and that Little Joe's car was a Buick Riviera 'black over gold, black over tan.' Twenty minutes later, around 1:55 A.M., one officer drove the informer past Colden, and saw 'the vehicle [the informer] had described as defendant's vehicle,' and the informer said, 'There's Little Joe's car,' and 'When you get him make sure you check underneath the glove box. That is where he keeps the stash and the gun, or he will have it with him.' The vehicle

was locked and they did not check the interior (after defendant's arrest his gun was found in the car; no heroin was found in the vehicle). They drove out of the alley onto Colden where the informant got out of the car and left on foot; the officer then parked several doors from Colden and with his partner went to the apartment, effected forcible entry, arrested the occupants and searched the premises.

"In addition to the foregoing the informant told the officer that he personally knew the people in the apartment, and upon arriving at the address pointed out to the officer the apartment in which defendant was staying; that the people in 'this' apartment had narcotics for sale—they 'kept it real close by the bedroom, and it was all heroin; they didn't have anything else . . .'; that Little Joe 'would be carrying the stuff [heroin]'; that the people in the apartment had guns and he had seen those guns himself. . . . While the officer testified that the informer did not tell him he had been in the apartment, he did not testify that the informer told him he had not been there." (*People* v. *Bryant*, 5 Cal. App. 3d 563, 85 Cal. R. 388.)

Is this arrest lawful?

6. An officer testified that in the latter part of April he received information from a tested informer that a person named "Sluggo," residing at a location on Piedmont Street, was engaged in the sale of narcotics, and that these sales took place in a park across the street from that address.

The officer also had personal knowledge that defendant had used narcotics because he had arrested him a year ago in front of the Piedmont Street address. A conviction for being under the influence of narcotics resulted from that arrest. The officer had also received information from his watch commander that a private citizen had come to the police station and reported that narcotics were being sold at the Piedmont address.

The next day, the officer saw defendant at a telephone booth across the street from the park the informer had mentioned and from defendant's alleged place of residence. At the time the officer was patrolling the area in plain clothes in an unmarked vehicle. He saw four individuals, three of whom had just left a vehicle. One of the three was known to him as a narcotics user. As the officer approached, the three persons who had left the car went in different directions. Two went into the park, the known user walked across the street and the driver left the scene. The driver was interrogated and found to be a "parole violator for a narcotics violation." The officer then returned to the park where he observed the defendant and another individual seated on a park bench. As the officer made a U-turn, defendant and his companion left the bench and walked farther into the park. The officer left his vehicle and went into the park on foot and approached the defendant. Defendant's right hand went to his sweater pocket and "fumbled" in it. Defendant attempted to flee the officer but was apprehended.

Was there sufficient corroboration here?

7. In his affidavit, a police officer stated that he had received information from a special agent of the Federal Bureau of Customs that they

had opened a parcel addressed to the defendant on East Main Street in Santa Paula, and that the parcel contained marijuana.

Later, the officer spoke by telephone to the agent who had opened the aforementioned parcel; the agent indicated that he had shipped the parcel in a locked mail pouch by registered mail to a postal inspector.

The officer spoke with the postal inspector, in Los Angeles, who verified that he had received the parcel. The inspector advised the officer that he had opened the package and that it contained marijuana.

"The inspector further advised that he had removed a sample of the material and placed it in a sealed envelope, and resealed the parcel. Both the sealed parcel and the sealed envelope containing the sample were forward by registered mail to the assistant postmaster at Santa Paula. The officer received the sealed envelope and had it analyzed as marijuana. . . .

"On that same day the officer was advised by the assistant postmaster at Santa Paula that the original parcel would be delivered to the East Main Street address between the hours of 9 and 10 A.M.

"The officer concluded his affidavit with an averment that he had personal knowledge that the defendant resided at the Main Street address." (*Alvidres* v. *Superior Court*, 12 Cal. App. 3d 575, 90 Cal. R. 682.)

Can a magistrate issue a warrant prior to the time the parcel will arrive at the house?

8. In California, the Legislature has provided three alternative methods for obtaining search warrants. Penal Code section 1526 allows oral testimony to substitute for the written affidavit; section 1528 authorizes telephonic search warrants; section 1529 authorizes written affidavits:

Section 1526.

(a) The magistrate may, before issuing the warrant, examine on oath the person seeking the warrant and any witnesses he may produce, and must take his affidavit or their affidavits in writing, and cause same to be subscribed by the party or parties making same.

(b) In lieu of the written affidavit required in subdivision (a), the magistrate may take an oral statement under oath which will be recorded and transcribed. The transcribed statement shall be deemed to be an affidavit for the purpose of this chapter. In such cases, the recording of the sworn oral statement and the transcribed statement shall be certified by the magistrate receiving it and shall be filed with the clerk of the court.

Section 1528.

(a) If the magistrate is thereupon satisfied of the existence of the grounds of the application, or that there is probable cause to believe their existence, he must issue a search warrant, signed by him with his name of office, to a peace officer in his county, commanding him forthwith to search the person or place named, for the property or things specified, and to retain such property or things in his custody subject to order of the court. . . .

(b) The magistrate may orally authorize a peace officer to sign the magistrate's name on a duplicate original warrant. A duplicate original warrant shall be deemed to be a search warrant for the purposes of this chapter, and it shall be returned to the magistrate. . . . In such cases, the magistrate shall enter on the face of the original warrant the exact time of the issuance of the warrant and shall sign and file the original warrant and the duplicate original warrant with the clerk of the court. . . .

Section 1529.

The warrant shall be in substantially the following form:

County of . . . .

The people of the State of California to any sheriff, constable, marshal, or policeman in the County of . . . . :

Proof, by affidavit, having been this day made before me by (naming every person whose affidavit has been taken), that (stating the grounds of the application . . . or, if the affidavit be not positive, that there is probable cause for believing that . . . . stating the ground of the application in the same manner), you are therefore commanded, in the daytime (or at any time) of the day or night, as the case may be, . . . to make search on the person of C. D. (or in the house situated . . . . , describing it or any other place to be searched, with reasonable particularity, as the case may be) for the following property: (describing it with reasonable particularity); and if you find the same or any part thereof, to bring it forthwith before me (or this court) at (stating the place).

Given under my hand, and dated this . . . . day of . . . . , A.D. 19. . . . .

E. F., Judge of the Justice Court (or as the case may be).

Chapter Six

Search Incident to Arrest

As a general rule, all searches must be conducted under the authority of a warrant unless there is some basis for a warrantless search. There are only a few recognized exceptions to the warrant requirement, but a warrantless search incidental to a lawful arrest is the most important. The courts have approved a search of an arrestee without a warrant because of demonstrated needs for such a rule. The rationale is that an officer can search an arrestee without a warrant to prevent escape, assault, or the destruction or concealment of evidence. Protection of the arresting officer and prevention of the loss of evidence are the twin underpinnings to a warrantless search of the person incidental to an arrest.

It should be noted that the full search of a person incident to his arrest should be distinguished from a limited search of a person incident to his detention (see Limited Search—the Frisk in chapter 2). The purpose of the frisk is to neutralize the possibility of an assault on the officer—not to discover otherwise seizable evidence. A detention is not an arrest, and consequently the warrantless frisk is limited to a weapons search only. If an arrest is made, a search for weapons as well as evidence related to the offense is justified, because if there is a strong suspicion that a person committed a crime (which is not the test for detention), it is reasonable to search his person, not only for weapons but for the proof of the crime itself. Whether the interference with a person's mobility constitutes a detention or an arrest will depend on what the officer said and did at the time. (See chapter 3, Arrest.)

Dispensing with the requirement of the warrant to search the person at the time of the arrest is entirely reasonable. The arrest itself deprives a person of his freedom of movement in any event, and searching his person under such a circumstance involves no more serious invasion of his privacy. Moreover, the justification for the warrantless search is based partly on the assumption that the arrestee will be booked in a jail facility where a full search is obviously necessary to prevent the introduction of weapons or contraband into jail. By searching in the field, the officer anticipates the booking search. But not all "arrests" in the field contemplate booking and custody. What difference does this factor make?

The First Requirement: Relatedness

Although the actual terminology differs, most jurisdictions do not consider the issuance of a traffic citation as an arrest in the traditional sense. Usually there is no search of the motorist; no custody is contemplated in the absence of injury to person or property; no booking is foreseen; and, most importantly, no evidence of the traffic offense will be yielded that would relate to the cited offense. Under these circumstances, the theoretical justification for a search incidental to an arrest disappears. Absent any concern about his safety, the officer cannot accelerate a booking search that will not occur. Nor could the motorist conceal or dispose of any evidence related to the traffic offense, because there would be no incriminating evidence in any event. Thus, the first limitation on the right of the officer to search incidental to an arrest: the search must be reasonably related to the arrest. In most cases, a search incidental to a traffic citation would be impermissible.

This principle applies only if there are no other circumstances involved in the issuance of the citation. If additional factors emerge, the officer may escalate his right to search provided that his search is reasonably related to the new circumstances. If there is some basis for believing that the motorist is armed and dangerous, a limited search of his person is authorized. If the investigation reveals the commission of a misdemeanor or a felony, further searching authority may be justified.

Consider other situations that may occur. Suppose that the officer arrests the driver for a traffic offense, and a statute authorizes custody rather than the mere issuance of a citation. Or, suppose that the officer determines that a traffic warrant is outstanding against the traffic violator. In either case, the officer intends to take the driver into custody. What is his searching authority now? Keeping in mind that a search must be for evidence reasonably related to the arrest, custody alone would not alter the rule. No more evidence of the traffic offense would be admissible if the suspect were arrested than if he were released. The only rationale for allowing a search of the traffic violator being taken into custody is the safety of the officer. Transporting anyone in a police car reasonably escalates the potential for resistance or violence, so that the officer can take some protective measures for his welfare even if he does not entertain a reasonable basis for believing the arrestee is armed and dangerous. The circumstances demand the use of minimum security measures; at least a search for weapons would be reasonable although a thorough search might not.

Can a thorough field search of the person be justified on the theory that the search is an anticipatory booking search? The answer will depend largely on the state's statute. Many states have initiated comprehensive legislation regulating the detention and arrest of traffic violators. If the statute requires the officer to deliver the arrestee to a magistrate, or to an officer authorized to admit the violator to bail, no real custody is contemplated. The violator is detained lawfully, but to be delivered to a magistrate—not a jail cell. If the violator will not be jailed, he will not be "booked" and the booking search will not occur. Again, a field search cannot anticipate a booking search that will not occur.

This analysis assumes that only a traffic violation, or a warrant for a previous traffic violation, is involved. If investigation reveals a different offense, the searching authority may increase. Or if the circumstances of the violation involve alcohol, drugs, or injury to person or property by means of the automobile, the officer's searching authority of the person—and his vehicle—may be extended.

The rule that a search must be reasonably related to the arrest is exemplified in the arrest of a motorist for driving under the influence of alcohol. An arrest for this misdemeanor would authorize the search of his person for evidence related to the offense, i.e., flasks or bottles of liquor. As will be seen later, a search of the vehicle itself would also be authorized in order to discover evidence of alcohol; or a search of the person and vehicle would also be authorized to discover any drugs that may have contributed to the motorist's erratic driving. Conversely, a search of a motorist's person, if he were arrested for misdemeanor reckless driving, would not yield any evidence of reckless driving. Absent any custody as a consequence of the driving, no search of the person or vehicle for evidence of the offense would be fruitful.

In the case of felony arrests, generally an arrestee may be searched thoroughly for weapons and evidence regardless of the particular felony. This rule could be challenged if the specific felony was not committed by force or violence, and no evidence of the crime would conceivably be concealed on the person, i.e., the theft of a valuable painting. But the vast majority of arrests for felonies automatically justify a search of the person for weapons and evidence. And in most cases, an arrest for a felony automatically authorizes jail custody, in which case a booking search would be perfectly proper.

The Second Requirement: Contemporaneity

The second limitation on the right to search incidental to arrest is that the search must be contemporaneous in time with the arrest and in the same place. This rule requires an officer to conduct his warrantless search at approximately the same time as the arrest and at substantially the same place. This rule harmonizes with the theory that a warrantless search of the person incidental to his arrest is justified to prevent assault or destruction of evidence. Once these purposes have been achieved, the reason for the warrantless search elsewhere or at a later time disappears. Any further search would require a warrant. The rule of contemporaneity also exists to prevent using the arrest as a pretext to conduct an unlimited search. By circumscribing the time and place of the search, a general and unlimited search is prohibited.

If a person is arrested while walking on the street, the only principle that applies to a search of his person is the requirement that the search must be for evidence reasonably related to his arrest. Such a search is obviously at the same time and place. If a person is arrested in or near a vehicle, however, the issues become twofold: Is a search of his person justified? Is a search of his vehicle justified? The answer to the first question depends on whether the search is for evidence reasonably related to the arrest. The answer to the second question depends on this principle and also on the issue of contemporaneity. Specifically: Is a search of the vehicle, as an incident of the occupant's arrest, conducted at the same time and place?

If the only basis for the search of the vehicle is the arrest of the occupant, the court will assess the validity of the arrest first. If there is a basis for the arrest, the second question is whether the search of the vehicle—which we assume will be for evidence reasonably related to the arrest—is substantially contemporaneous with the arrest in time and in the same place. If the search of the vehicle is conducted on the street immediately after placing the defendant in custody, the rule of contemporaneity is satisfied. More difficult cases arise when the defendant is separated from the vehicle and the car is searched at a later time and in a more convenient location—usually a police facility. Consider the following problems:

1. Officers observe the defendant drive up to his apartment, exit, and walk away from the car. As the defendant reaches the door to his apartment, officers lawfully arrest him. The officers return to the car and search it.

2. Officers observe the defendant driving his car on a public street and arrest him pursuant to a validly issued arrest warrant charging unlawful possession of narcotics. As they commence the search of the car, a large crowd forms and threatens injury to the officers. The officers tow the car away and search it shortly afterwards at the impound garage.

3. Officers arrest the driver of a car based on probable cause to believe that he had committed a felony. They observe two new television sets sitting on the back seat of the vehicle, each bearing the original price tag. Reluctant to remove the sets for fear of disturbing possible fingerprints, officers impound the car. Several days later police technicians enter, remove the sets, and examine them for fingerprints.

4. Officers arrest the defendant in Louisiana for a murder he allegedly committed in California. The murder was committed inside the car itself. Lacking jurisdiction to prosecute, the arresting officers transfer the vehicle to a freight car, seal it, and route the car to the demanding jurisdiction. On arrival, the vehicle is removed from the freight car and searched. Chemical analysis reveals incriminating evidence.

5. Officers, armed with a murder warrant, arrest the defendant. The arrest occurs when officers see him standing next to his car. Believing that there is incriminating evidence inside the car and that this evidence can be removed only by chemical analysis, officers seal the car and request an expert to subject the car to laboratory inspection. Several days later, chemists enter and remove incriminating evidence.

6. Officers attempt to arrest the defendant, whom they observe driving his car. The defendant abandons his car and flees. Being unable to apprehend the defendant, officers return to the car and search it, seizing incriminating evidence. Several days later the defendant is arrested.

The single thread that runs through these examples is the obvious reasonableness of the officer's conduct. None of the searches suggests an indifference to constitutional rights or an exercise of arbitrary police authority. In each case, the vehicle was searched after the occupant's personal liberty had been breached by arrest, and in all cases an immediate and thorough search at the time of arrest would have been justified. Yet the defendant has been separated from the car, and the search lacks contemporaneity.

1-A. Although there is a tendency to apply the exclusionary rule mechanically, most courts have indicated that the Fourth Amendment is a rule of reasonableness. Despite the general rule that all searches must be contemporaneous in time and substantially identical in place (to avoid the possibility of an arrest justifying any kind of search), most courts have held that the rule of contemporaneity requires the search to be *substantially* contemporaneous in time and in the same place as the arrest. If the defendant is arrested near his car, a search of the car would be substantially contemporaneous. As long as there is some evidence that the defendant exercised control over the vehicle, an arrest of the defendant in the near vicinity of his car will justify an otherwise lawful search of the vehicle.

2-A. Whether a search is contemporaneous with an arrest depends on the totality of circumstances. This rule lacks the precision of arithmetic, but it does provide the officer with an opportunity to develop those facts and circumstances that prevent or interfere with the usual requirement of an immediate search. Thus, an officer confronted by a threatening crowd need not press forward with his search while simultaneously pondering the prospect of assault. Under such circumstances, removing a car from the scene of arrest and subjecting it to search a short time later is quite reasonable. The officer had the right to search the car incidental to the arrest, but was foreclosed from executing his right to search by circumstances beyond his control. By commencing his search at the location of arrest, discontinuing the search and resuming the search as soon as possible thereafter, the officer established that his search was not delayed capriciously; rather the search was commenced, discontinued briefly, and resumed shortly thereafter.

3-A. Courts have encouraged law enforcement agencies to rely on scientific evidence as much as possible. This category of evidence is often most compelling and most reliable. But such evidence is also often difficult to obtain. When officers delay a search because they lack the skills or the facilities to conduct scientific tests, the court will frequently approve a delayed search of the vehicle. Thus, when officers observe new television sets with price tags affixed lying in the back seat of a car, the possibility of fingerprints on the sets is substantial. Although officers could remove the sets immediately in the street, such a course would not be reasonable. Aside from the inconvenience of transferring the sets from one vehicle to another, the potential loss of latent prints is increased. Courts would undoubtedly note that the officers did have the right to seize the sets at the moment of the arrest, but merely delayed executing that right until the circumstances allowed for removal at the laboratory.

4-A. Similarly, if the defendant is arrested in a car that was an instrumentality of the crime of murder itself, officers could seize the car incidental to the arrest. Not only could the delayed examination of the car be justified under the previous theory, but also the entry by lab technicians can be considered constitutionally reasonable on the ground that the car was evidence of the crime itself and, like guns, contraband, or stolen property, could be seized as evidence. The entry of the car by lab personnel would not be a "search" at all because the car was evidence in police custody and could be subjected to examination just like any other piece of evidence. Such a theory is only sustainable if the vehicle is an instrumentality of the crime itself and not used as a mere carrier of seizable evidence.

5-A. If officers desire to search a car incidental to an arrest, but desire to delay the search to facilitate laboratory examination, precautions should be taken to indicate the reasonableness of this conduct. Reports should clearly state the reasons why no immediate search was undertaken (i.e., lack of skilled personnel and facilities); that, for these reasons, no entry of the vehicle was attempted; that the vehicle was sealed; that an entry was attempted as soon as possible by lab personnel (preferably in the presence of the arresting officer or the investigating officer).

6-A. If officers establish probable cause to arrest for a felony, thereby simultaneously authorizing an incidental search of the arrestee, that right cannot be frustrated by an arrestee's escape. Even if the prospective arrestee's absence eliminates the theoretical need to search the car for weapons and destructible evidence, the car *could* have been searched if an arrest were effected. The suspect's flight cannot immunize his car from search. In many cases the defendant, when arrested, will contend that the officers also lacked the initial probable cause to arrest.

Alternative theories exist to validate a search of the car. There is a clear indication by the U.S. Supreme Court that if there is probable cause to search or seize the vehicle itself—regardless of probable cause to arrest the occupants—the car may be entered and searched without a warrant at a time and place remote from the arrest. This rule requires evidence of probable cause to believe that the car was used as an instrumentality of the crime or contained seizable evidence. This subject will be discussed separately (see Probable Cause to Search a Motor Vehicle in chapter 8, Searches without Warrants).

Impound Search

A frequent police practice is to inventory the contents of a vehicle after the driver has been arrested. Such an inventory is conducted at a police facility to allow a thorough search under reasonably safe conditions. If the inventory reveals the presence of seizable evidence, may the items be admitted in court?

Not all courts have agreed on the answer. One argument upholds the right of police officers to inventory the contents of a car to safeguard possible valuables and negate the prospect of civil suits against the law enforcement agency for loss or theft of property. Under this rationale, any seizable evidence yielded by the investigation should be admitted.

The counterargument contends that the inventory search is simply not a contemporaneous search and that inventories are unlimited searches for anything that may be discovered. Such searches cannot be sanctioned under "search incident" theory because any danger to the officer's safety or possible destruction of evidence is unlikely in the absence of the arrestee. Lacking this justification, only a search warrant would authorize the search. Moreover, says the California Supreme Court, almost no civil liability attaches to an agency that involuntarily assumes custody of property. Only slight precautionary measures are necessary to avoid civil liability.

The status of impound searches may vary in state and federal jurisdictions and their lawfulness may depend on either of two factors: the reason for the driver's custody, or the basis for the car's custody. In the former case, if the court applies the rule that a search of the car must be for evidence reasonably related to the arrest of the driver or occupant, an officer can determine whether the search of the car would reasonably yield such evidence. Thus, an arrest of a motorist on a traffic warrant would not automatically justify an impound search, because no evidence related to that offense would be found inside the car. If evidence related to the arrest could be conceivably inside the car, the officer must be able to sustain any later (noncontemporaneous) search on one of the theories discussed earlier. In other cases, the custody of the car itself may justify a search of the interior without reference to an arrest. For example: a car impounded as evidence for use in a subsequent forfeiture proceeding against the car for transporting contraband. In such a case, police retain the car as the subject of the crime.

As will be discussed later (chapter 8, Searches without Warrants—Probable Cause to Search a Motor Vehicle), an arrest of a car's occupants for robbery in which the car was used as an instrumentality of the crime would provide probable cause to search the car itself. Probable cause to search the car in custody would remain independent of the arrest.

The Third Requirement: Limited Scope

The rule of contemporaneity applies to searches of houses as well as to those of persons and vehicles. Because searches of dwelling houses are considered the most serious invasion of privacy, the courts have insisted that a search of a person's house incidental to his arrest can be conducted only if the person is arrested inside his house and the search is made at the same time. In *Vale* v. *Louisiana*, the U.S. Supreme Court emphasized this rule.

Possessing two warrants for the defendant's arrest, and having information that he was residing at a specified address, officers proceeded there in an unmarked car and set up a surveillance of the house.

"After approximately 15 minutes the officers observed a green 1958 Chevrolet drive up and sound the horn and after backing into a parking place, again blew the horn. At this juncture the defendant, who was well-known to the officers having arrested him twice in the previous month, was seen coming out of the house and walking up to the passenger side of the Chevrolet where he had a close brief conversation with the driver; and after looking up and down the street returned inside of the house. Within a few minutes he reappeared on the porch, and again cautiously looked up and down the street before proceeding to the passenger side of the Chevrolet, then leaned through the window. From this the officers were convinced a narcotics sale had taken place. They returned to their car and immediately drove toward the defendant, and as they reached within approximately three car lengths from the defendant he looked up and, obviously recognizing the officers, turned around, walking quickly toward the house. At the same time the driver of the Chevrolet started to make his get-away when the car was blocked by the police vehicle. The three officers promptly alighted from the car, whereupon two of the officers called to the defendant to stop as he reached the front steps of the house, telling him he was under arrest. The third officer, at the same time, saw the driver of the Chevrolet, whom the officers knew to be a narcotic addict, place something hurriedly in his mouth. Because of the transaction they had just observed they informed the defendant they were going to search the house."

The search of a rear bedroom revealed a quantity of narcotics.

"A search may be incident to an arrest only if it is substantially contemporaneous with the arrest and is confined to the *immediate* vicinity of the arrest. If a search of a house is to be upheld as incident to an arrest, that arrest must take place *inside* the house, not somewhere outside—whether two blocks away, twenty feet away, or on the sidewalk near the front steps. Belief, however well founded, that an article sought is concealed in a dwelling house furnishes no justification for a search of that place without a warrant." (*Vale* v. *Louisiana.*)

Suppose that officers delay an arrest to allow a suspect to enter his home. Once the suspect is inside, the officers enter, arrest, and search the entire house. The search is indeed conducted at the same time and place as the arrest. Yet the wholesale search of a person's house does not square with other Fourth Amendment principles, and in *Chimel* v. *California,* decided in 1970, the U.S. Supreme Court severely restricted the right of officers to search a house as an incident of the suspect's arrest inside.

To understand the *Chimel* case, other constitutional principles must be set in context. One of the principal and well-established Fourth Amendment rules was the requirement that a house may never be searched without a warrant, even if there is probable cause to believe seizable evidence is inside. Thus, if the house were unoccupied when the officers entered, no search could be undertaken in the absence of a warrant. If the suspect was arrested several miles from his house, no warrantless search of his quarters could be justified as an incident of his arrest under the "search incident" theory, because there would be no need to avert assault or prevent destruction or loss of evidence. If the house of the arrestee could not be searched if he were arrested away from his quarters, why should his house be subjected to search merely because he was arrested inside? Once the suspect was in custody, no assault or loss of evidence inside the house was likely. The mere accident of an arrest effected inside the house should not expand a right to search that would have been otherwise unlawful had the suspect been arrested outside the house.

In *Chimel* v. *California,* the court applied such reasoning to the following facts: Officers, holding a warrant for the defendant, knew where he worked and where he lived. They chose not to arrest him at his place of business, but instead waited until he came home. After Chimel was inside his house, officers entered, placed him under arrest, and searched the entire house. Incriminating evidence was discovered, and on that evidence Chimel was convicted of burglary.

On his appeal, the U.S. Supreme Court reviewed past decisions that had seemingly authorized the search of an entire house as an incident of the defendant's arrest. The Court modified the rule of contemporaneity by deciding that henceforth the search of a house incidental to the arrest of an occupant would be limited in its scope. The Court said:

> When an arrest is made, it is reasonable for the arresting officer to search the person arrested in order to remove any weapons that the latter might seek to use in order to resist arrest or effect his escape. Otherwise, the officer's safety might well be endangered, and the arrest itself frustrated. In addition, it is entirely reasonable for the arresting officer to search for and seize any evidence on the arrestee's person in order to prevent its concealment or destruction. And the area into which an arrestee might reach in order to grab a weapon or evidentiary items must, of course, be governed by a like rule. A gun on a table or in a drawer in front of one who is arrested can be as dangerous to the arresting officer as one concealed in the clothing of the person arrested. *There is ample justification, therefore, for a search of the arrestee's person and the area "within his immediate control"—construing that phrase to mean the area from within which he might gain possession of a weapon or destructible evidence.*
>
> *There is no comparable justification, however, for routinely searching rooms other than that in which an arrest occurs—or, for that matter, for searching through all the desk drawers or other closed or concealed areas in that room itself.* Such searches, in the absence of well-recognized exceptions, may be made only under the

authority of a search warrant. The "adherence to judicial processes" mandated by the Fourth Amendment requires no less.

The *Chimel* case thus places a third limitation on a warrantless search incidental to a lawful arrest: the search must be limited to the area under the immediate control of the defendant. What are the boundaries of this term? Consider this example:

The defendant was lawfully arrested while sleeping on a bed in her home. "The officer then directed defendant to remove herself from the bed; and, without having to move any bedding or clothing, he looked under the bed with his flashlight and saw a brown paper sack. The sack was open, and he observed a small piece of cellophane sticking out of it. As a qualified expert on the packaging and use of benzedrine, he believed that the bag might contain dangerous drugs. He thereupon removed the bag and discovered that it contained benzedrine tablets. He then placed defendant under arrest.

"Even under the restrictions imposed by *Chimel,* however, the officer's search did not exceed the permissible scope. Under the *Chimel* rule it is entirely reasonable for the arresting officer to search for and seize any evidence . . . [within] the area into which an arrestee might reach in order to grab . . . evidentiary items. . . . When the defendant was sitting on the bed, the area under it was within 'the area into which [she] might [have] reached in order to grab . . . evidentiary items.' " (*People v. King.*)

Under the *Chimel* rule, a thorough search of a house as an incident of an arrest may only be conducted under the authority of a search warrant. The Court in *Chimel* also harmonized their rule governing the scope of a search incidental to an arrest with rules affecting other kinds of searches. The Court said that in analyzing searches and seizures generally, the inquiry should be twofold: (1) Is there a reasonable basis for the search? and (2) If so, is the scope of that search reasonably related to the reason for the initial intrusion? This rule governs the search of a person, his car, and his house. Thus, if there is a reasonable basis for stopping a person, the frisk, i.e., search, is related to the original detention because of the need to neutralize potential danger. The scope of the search, i.e., a limited pat-down, reasonably relates to that end. Similarly, any search of an automobile will be measured by the reasons for the original detention. If the original detention was for a traffic violation, no search of the car would be reasonably related to the traffic offense. If some other offense is discovered after the stop, the scope of any search must be reasonably related to such offense. And finally, a search of the house itself would exceed the scope of a search incident to arrest of the suspect inside— for whatever offense—because custody would foreclose any danger to the officer or destruction of evidence. A full search of the person—at least for a felony arrest—would be authorized whether an arrest was made of a pedestrian, a motorist, or a household occupant. Beyond that, a warrant might be necessary.

The full implications of the *Chimel* decision remain to be explored. If seizable evidence is seen in plain view inside the house where officers have made an arrest, the object may be seized under the "plain view" doctrine (see chapter 4, Search). A more difficult question arises when officers enter rooms other than where the arrest is made and observe evidence in plain view. If the officers had some basis for being in an adjoining room—perhaps because of the suspect's flight or because there was a reasonable basis to believe confederates were present—any evidence in plain view could lawfully be seized. If curiosity was the officers' only object, the courts would probably reach the opposite result. In some cases the kind of crime arrested for may define the area into which officers might enter. For example:

"Police officers were told by an informant that defendant, his mistress and others were engaged in large scale dealings in heroin. They arranged with the informant to purchase an ounce of heroin from defendant. After that transaction, defendant departed for his home and the informant returned to the police officers, gave them a condom of heroin that he claimed he had received from defendant, told them of his conversations with defendant, including the information that defendant had gone home to await the arrival of some potential buyers.

"The officers then proceeded to defendant's home and arrested him in the living room of the house. After the arrest, one officer went into the kitchen, where he observed a large quantity of heroin, together with other supplies and equipment commonly used to package heroin for sale. A search of the house for other occupants was unavailing. The defendant contended that the search of the kitchen exceeded the allowed scope of *Chimel*.

"In this case, the officer had a right to enter the kitchen to look for possible confederates of the defendant. The informant had told the officers that defendant was living with a woman, that other persons frequented the apartment, and that a buyer was expected momentarily— in fact that defendant had gone home to meet that buyer. Even if the sale by the defendant to the informant was not sufficient corroboration to make him thereafter a 'reliable' informant, it is clear that the officers had information as to other persons which it was their right, and their duty, to follow up. Having arrested defendant, it was not unreasonable for them to walk through the house to see if others were there and, if found, at least to interrogate them. To walk through an open doorway, in pursuit of such an investigation, is not the kind of excessive invasion of privacy that *Chimel* is designed to prevent; it is merely basic police investigation of information received. If the officer lawfully entered the kitchen, his observations thereafter were not a 'search' within the definition of the term." (*Guevara* v. *Superior Court.*)

The courts, however, are likely to scrutinize entry of adjacent rooms. In order for the officer to avail himself of the "plain view" theory, he must establish his "right to have his view." The courts would not approve entry and search of rooms adjoining the arrest in the absence of an articulable reason for the officer to enter those rooms.

Although the Supreme Court in *Chimel* attempted to define the area that could be searched incidental to an arrest inside a dwelling house, the Court left the door open for a flexible approach to circumstances that present themselves to an officer at the time of an arrest. Part of that determination depends on who the suspect is and what crime he has committed. And more latitude will be allowed depending on the nature of the evidence seized. If there is a reasonable basis for believing that guns are present on the premises, officers will be allowed a wider area of discretion than if marijuana is involved. In most arrests, the officers' attempt to maximize their safety, and an explanation of those steps, will satisfy the Court that the officers were acting reasonably.

The "search incident" theory was one of the first exceptions carved out of the general rule requiring all searches to be conducted pursuant to warrant. The twin needs—officer safety and preserving evidence—were apparent. But the right to search incident to an arrest was always an exception to the general rule. As time passed, however, the exception threatened to swallow the rule. For example, an "arrest" for a traffic citation would theoretically allow an "incidental search" of the person and his car. Thus, the rule requiring a search to be reasonably related to the arrest emerged. Another example: if the defendant was arrested in Miami, his car could theoretically be searched in Tampa for evidence reasonably related to the arrest. Thus the rule emerged requiring searches to be not only for evidence reasonably related to the arrest, but also contemporaneous. Finally, *Chimel* requires the search to be limited to the area under the arrestee's control.

All these apparent restrictions on searching authority relate directly back to the rule prohibiting searches without a warrant. What had happened was that the arrest was invoked as justification for a search without a warrant. But *Chimel* clearly reaffirms the old rule requiring searches to be conducted pursuant to warrant. An arrest cannot bootstrap itself to permit an otherwise unreasonable search. The courts will no longer assume that an arrest authorizes an automatic search. The nature of the seizure will delineate searching authority.

Another method of analyzing the search-incident-to-arrest theory: The arrest, whether traffic stop, detention for investigation of criminal activity, misdemeanor, or felony, confers on the officer a "right to search." Once the "right to search" is established, the extent, or scope, of that right must be determined. If the officer establishes his right to arrest, he correspondingly establishes his right to search. But the kind of arrest he effects will mark the boundaries of the search. The scope of the search must bear some reasonable relationship to the reason for the seizure. Nowhere is this principle better illustrated than in stop and frisk. The temporary detention of a person (the right to seize) authorizes only a search that is limited in scope, i.e., removal of weapons.

Cases and Materials

Chimel v. *California*, 395 U.S. 752, 89 S. Ct. 2034, 23 L. Ed. 2d 685.

Guevara v. *Superior Court*, 7 Cal. App. 3d 531, 86 Cal. R. 657.

Mozzetti v. *Superior Court*, 4 Cal. 3d 699, 484 P. 2d 84 (impound searches).

People v. *Block*, 6 Cal. 3d 239, 499 P. 2d 961 (house).

People v. *King*, 5 Cal. 3d 458, 487 P. 2d 1082.

People v. *Superior Court* (Kiefer), 3 Cal. 3d 807, 478 P. 2d 499.

Preston v. *United States*, 376 U.S. 364, 84 S. Ct. 881, 11 L. Ed. 2d 777.

Stoner v. *California,* 376 U.S. 483, 84 S. Ct. 889, 11 L. Ed. 2d 856.

Vale v. *Louisiana*, 399 U.S. 30, 90 S. Ct. 1969, 26 L. Ed. 2d 409.

1. Around 11 P.M., officers observed a female, who appeared to be a minor, walking slowly on a city street in an area frequented by prostitutes. One of the officers suspected this person of being a prostitute and described her walk as a "prostitute walk" or "prostitute stroll." The officers drove around the block and, on seeing her again, stopped and questioned her. They ascertained that her name was Nancy C. and that she was sixteen. She indicated to the officers that she was coming from a nearby club—which does not admit persons under twenty-one—and she had been staying with someone who was known to one of the officers as a prostitute. Finally, she said she was on her way to the bus depot to meet a friend. The minor was arrested for violation of a local curfew ordinance and was booked at city jail. During the booking, her purse was searched, and a bag appearing to contain marijuana was discovered. Will this search be reasonable as an incident of the minor's arrest for violation of a county ordinance? (*In re Nancy C.*, 28 Cal. App. 3d 747, 105 Cal. R. 113.)

2. The defendant is arrested for being drunk in a public place. A cursory search reveals no weapons, and the officer does not believe the arrestee is armed or dangerous. Instead of confining him to the city jail, the officer transports the inebriate to a detoxification facility authorized

under a state statute. On arrival, a thorough search of his person reveals contraband. At trial, the defendant contends that any search of his person prior to commitment in a civil facility is unlawful, or, in the alternative, even if the search is reasonably related to the need for security in the facility, any evidence secured from his person should not be admitted in a subsequent criminal trial.

What should be the result?

(*People* v. *Superior Court* (Colon), 29 CA 3d 397.)

3. The defendant sold heroin to a police informant in the presence of a deputy sheriff in the defendant's car in a parking lot. Two weeks later, two officers assigned to the narcotics bureau went to the defendant's residence to serve a warrant for the defendant's arrest on the charge of selling heroin relating to the sale. The officers entered the house and proceeded to the front room, where the defendant was arrested. The officers then searched defendant's apartment and found a red balloon containing heroin in a light fixture on a bedroom wall.

Assuming this search was properly incident to the arrest, was it lawful? What evidence, if discovered, would be reasonably related to the offense of sale committed two weeks earlier?

4. Officers lawfully arrested several suspects inside a house for possession of alcohol. One officer observed that at least four of the six suspects had dilated eyes and pupils and an odor of marijuana upon their breath. "We went upstairs 'to see if there were any other people in the house.'" He testified that 'because of the number of defendants in the house, I believed there was a possibility of more defendants' upstairs. The house was 'quite large,' containing three or possibly four bedrooms. Lights were turned on to illuminate the stairs leading to the second floor and the upstairs hallway. On the second floor, he looked in one bedroom, a bathroom, and then a second bedroom. The light in the second bedroom was off and the door partially open. He turned on the light, looked behind the door to see if anyone was hiding there, and then surveyed the room. He then observed a clear plastic vial lying in plain sight on the table containing marijuana.

"Was the search of the upstairs lawful?" (*People* v. *Block*, 6 Cal. 3d 239, 499 P. 2d 961.)

5. Officers contacted the defendant who, in an inebriated state, informed them his car had just been involved in an accident. The car was discovered in a severely damaged condition just off the roadway. After towing the car away to a private garage, officers drove the defendant to the police station and placed him under arrest for driving under the influence of alcohol.

Upon learning the defendant was a police officer, the arresting officer attempted to locate his service revolver, which they believed he kept in his possession. One officer returned to the yard where the disabled car had been towed and searched the interior of the car and glove compartment. Unsuccessful in his quest, he unlocked the trunk and discovered evidence of a homicide. The evidence revealed that the arrest and search took place in a rural community and no facilities were available to guard the vehicle from intrusion by others. The officer further testified that he searched the car only to locate a potential lethal weapon.

The driver's custody was based upon an arrest for driving under the influence of alcohol, but the search cannot be sustained as incident to the arrest because it was conducted at a time and place remote from the arrest. Because the homicide was unknown to the officer prior to the search, no independent probable cause existed to search the vehicle. What reasons, if any, make this search reasonable? *Cady* v. *Dombrowski,* 41 Law Week 4995 (June 1973).

Chapter Seven

Consent Searches

The courts have held that a constitutional right may be surrendered if it is surrendered knowingly and voluntarily. The Fourth Amendment is no exception to this rule, and officers may request consent to search a person, a car, or a dwelling house. Officers do not have the right to enter or search anyone's home in the absence of probable cause to arrest, an arrest warrant, a search warrant, or some evidence of an emergency, but they can request permission to enter a car or a dwelling house. Because there is no "right" to conduct a consent search, the lawfulness of the ensuing search depends on the decision of the person whose consent is sought. Before approving a consent search, the court will examine the circumstances in which consent was granted.

Questions of Consent

The initial inquiry is into the fact of consent itself. The consenting party must expressly or impliedly consent to the search. In all cases, this issue will become a matter for the trial court to determine. Typically the officer will testify that he asked for and received consent; the defendant will deny it. The court must determine where the truth lies. Although it is not essential, the case is clearly stronger if the consenting party expressly authorizes the search than if the prosecution must rely on consent implied from the circumstances. A householder who retreats silently from an open door when confronted by officers may be either inviting entry or merely acquiescing to a display of authority.

The general rule is that the validity of a consent search depends on all the facts and circumstances of the case. The contours of such a rule are obviously imprecise for mathematical purposes. The officer must establish that the defendant in fact consented and that the consent was voluntary. These elements must be proved by the prosecutor. The court will review numerous factors: the time of day; the location; the number of officers; the number of occupants at the house; the language and tone of the request; the nature of the response; whether the defendant was in custody or not at the time the consent was requested; whether there was any detention prior to the request; whether any false or misleading statements were made by the officer. These are the facts and circumstances relevant to a determination of voluntariness that the prosecution must consider in proving consent.

Involuntary Consent

Officers arrested the defendant (with adequate probable cause) on the street. The officers testified that they asked him if he had any more narcotics at his house and that the defendant said he did not. "I asked him if we could look, and he asked me if I had a search warrant. I stated I did not have a search warrant, and I would not need one if he would give me consent, at which time he gave me consent. Officers took the defendant with them in their car and started toward his house. The officers asked defendant where he lived, and the defendant said that he lived on Tamarind Street. He was asked if he was sure, and then said 'All right. You guys know where I live.' When they arrived at his house, defendant said, 'I don't live here; I live over here,' and pointed to the house next door. He knocked on the door, and his aunt let him and the officers in. The officers asked defendant's aunt if he lived there and she said, 'No, he lives across the way.'

"The officers took defendant to his house and asked him again if he had any narcotics in the house. The defendant said, 'All right, I will tell you where they are.' He directed the officers to his mother's house on Tamarind Street and told them that there were narcotics on a rafter in the garage. The officers looked and found nothing. They then took defendant back to his house and searched the house in his presence. They discovered a quantity of heroin. . . .

"To protect his right to object to an unreasonable search or seizure a defendant need not forcibly resist an officer's assertion of authority to enter his home or search it or his person, but if he freely consents to an entry or search, or voluntarily produces evidence against himself, his constitutional rights are not violated and any search or taking of evidence pursuant to his consent is not unreasonable. . . . In the present case, the testimony of the officer dispels any inference that might otherwise have been drawn from defendant's words of consent that he freely and voluntarily consented to the search of his home.

"Although not conclusive, a circumstance of particular significance was the defendant's custody at the time of the request for his permission to search, for where he has submitted to arrest, or is in jail, he knows that he is virtually powerless to prevent the search. In the present case, defendant was not only under arrest, but he was handcuffed at all times until he was finally taken to jail several hours after his arrest, and he had no choice but to go wherever the officers took him. He knew that the officers wished to search his home and that if they did so they would find evidence against him. He repeatedly attempted to lead the officers away from his home, and after these efforts failed, he was neither asked to nor did he express his consent to the search of his home. The most that can be inferred is that defendant sought to placate the officers and hoped that by agreeing to the search of other premises, he would forestall the search of his home and the discovery of incriminating evidence ... Defendant was under no duty to assist the officers in securing evidence against him. Since the search was not incident to his arrest, he had the right to have a magistrate determine whether there was reasonable cause to search his home and whether a search warrant should therefore issue." (*Castaneda* v. *Superior Court.*)

" 'X,' together with three companions, were travelling in an automobile owned by one of them. About 3:30 P.M., an officer observed the automobile going up a hill in the middle lane of a three-lane highway. Because the car was towing a trailer in the wrong lane, the officer signalled 'X' to pull over to the side of the road. 'X' complied.

"The officer walked back to the car and asked 'X' for his driver's license. 'X' answered that he did not have a driver's license or any identification because his wallet had been stolen a short time before. The officer directed him to get out of the automobile and to proceed to the front of the patrol car.

"After ordering 'X' to remain at the patrol car, the officer returned to the car to question its other occupants. He asked them for identification and was apparently satisfied with the identification produced by two of them. The third, a woman, produced a Canadian passport. The officer noticed that her speech 'was a little bit erratic' and thought that 'she was under the influence of something.' He had her step out of the vehicle and proceed to the front of the patrol car. At the same time, he ordered 'X' to return to the car and sit in the driver's seat. The officer asked the woman if she was under the care of a doctor; she replied that she was.

At this point she searched through her purse for further identification. As she did so the officer saw a gold cigarette case which he thought looked like a wallet.

"He asked her 'if she cared if I looked at it' and she replied in the negative and handed the case to him. He ordered her to open it, looked inside and saw marijuana.

"After arresting her, the officer radioed for assistance. . . .

"The officer went back to the car and advised its three occupants that the woman had been arrested and that he 'was going to check them.' The officer ordered the men to get out of the car so they could be frisked. As he prepared to frisk one occupant, whom he had previously learned to be the owner of the car, the officer asked him 'if he cared if I checked the vehicle and he stated no. . . .' "

Under the left-front-bucket seat the officer found marijuana.

As a matter of law, was the consent to the search of the owner's car involuntary? "The circumstances under which consent was given appear from the uncontradicted evidence to be highly coercive. The car which he owned and in which he had been riding, had been stopped by a highway patrol officer who ordered first the driver and then the woman to get out of the vehicle and go with him to the patrol car. The driver was then sent back to the car and ordered to remain in the driver's seat. The woman was detained in the patrol car. For approximately 30 minutes nothing further happened. The owner and his companions were given no explanation for the delay. Later, the officer informed the owner that the woman had been arrested and that the other three occupants of the car were going to be 'checked out.' The officer then ordered the owner to get out of the automobile so that he could be searched and asked whether the owner cared if the officers checked the car. At no time was the owner informed by any of the officers that he could effectively refuse consent." (*People* v. *Superior Court* [Casebeer].)

In both these cases, the officer testified that the person verbalized his consent, i.e., the fact of consent was proved, yet in each case other facts and circumstance rebutted the voluntariness of the consent. In the first example, the defendant's conduct impliedly negated his alleged consent. In the second example, the atmosphere in which consent was obtained was highly coercive. Each case illustrates facts that rebut any testimony that the consent was voluntary.

Because the very presence of police officers carries with it an implication of authority, the courts also hold that a consent search cannot be approved if obtained by submission to a display of authority. To many citizens, police officers possess unlimited power that cannot be thwarted. The mere presence of uniformed and armed police officers at a householder's door implies a display of authority difficult to defy.

On the highway, the solitary motorist who is detained for a traffic violation nervously confronts the helmeted and armed motor officer. Refusing to grant consent to a search of his vehicle may seem foolhardy to most citizens.

If the occupant submits to a display of authority, his consent is involuntary, and any evidence seized is inadmissible. For example, in *Bumper* v. *North Carolina,* officers confronted an elderly woman in her home and informed her that they possessed a search warrant. She told the officers to "go ahead." At trial, no search warrant was offered in evidence, and the prosecution relied on consent. The U.S. Supreme Court held that consent could not be presumed when induced by an apparently false statement. In addition, the officers' assertion of their right to enter based on the authority of the warrant required the occupant to submit. Without proof of the warrant, the search was the unlawful product of an involuntary consent.

Most officers are aware of the need to advise a suspect of his right to counsel and silence before interrogation may begin. Under the *Miranda* decision, the U.S. Supreme Court held that in order for a suspect to surrender his right to silence, guaranteed by the Fifth Amendment, and his right to counsel, guaranteed by the Sixth Amendment, he must be informed of those rights. Unless he understands that the Constitution extends these rights to him, he cannot knowingly waive them. Under the Fourth Amendment, however, the U.S. Supreme Court has held that an officer need not inform a person of his right to refuse consent (a right which he does enjoy). Failure to advise a person of his right to refuse consent will not void the ensuing search, but it may be relevant in determining whether the defendant's consent was voluntarily given.

Joint Occupancy

A question frequently presented involves a search of premises jointly occupied. For example:

Two officers arrested the defendant in an apartment. The officers searched the apartment, but found no narcotics or other contraband. They searched the defendant and found a key and a rent receipt for an apartment No. 212. The defendant denied knowledge of the receipt. "Having ascertained that apartment No. 212 was on West 87th Street, the officers told defendant they were going to take him there. Defendant then admitted that he had rented the apartment the preceding night. An officer asked the defendant who was in apartment No. 212 and defendant said no one. The officers asked if he had any 'junk' in there and he said no. They asked if they could go down and take a look and the defendant said, 'All right, go ahead.' The officers took the defendant to the apartment and knocked on the door. After some delay the [codefendant] asked who was there. The officers asked defendant to say it was he, but he refused to do so." One of the officers demanded entry, and the codefendant opened the door. The officer testified that she had a hypodermic needle attached to an eye dropper in her left hand. The officers arrested her and searched the apartment. They found heroin.

"The search of the apartment cannot be justified on the ground that defendant consented to it. It is true that one of the officers testified that defendant responded, 'All right, go ahead,' when the officer suggested they go to the apartment and take a look. But his subsequent refusal to assist the officers in gaining access to the apartment establishes that his apparent consent was not voluntarily given. Moreover, even if defendant had voluntarily consented to the search, his consent could not justify the invasion of his joint occupant's privacy that occurred when the officer demanded that the door be opened."[1] (*People* v. *Shelton.*)

Generally speaking, a cotenant on the premises may admit anyone. If a cotenant freely admits officers to jointly shared quarters, the absent cotenant cannot legally object. Once inside, the cotenant can further consent to a search of jointly shared areas, but not to a search of property belonging exclusively to the other absent tenant. But if both cotenants are on the premises, a consenting cotenant cannot approve of the search of jointly shared areas over the objections of the other cotenant. The consenting cotenant can then only approve the search of property exclusively his own. If officers obtain consent to search the quarters of a jointly occupied apartment from the tenant while he is away from the premises, they cannot enter, unless there is probable cause to arrest, over the objections of a tenant occupying the premises. A cotenant away from the premises impliedly authorizes the occupying tenant to admit or deny anyone entry.

Apparent Authority

The courts have also approved consent searches by those who have apparent authority to consent. For example: The defendant is a

---

1. "The search cannot be justified on the ground that the officers had reasonable cause to arrest the co-defendant before they demanded that she open the door. Although the officers apparently knew that the co-defendant was at the apartment, they did not know that she was also a user or was involved with defendant in the narcotics. Thus, even if the officers had reasonable cause to believe that defendant had narcotics in the apartment, they had no reasonable cause to believe that his possession, if any, was shared with co-defendant. Before they demanded that the door be opened, they knew only that a woman was in an apartment where defendant may have stored narcotics. Such association between a suspect and even a known criminal by itself is not reasonable cause for an arrest and search." (*Shelton.*)

guest in a private residence. In the defendant's absence, the homeowner allows the police to search the guest's room, where they find narcotics. When officers act in good faith with the consent and at the request of a homeowner in conducting a search, evidence they obtain cannot be excluded merely because the officers may make a reasonable mistake as to the extent of the owner's authority. Although sometimes criticized, the rule that a search is not unreasonable if made with the consent of a third party whom the police reasonably and in good faith believe has authority to consent to their search has been regularly reaffirmed.

The rule governing searches based on consent by a third party is: A search is not unreasonable if made with the consent of a third party whom the police reasonably and in good faith believe has authority to consent to their search. The operative word in the rule is "reasonably"; thus, there must be some objective evidence of joint control or access to the places or items to be searched that would indicate that the person authorizing the search has the authority to do so. The good-faith–mistake rule does not apply where the third party makes clear that the property belongs to another.

The good-faith rule also does not apply where the relationship of the third party and the defendant makes clear that the defendant has not authorized the third party to act as his agent. Thus, in *Stoner v. California,* the Supreme Court, in holding that a room clerk could not consent to the search of a guest's room, and rejecting the "claim that the search was reasonable because the police, relying upon the night clerk's expressions of consent, had a reasonable basis for the belief that the clerk had authority to consent to the search," stated: "There is nothing in the record to indicate that the police had any basis whatsoever to believe that the night clerk had been authorized by the [occupant of the room] to permit the police to search [his quarters]."

Evidence of apparent authority may emerge from the relationship of the parties (father-son; householder-guest) or from the circumstances of the case. Whether apparent authority exists is a question of fact determined in part on the reasonable good-faith belief of the officers. But some legal relationships preclude any apparent authority of a third party to authorize consent, even though they may possess some evidence of that authority. For example, hotel clerks, motel clerks, or landlords who possess keys to individual living units cannot authorize entry and search. Payment of the rent carries with it the right to exclusive occupancy for the term prescribed and, absent permission to enter by the guest, no entry by others is authorized except in the normal course of housekeeping or maintenance.

Consent searches are legally vulnerable because of the variety of attacks available to the defendant. When officers rely on consent to search, they must realize the legal weaknesses of their position. Only by carefully adhering to the guidelines for obtaining a lawful consent will they enhance their chance for success in court. Courts look critically on consent searches, and many observers predict the day when officers will be denied the right to conduct consent searches without some clear justification for their use.

In determining from all the facts and circumstances whether the consent was valid, the court will not isolate the alleged consent from the context of the situation. If the acts prior to consent are illegal, they taint any further search. For example, if consent is obtained after an arrest that lacks probable cause, the illegal arrest taints the consent and voids it. Officers cannot rescue an unlawful arrest by a subsequent act of consent (see Chapter 10, Fruit of the Poisoned Tree—Other Limitations on Admissibility of Evidence). The consent depends too heavily on the arrest to be considered truly voluntary. Similar reasoning would be applied to illegal detentions or illegal entries. Any consent secured after these illegal acts cannot be voluntary.

In the case of a dwelling house, consent to enter does not authorize consent to search. The entry must be freely granted, but, once granted, does not automatically bestow any further authority. Once consent to enter has been obtained, the scope of that entry must be reasonably related to the consent bestowed. In most cases, officers are seeking only interviews—not evidence—and consent to entry for that purpose does not include consent to search. The consenting party may not only restrict the scope of his consent; he may also withdraw his consent at any time.

For example: "A police officer observed defendant sitting in his car at 2 A.M. and questioned him because of the hour and the area where frequent arrests had been made for burglaries and narcotic violations. The officer had no warrant nor any further information regarding the defendant or his car, other than that it was registered in another name but was not listed as stolen. Both the defendant and the officer testified that the defendant was cooperative when the defendant was first asked to identify himself. Both testified that the defendant allowed the officer to look around inside the vehicle. The officer then searched the front seat area and the glove compartment. The officer then asked to look in the trunk of the car. There was no key to the trunk and it was not locked. The defendant told the officer that the trunk contained a spare tire, car battery and some tools. The officer testified that he had defendant lift the trunk lid. The defendant testified that the officer opened the trunk and began to examine the contents. Defendant testified that the investigation to this point had taken about 15 minutes and that he was becoming concerned about the delay and harassment of the investigation.

"At this point the defendant asked the officer what he was looking for and told the officer to stop his search because he felt he was being harassed. The officer testified that, in fact, he did not know what he might find, but that he intended to, and did, continue his search despite the defendant's objection. The contraband introduced as evidence in the trial, over appropriate objection by the defendant, was subsequently found concealed under a rag on top of a car battery stored in the truck."

The court saw no reason why the defendant could not withdraw his consent previously given. (*People* v. *Martinez.*)

Cases and Materials

Bumper v. *North Carolina*, 391 U.S. 543, 88 S. Ct. 1788, 20 L. Ed. 2d 797.

Castaneda v. *Superior Court*, 59 Cal. 2d 439, 380 P. 2d 641.

Chapman v. *United States*, 365 U.S. 610, 81 S. Ct. 776, 5 L. Ed. 2d 828.

People v. *Martinez*, 259 Cal. App. 2d Supp. 943, 65 Cal. R. 920.

People v. *Shelton*, 60 Cal. 2d 740, 388 P. 2d 665.

People v. *Superior Court* (Casebeer), 71 Cal. 2d 265, 455 P. 2d 146.

People v. *West*, 3 Cal. 3d 595, 477 P. 2d 409.

Schneckloth v. *Bustamonte,* U.S. Supreme Court, June 4, 1973.

State v. *Commonwealth*, 246 S.W. 449 (Kentucky).

State v. *Johnson*, 427 P. 2d 705 (Washington).

Stoner v. *California*, 376 U.S. 483, 84 S. Ct. 889, 11 L. Ed. 2d 856.

1. Officers are invited into the home by the defendant. While inside, officers question the defendant about a crime and ask if they can "look around." The defendant agrees. One of the officers opens a dresser drawer and discovers evidence of a crime.

Is the defendant's consent to "look around" equivalent to a consent to "search"?

2. Officers stop the defendant's vehicle for commission of a minor traffic violation. Even though the defendant produces satisfactory identification and does not appear to be under the influence of any drug or alcohol, the officer asks whether he may search the vehicle.

Assuming that the defendant is not otherwise suspected of any crime, must the officer have a reasonable basis to request a consent search? In other words, must there be "probable cause" to request a person to consent to a search?

Chapter Eight

Searches without Warrants

Although searches incidental to arrest constitute the vast majority of warrantless searches, there are several other exceptions to the rule that all searches must be conducted under the authority of a search warrant.

Probable Cause to Search a Motor Vehicle

The motor vehicle is a mixed blessing: indispensable to the citizen for business and recreation, yet often essential to the criminal engaged in his unlawful enterprise; a source of transportation, yet a weapon of destruction when driven by a drunken driver. For obvious reasons, all state legislatures have heavily regulated the ownership and use of vehicles. Many of the regulations concern theft or damage to vehicles. Other statutes regulate the conduct of the driver.

When a police officer detects a statutory violation involving a vehicle, his detention of the motorist to issue a citation often reveals the commission of a different or more serious criminal offense involving either the driver, the vehicle, or both. In such cases, the arrest and possible search of the persons in the car and the possible search of the car itself involve the constitutional protections of the Fourth Amendment. How have the courts responded?

Note that there is a constitutional distinction between entry of a vehicle and search of a vehicle. In some cases, the officer is not attempting to search, i.e. "discover items concealed from view," but is only attempting to verify ownership of the vehicle or perhaps determine the status of a sleeping or possibly injured occupant. If, during a lawful entry, he observes seizable evidence in plain view, the courts will not exclude it. If the initial entry is reasonable under all the circumstances and not a subterfuge to search, the officer may escalate his right to search according to the circumstances.

In large part the courts have recognized the automobile's unique characteristic of mobility. In analyzing the search of a person, the courts require the initial interference with personal freedom be evidenced by probable cause to arrest. For a search of a house, a search warrant is usually required. But in the case of automobiles, the courts have developed the doctrine of "probable cause to search a motor vehicle" without the necessity of an arrest and absent a search warrant. The doctrine of probable cause to search holds that whenever there is probable cause to search a motor vehicle, no arrest or warrant is necessary. This doctrine requires officers to develop probable cause to believe that the car contains stolen property, contraband, evidence or fruits of a crime, or that the car is an instrumentality of the crime itself, e.g., the car was used as an instrument of assault or was involved in the negligent injury of a pedestrian.[1] The same standard of probable cause that governs the arrest of a person or the issuance of a search warrant prevails, and officers must comply with the rules of observational probable cause and informational probable cause.

In terms of the circumstances justifying a warrantless search, the Supreme Court in particular has long distinguished between an automobile and a home or an office. In *Carroll* v. *United States*, the issue was the admissibility in evidence of contraband liquor seized in a warrantless search of a car on the highway. After surveying the law from the time of the adoption of the Fourth Amendment onward, the Court held that automobiles and other conveyances may be searched without a warrant in circumstances that would not justify the search without a warrant of a house or an office, provided that there is probable cause to believe that the car contains articles that the officers are entitled to seize. The Court expressed its holding as follows:

"We have made a somewhat extended reference to these [federal] statutes to show that the guaranty of freedom from unreasonable searches and seizures by the Fourth Amendment has been construed, practically since the beginning of the Government, as recognizing a

---

1. Classification of the crime may be important. If the crime were a misdemeanor, officers might need an arrest warrant for the driver because the crime was not committed in their presence. But a warrant would not be required for the seizure and search of the car.

necessary difference between a search of a store, dwelling house or other structure in respect of which a proper official warrant readily may be obtained, and a search of a ship, motor boat, wagon, automobile, for contraband goods, where it is not practicable to secure a warrant because the vehicle can be quickly moved out of the locality or jurisdiction in which the warrant must be sought.

"Having thus established that contraband goods concealed and illegally transported in an automobile or other vehicle may be searched . . . without a warrant, we come now to consider under what circumstances such search may be made. Those lawfully within the country, entitled to use the public highways, have a right to free passage without interruption or search unless there is known to a competent official authorized to search, probable cause for believing that their vehicles are carrying contraband or illegal merchandise. . . . The measure of legality of such a seizure is, therefore, that the seizing officer shall have reasonable or probable cause for believing that the automobile which he stops and searches has contraband liquor therein which is being illegally transported."

The Court also noted that the search of an automobile on probable cause proceeds on a theory wholly different from that justifying the search incident to an arrest: "The right to search and the validity of the seizure are not dependent on the right to arrest. They are dependent on the reasonable cause the seizing officer has for belief that the contents of the automobile offend against the law."

Neither *Carroll* nor other cases decided by the Supreme Court require or suggest that in every conceivable circumstance the search of an automobile even with probable cause may be made without the extra protection for privacy that a warrant affords. But the circumstances that furnish probable cause to search a particular auto for particular articles are most often unforeseeable; moreover, the opportunity to search is fleeting since a car is readily movable. Where this is true, as in *Carroll*, if an effective search is to be made at any time, either the search must be made immediately without a warrant or the car itself must be seized and held without a warrant for whatever period is necessary to obtain a warrant for the search.

In enforcing the Fourth Amendment's prohibition against unreasonable searches and seizures, the Court has insisted on probable cause as a minimum requirement for a reasonable search permitted by the Constitution. As a general rule, it has also required the judgment of a magistrate on the probable-cause issue and the issuance of a warrant before a search is made. Only in exigent circumstances will the judgment of the police as to probable cause serve as a sufficient authorization for a search. *Carroll* holds a search warrant unnecessary where there is probable cause to search an automobile stopped on the highway; the car is movable, the occupants are alerted, and the car's contents may never be found again if a warrant must be obtained. Hence an immediate search is constitutionally permissible. Thus, the first issue is whether there is probable cause.

"During a local labor dispute, a car was seen to drive past the home of a nonstriking employee. Shots were fired from the car at or into the home. The occupant of the house was standing in the front yard and fired back at the car with a pistol, and thought his first shot hit the back of the car. He informed the Sheriff by telephone only of the shooting by occupants of the car. Soon after, a deputy sheriff contacted by the Sheriff on his radio and presumably told of the crime, spotted a suspicious car and began following it. The car raced away but was stopped by another policeman notified of a speeding car. The stopped car, which contained the defendant, was taken to jail. While defendant was waiting inside the jail, policemen searched the car. Under the front seat they found an air rifle.

"While the record was not entirely clear, defendant appears to have been arrested for reckless driving. Whether or not a car may constitutionally be searched 'incident' to arrest for a traffic offense, the search here did not take place until defendant was in custody inside the courthouse and the car was parked on the street outside, and under such circumstances a search is too remote in time or place to be incidental to the arrest.

"In this case there is no indication that the police had purported to impound or to hold the car, or that they were authorized by any state law to do so, or that their search of the car was intended to implement the purposes of such custody. Here the police seem to have parked the car near the courthouse merely as a convenience to the owner. The record here did not contain evidence that the Sheriff or deputy sheriff or the officers who assisted in the search had reasonable or probable cause to believe that evidence would be found in defendant's car. The deputy sheriff had not been told that the occupant of the house had identified the car from which shots were fired. He testified: 'All I got is just that it would be an old make model car. Kinda old make model car.'

"The record also contains no suggestion that the occupant of the house told the Sheriff or deputy sheriff or any other law enforcement official that he had fired at the car or that he thought he had hit it with one bullet. As far as this record shows, the deputy knew only that the car he chased was 'an old make model car,' that it speeded up when he chased it, and that it contained a fresh bullet hole. The evidence was insufficient to justify a conclusion that the defendant's car was searched with 'reasonable or probable cause' to believe the search would be fruitful." (*Dyke* v. *Taylor, etc.*)

In determining the lawfulness of a search of a car on probable cause, a variety of fact situations occur and it is useful to categorize them: (1) unoccupied vehicles; (2) occupied vehicles; and (3) occupied and abandoned vehicles.

Unoccupied Vehicles

Police began an investigation into the murder of a young girl. "During the ensuing two and a half weeks, the State accumulated a quantity of evidence to support the theory that it was the defendant Coolidge who had killed the girl. The results of the investigation were presented at a meeting among the police officers working on the case. At this meeting, it was decided that there was enough evidence to justify the arrest of defendant on the murder charge and a search of his house and two cars.

"The police arrested defendant in his house. Some time later, the police called a towing company, and about two and a half hours after defendant had been taken into custody his car was towed to the police station. At the time of the arrest the car was parked in the driveway, and although dark had fallen, it was plainly visible both from the street and from inside the house where defendant was actually arrested. The car was searched and vacuumed.

"At defendant's subsequent jury trial on the charge of murder, vacuum sweepings, including particles of gun powder taken from the car, were introduced in evidence against him as part of an attempt by the State to show by microscopic analysis that it was highly probable that the girl murdered had been in defendant's car."

In this case, *Coolidge* v. *New Hampshire*, the Court again reviewed its earlier cases on the search of automobiles based on probable cause. They repeated the constitutional difference between a search of a store, dwelling house, or other structure in which a warrant readily may be obtained for contraband goods, and a search of an automobile, where *it is not practicable to secure a warrant* because the vehicle can be quickly moved out of the locality or jurisdiction in which the warrant must be sought. These exigent circumstances justify the warrantless search of an automobile *stopped on the highway*, where there is probable cause, because the car is movable, the occupants are alerted, and the car's contents may never be found again if a warrant must be obtained. The opportunity to search is fleeting.

"In this case, the police had known for some time of the probable role of the car in the crime. The defendant had been aware that he was a suspect in the murder, but there was no indication that he meant to flee. He had already had ample opportunity to destroy any evidence he thought incriminating. There is no suggestion that, on the night in question, the car was being used for any illegal purpose, and it was regularly parked in the driveway of his house. The opportunity for search was thus hardly 'fleeting.' The objects that the police are assumed to have had probable cause to search for in the car were neither stolen nor contraband nor dangerous.

"When the police arrived at the house to arrest him, two officers were sent to guard the back door while the main party approached from the front. Defendant was arrested inside the house, without resistance of any kind on his part, after he had voluntarily admitted the officers at both front and back doors. There was no way in which he could conceivably have gained access to the automobile after the police arrived on his property.

"The word 'automobile' is not a talisman in whose presence the Fourth Amendment fades away and disappears. There is nothing in this case to invoke the meaning and purpose of the rule—no alerted criminal bent on flight, no fleeting opportunity on an open highway after a hazardous chase, no contraband or stolen goods or weapons, no confederates waiting to move the evidence, not even the inconvenience of a special police detail to guard the immobilized automobile. There is no way this can be made into a case where it is not practicable to secure a warrant, and the 'automobile exception,' despite its label, is simply irrelevant. Here there was probable cause, but no exigent circumstances justified the police in proceeding without a warrant. The later search at the station house was therefore illegal."

It should be noted that the Coolidge case was subscribed to by only four members of the Supreme Court. The fifth justice concurred in the ruling, but did not concur in the reasoning that, under these circumstances, a warrantless search of an unoccupied car, absent an emergency, is unreasonable. As a consequence, some disagreement exists as to the impact of the decision. For example: Some jurisdictions hold that a car may be seized contemporaneous with an arrest if the car itself is evidence of the crime—as it would be in the case of kidnapping, robbery, or murder—if there is evidence that the car was used as an instrumentality of the crime of murder. This doctrine, coupled with the "plain view" rule, allows the officers to seize evidence that comes within their plain view. Thus, if the subject car is observed on the street, i.e., in plain view, and there is probable cause to believe that it is the instrumentality of a crime, a seizure of the car would be reasonable without a warrant. Any subsequent search would not be a delayed search because the police are authorized to subject evidence lawfully in their custody to inspection at any time. The search is not an impound search—it is an inspection of evidence.

Occupied Vehicles

If probable cause is established, the doctrine applies whether the initial search is of an occupied car in the street or of a car removed from the street and searched later after the arrest. Yet, the nature of the original custody becomes crucial. If the car was removed from the street after an arrest and searched at the police garage, the validity of the search will be judged by the reasons for the original removal. A car removed from the street after an arrest of the occupants on traffic warrants could not be searched because probable cause to believe that the car contains evidence of a crime is lacking. Even if officers are statutorily authorized to impound vehicles and inventory contents, the results of the inventory may not be admissible unless the inventory search is based on probable cause to search the car independent of inventory.[2] Statutorily, officers may be authorized to inventory the contents of a stored vehicle, but constitutionally speaking, the successful results of such a search may not be admissible in evidence.

"A service station was robbed by two men, each of whom carried and displayed a gun. The robbers took the currency from the cash register; the service station attendant was directed to place the coins in his right-hand glove, which was then taken by the robbers. Two witnesses, who had earlier noticed a blue compact station wagon circling the block in the vicinity of the station, then saw the station wagon speed away from a parking lot close to the station. At the same time, they learned that the station had been robbed. They reported to police, who arrived immediately, that four men were in the station wagon and one was wearing a green sweater. The attendant told the police that one of the men who robbed him was wearing a green sweater and the other was wearing a trench coat. A description of the car and the two robbers was broadcast over the police radio. Within an hour, a light blue compact station wagon answering the description and carrying four men was stopped by the police about two miles from the station. Defendant was one of the men in the station wagon. He was wearing a green sweater and there was a trench coat in the car. The occupants were arrested and the car was driven to the police station. In the course of a thorough search of the car at the station, the police found concealed in a compartment under the dashboard two .38-caliber revolvers and a right-hand glove containing small change.

"The police obviously had probable cause to believe that the robbers, carrying guns and the fruits of the crime, had fled the scene in a light blue compact station wagon which would be carrying four men, one wearing a green sweater and another wearing a trench coat. There was probable cause to arrest the occupants of the station wagon that the officers stopped; just as obviously was there probable cause to search the car for guns and stolen money. Arguably, because of the

---

2. The California Supreme Court has held that peace officers who become involuntary recipients of vehicles need only exercise a slight amount of care to immunize their department from charges of negligence.

preference for a magistrate's judgment, only the immobilization of the car should be permitted until a search warrant is obtained; arguably, only the "lesser" intrusion is permissible until the magistrate authorizes the 'greater.' But which is the 'greater' and which the 'lesser' intrusion is itself a debatable question and the answer may depend on a variety of circumstances. [The Court saw] no difference between on the one hand seizing and holding a car before presenting the probable-cause issue to a magistrate and on the other hand carrying out an immediate search without a warrant. Given probable cause to search, either course is reasonable under the Fourth Amendment." (*Chambers* v. *Maroney*.)

Probable cause to search a motor vehicle allows the officer to detain and search an occupied car even if there is no probable cause to arrest the occupants. In most cases, probable cause to search will be substantially the same probable cause to arrest the occupants—in which case the validity of the search may be sustained on the theory of search incident to arrest. But the added advantage of probable cause to search a motor vehicle arises when officers desire to remove the vehicle to search at a different time and place. Under "search incident" theory, a search at a later time and place is not contemporaneous with the arrest and is therefore unlawful. But the U.S. Supreme Court has held that if the officers had probable cause to search the vehicle at the time the occupants were arrested, that same probable cause continues even after the arrest. The court held that since the occupants were already arrested and their right of privacy personally invaded, the delayed search of the vehicle in which they were riding at the time of arrest would not be sufficient additional violation of their personal security to require a warrant. But this doctrine applies only when probable cause to search the car existed at the time of arrest. Absent probable cause to search the motor vehicle, any later impound search would be unauthorized without a warrant—except, of course, as to evidence in plain sight.

Developing probable cause to search a motor vehicle can include evidence of the observation of a traffic violation or vehicle equipment violation; or it can rest on a reasonable suspicion that the car or its occupants are involved in criminal activity. Whether the initial stop is statutorily authorized because a misdemeanor has been committed in the officers' presence, or whether a detention for investigation is constitutionally authorized, officers can always request display of the driver's license and evidence of vehicle ownership. The results of this inquiry may be the first step in establishing probable cause. Thereafter, the officers may view the interior of the vehicle as well as the actions of the occupants to determine whether any additional evidence of criminality is present. The conduct and demeanor of the driver and passengers are relevant, and answers to preliminary questions are permitted under the *Miranda* decision. A radio check is also proper. From a combination of circumstances the officer can either build his case for probable cause or dispel the thought of arrest. If he detects the odor of alcohol and ultimately arrests the driver for driving under the influence of it, a search of the car would be authorized as an incident of the arrest. If he detects the odor of marijuana, he could enter and search the car without arrest—based on probable cause to believe the car contains contraband—and the results of this search govern whether or not an arrest is in order.

Despite the rule that a motor vehicle may be searched without a warrant based on probable cause to believe that the car contains evidence of a crime or is an instrumentality of the crime, officers who impound such vehicles for a later search should search as soon after the arrest as possible. An extensive delay in searching may lead the court to ask why a search warrant could not be obtained when time clearly allowed.

Occupied and Abandoned Vehicles

Just as unoccupied or occupied cars may be searched without a warrant, a car occupied and abandoned may also be searched without a warrant. The flight of a suspect from the car cannot frustrate a search of the vehicle as long as probable cause to search the car exists. Cars abandoned after their use as an instrumentality in the commission of a robbery may therefore be entered and searched immediately after discovery, without a warrant, even if there is no pressing emergency or officers are not in hot pursuit—factors that may also justify search of the car without a warrant (see the section Emergency Searches in this chapter).

The Doctrine in Perspective

By treating the automobile as a separate entity, the U.S. Supreme Court has attempted to modify the explicit demands of a warrant required for the search of a house. But the rule that a car may be searched without a warrant based on probable cause to believe the vehicle contains seizable evidence cannot always excuse the requirement of a warrant. The leading case, *Chambers* v. *Maroney*, approving the warrantless search of cars based on probable cause, involved the arrest of its occupants for robbery and a later search at a police facility. Probable cause to search the car as an instrumentality of the crime existed at the time of the arrest of its occupants. Their privacy was already invaded, and an incidental search of the car was not deemed sufficient to justify a warrant. And under well-established rules, the car could be searched for evidence of the robbery at the time and place of arrest. Delaying the search was deemed immaterial when the right to search already existed at the time of arrest.

But in *Coolidge* v. *New Hampshire*, the Court refused to apply the doctrine under almost similar circumstances. The defendant was arrested in his house after a lengthy investigation, and his car, parked nearby, was searched without a warrant. The court held that even if probable cause existed to believe seizable evidence was in the car, a warrant should have been obtained. The car had been subject to investigation for some period of time; at the time of arrest, the car was unoccupied and immobile; no emergency existed to excuse the warrant. Thus, no justification appears for the initial intrusion without a warrant. If the car had been occupied at the time of the arrest, the result might have been different. Unoccupied cars, therefore, may not always be searched without a warrant absent some other justification or evidence of emergency.

Another unresolved issue affecting the search of vehicles involves the rationale of the *Chimel* decision. Although *Chimel* resolved the scope of a search incident to an arrest effected inside a dwelling house, the rationale could arguably apply to cars. If the scope of a search incidental to arrest was limited to the person of the arrestee and the area within his immediate control, why not apply a similar rule to the search of vehicles? In fact, once the driver or his passenger has been removed from the vehicle, any possible danger from assault or any loss of evidence is substantially reduced. Perhaps the search of the interior of the car for evidence related to the arrest would be reasonable. But a search of a closed trunk would not necessarily be included.

On balance, the *Chambers* case would probably prevail, i.e., once the occupants have been arrested, little significance can be attached to a further invasion of their privacy in searching the trunk. This rule is at least valid when there is probable cause to search the vehicle at the time of the arrest. If the occupants were arrested for a felony and merely occupying the vehicle for transportation, the car itself would not necessarily be the instrumentality of the crime.[3] In which case no probable cause to search the car exists independent of the arrest of its occupants. But the arrest itself may authorize a search of the car or the trunk of the car without a warrant, notwithstanding the language of *Chimel*.

Search of Goods in Transit

The doctrine of probable cause to search a motor vehicle without a warrant rests largely on the assumption that the factor of mobility

---

3. In burglary, for example, the crime is complete when the burglar enters the dwelling house with the requisite criminal intent. Transporting the stolen property is only incidental. In robbery, however, asportation of the goods is usually a part of the crime, and the crime is not complete until the goods are reasonably secure in the thief's custody.

transcends the rule that all searches must be conducted under authority
of a warrant. When the Fourth Amendment was adopted, searches of
cars were not contemplated, but searches of goods moved in the course
of transportation by boat, wagon, or other conveyance were common.[4]
Because goods were easily removable before a warrant could be obtained, the U.S. Supreme Court early in constitutional history held that
the usual requirement of a warrant to seize contraband goods in transit
may be dispensed with as long as probable cause to search the goods
exists. Modern transportation methods do not differ, analytically
speaking, from colonial travel. But nowhere do Fourth Amendment
problems appear more clearly focused than on the issue of warrantless
searches of goods in transit.

"An air freight agent testified that defendant brought five cardboard cartons to the freight counter at the airport. Defendant stated he
wished to ship the cartons to Seattle; he described the contents as
'personal effects,' and gave the name 'L. McKinnon' as the consignor
and 'L. McKinnon' as the consignee.

"The agent had not seen the man before, but suspected that the
cartons contained contraband. After defendant left, the agent asked a
fellow employee to note the make and license number of defendant's
car. He then obtained his supervisor's permission to open one of the
cartons for purposes of inspection. In the presence of the supervisor
and other employees, he slit the tape on one of the cartons and put his
hand inside. Beneath some paper he felt brick-shaped packages of what
seemed to be soft tobacco or grass. He then lifted the lid of the carton,
took out one of the packages, and pinched it open. Upon finding that
it contained what he believed to be marijuana, he telephoned the
police.

"In response to the call, an officer arrived at the air freight
counter 20 or 30 minutes later. He looked at the air bill, then entered
a back room where the cartons had been placed. The carton that the
agent had inspected stood open on the floor; it contained a large brown
plastic bag, which was also open. As the officer approached the carton,
he saw inside a number of brick-shaped packages wrapped in red
cellophane. Each was 10 to 12 inches long, about 6 inches wide, and
2 to 3 inches thick. The officer formed the opinion that the substance
in the packages was marijuana. He proceeded to open one of the
packages and verified its contents.

"The officer next learned that a passenger by the name of 'L.
McKinnon' had a reservation on a flight due to leave for Seattle within
the hour. He obtained from the agent a description of the man who
had presented the cartons for shipment, together with the make and

4. But not first-class mail, which is afforded greater protection; *United States* v.
Van Leuween, 397 U.S. 249, 90 S. Ct. 1029, 25 L. Ed. 2d 282.

license number of his car. Shortly afterward the officer located the car in the parking lot, and arrested defendant as he entered it." (*People* v. *McKinnon.*) The defendant contended that the search by the officer could only be made with a warrant.

To begin with, the U.S. Supreme Court has repeatedly held that if probable cause exists to believe that a search will reveal seizable evidence, a warrant must be obtained—absent an emergency—unless the search is incidental to an arrest. The only other exception to the warrant requirement is a danger of immediate destruction, removal, or concealment of property intended to be seized. This Fourth Amendment protection from unreasonable searches and seizures applies to a search of "effects" as well as searches of houses and cars.[5] Thus, the contents of any container cannot be searched, absent consent, without compliance with the Fourth Amendment.

Cars have been excepted from the warrant requirement because their mobility enables someone to remove seizable evidence before a warrant can be obtained. But suppose that peace officers have probable cause to believe that a locked trunk, consigned for immediate air freight shipment, contains contraband. Can the trunk be searched without a warrant? The trunk and its contents are "effects" within the meaning of the Fourth Amendment. Does its potential removal from the airport dispense with the warrant requirement? At this point, the role of the Fourth Amendment becomes critical. One viewpoint holds that the police alternative is twofold: search the trunk immediately without a warrant, or, seize and hold the trunk until they can obtain a warrant. In the automobile search case of *Chambers* v. *Maroney*, the U.S. Supreme Court held that, in these circumstances, there is no constitutional difference between the alternatives facing the police. An immediate search without a warrant, said the court, is no greater an intrusion on the driver's right of privacy than is immobilization of the car until a warrant can be obtained; either course is reasonable under the Fourth Amendment. Under this reasoning, goods consigned to a common carrier for shipment are no less movable than an automobile, and the reasons for the rule permitting a warrantless search of a vehicle on probable cause are equally applicable to the search of goods in transit.

In response, the argument can be made that if indeed "effects" mean anything in the constitutional sense, then warrant protection must be afforded. The mobility of a car or other conveyance is the only distinguishing factor that allows a search without a warrant. Effects are immovable in themselves, and only if the goods are in the course of

---

5. "The right of the people to be secure in their persons, houses, papers, and effects against unreasonable searches and seizures, shall not be violated. . . ."

transportation, i.e., in a vehicle or other carrier capable of carrying them beyond the jurisdiction, may the "effects" be searched without a warrant. Manifestly, a trunk consigned for rail or air shipment is not within a vehicle, nor can it move under its own power.

Further, the only other basis for allowing a warrantless search of a vehicle is the arrest of its occupants, which would allow an incidental search. Since the original detention and arrest of the driver is a substantial invasion of his privacy in any event, a search of his vehicle is of little additional significance. But goods consigned for shipment are normally searched in the absence of, and remote from, any arrestee. The arrest, if one occurs, follows the search and is justified by what the search turns up. In this event, the search of the trunk is a classic example of the reason for the Fourth Amendment, i.e., probable cause to search requires a warrant, and an arrest cannot justify an incidental search not based on probable cause to arrest someone. Moreover, almost all "effects" are in fact movable, and the Fourth Amendment protection evaporates if the car search theories are applied.

This latter argument probably expresses the most accurate interpretation of the Fourth Amendment, but it fails to consider the element of goods "consigned for transportation." Thus, "effects" on the person, in the car, and in the dwelling house remain personal to the owner and entitled to full Fourth Amendment protection. But if the owner agrees to ship his effects on a common carrier, he cannot expect the same degree of protection. The mobility of such parcels is substantially equivalent to the mobility of an automobile. If so, no warrant is required for their search as long as probable cause exists.

Emergency Searches

Police work is intimately linked with emergency situations. With the exception of fire departments, no other job requires as much planning for emergencies as does law enforcement. Because a state of emergency is commonplace in police work, the courts have tailored the rules of arrest and search accordingly. Necessity often justifies an action that would otherwise constitute a trespass, as, when the act is prompted by a motive of preserving life or property and reasonably appears to be necessary for that purpose. Emergency entries and searches motivated by such goals need not be judged by usual Fourth Amendment standards. But the Fourth Amendment remains relevant, and the courts have placed boundaries around the doctrine of emergency. The emergency exception must be reasonably related to the situation that confronts the officer. Thus, the tests for emergency entry and search of a vehicle are not necessarily the same as for the entry of a house.

Vehicles: Generally speaking, the driver of an automobile, and the automobile itself, are entitled to Fourth Amendment protection. An officer who intends to detain a driver or search the car must testify to the reasonableness of his actions. If an officer observes an unoccupied car protruding onto the highway, his decision to enter the car and move it will be motivated by the need to remove a potential safety hazard. Since he makes no arrest, and no one can consent, his action can only be justified as an emergency entry. While inside, he can make an inspection to determine ownership of the vehicle. If he discovers seizable evidence during the course of his investigation, a warrantless seizure will be lawful. Of course, any search of the car not reasonably related to the safety objective would not be in response to the emergency; rather, it would be merely a general search and, therefore, unreasonable.

Another example of an emergency search of an unoccupied vehicle: Responding to the report of an armed robbery, officers discover the described vehicle shortly after the robbery has occurred. If an officer enters the vehicle, the entry and search would be reasonably related to the emergency situation. Officers are in hot pursuit of a fleeing suspect who has just committed a crime, and the need to identify and locate the suspect under these circumstances clearly creates an emergency that justifies the officers' warrantless entry.

In some cases, officers discover occupants of vehicles whose physical condition clearly warrants investigation. A limited entry of the vehicle to determine whether the occupant is sick or injured is clearly reasonable. Any seizable evidence discovered as a consequence of the entry for that purpose would not be the product of an unreasonable search. A general search for evidence, however, would not be reasonable.

Houses: The warrantless entry into a house in response to an emergency is also reasonable as long as there is some evidence of the emergency. The legal test of entry into a home is stricter than that of entry into a vehicle. Illustrative of this rule is the language of the U.S. Supreme Court in *McDonald* v. *United States*: "The presence of a search warrant serves a high function. Absent some grave emergency, the Fourth Amendment has interposed a magistrate between the citizen and the police. This was not done to shield criminals nor to make the home a safe haven for illegal activities. It was done so that an objective mind could weigh the need to invade the privacy in order to enforce the law. . . . We cannot be true to that constitutional requirement and excuse the absence of a search warrant without a showing by those who seek exemption from the constitutional mandate that the exigencies of the situation made that course imperative."

For example: A murder of a police officer occurred at a local department store. "An officer testified that he arrived at the store within minutes after the shooting and took charge of Mrs. W., one of the suspects involved and, as determined later, defendant's mistress. He explained, 'We were seeking the identity of the man who had accompanied her into the store.' In Mrs. W.'s purse he found her driver's license bearing her address. The officer asked her who lived with her at that address, and she said that Lee did, the man who had come into the store with her (i.e., the defendant). The officer then asked her if Lee would go back to that address, and she answered, 'I suppose he will. His clothes are there.' The officer instructed two uniformed policemen to stake out the premises.

"The officer questioned Mrs. W. further, his purpose being 'To attempt to identify the man that shot the officer.' She said she didn't know his real name, but that he had told her to call him 'Jim Snyder.' She gave a physical description of defendant, and the officer caused this description to be broadcast over police radio.

"At the station the officer asked Mrs. W. if she had any pictures of 'this Jim Snyder.' She said there were pictures of him at the house. The officer then asked her if there was anything else in the house to identify 'Jim Snyder,' and she answered there might be 'something in a bag or some bags.'

"The officer then spoke by telephone to other officers and instructed them to pick up the pictures of 'Jim Snyder' at the house and anything else that might aid in identifying him. Being aware, moreover, that the entire shooting incident had arisen out of an attempt by 'Jim Snyder' to pass a check of doubtful validity, he told them generally to bring in all identifying evidence in 'a forgery case or shooting case.' In the ensuing search the officers found and removed a photograph of defendant and Mrs. W., a box of .38 caliber ammunition, and other evidence.

"Although 'Jim Snyder' escaped from the scene, the manhunt began immediately. It was reasonable for the police to believe he might stop at his house before continuing his flight, to obtain clothes, money, or ammunition. This belief, in fact, was shared by Mrs. W., who communicated it to the police at that time.

"It was with this kind of danger in mind that officers took reasonable precautions in entering the house. They had received a radio message instructing them to enter that house, and informing them that the suspect had just killed two policemen at the store. Failing to obtain a key from the adjacent house of the landlord, the officer forcibly entered the suspect's residence. With drawn guns the policemen then searched the house for the suspect or 'for any evidence of the suspect's having been there and gone.'

"The law recognizes that fresh pursuit of a fleeing suspect who has committed a grave offense and remains dangerous to life and limb may constitute 'exceptional circumstances' sufficient to justify a search without a warrant. When the police determined the house was vacant, they were not required at that point to abandon their search for 'Jim Snyder' or his true identity. They were not compelled to close their eyes to the contents of the house, and their ensuing search was incidental to the purpose of their entry. While in the house, it was not unreasonable for the officers to look about them for evidence that would identify the suspect, thus far known to them only by one of his several aliases, or that would enable them to pick up his trail." (*People* v. *Smith*.) The evidence obtained by that search was properly admitted.

The emergency exception, however, cannot swallow the rule. At least two conditions must be met: first, officers must present evidence that their entry was motivated by an imminent and substantial threat to life, health, or property; second, the scope of any search incidental to the emergency must be strictly tied to, and related to, the need for the initial intrusion. By limiting the doctrine of emergency in this way, officers are free to respond fully to the situation confronting them while simultaneously preserving the citizen's privacy from unjustified invasion.

Emergency searches of the person normally include removal of blood from a suspected intoxicated driver, or an attempt to determine the cause of illness of someone who is either unconscious or unable to respond. In the latter case, a search of the pockets for medicine or other information is reasonable, and if seizable evidence is discovered, the objects are lawfully seized. But in the case of the removal of blood samples, a more difficult problem arises.

There are at least three constitutional objections to the admissibility of evidence seized by an intrusion of the body: first, removal of a blood sample violates a person's right to due process of law on the ground that such conduct is too shocking to tolerate; second, removal of a blood sample violates the privilege against self-incrimination; third, the entry into the blood stream constitutes a search within the meaning of the Fourth Amendment and requires a warrant.

As to the first objection, the courts have concluded that removing a blood sample in a medically approved manner is commonplace, and if administered by qualified personnel, is not violative of due process (see Chapter 13, Force to Obtain Evidence). Nor does removal of a blood sample violate the privilege against self-incrimination because the privilege only applies to verbal, i.e., testimonial, evidence, not real evidence. But the entry of the needle into the blood stream to extract blood is a "search" within the meaning of the Fourth Amendment. In order for it to be reasonable without a warrant, the search must be incidental to arrest or by consent. In many cases, the driver who is suspected of driving under the influence of alcohol can be placed under arrest, and the search for blood will be incidental to the arrest. But if the driver did not commit the act of driving under the influence in the officer's presence—a requirement for a misdemeanor arrest—the officer cannot place him under arrest for that offense. Arrest for "plain drunk" is the only alternative, if in fact the arrestee is drunk and not merely under the influence. Or, similarly, if the suspected inebriated driver is unconscious from an accident when officers arrive at the scene, no misdemeanor arrest could follow unless someone were injured. The injury might escalate the gravity of the offense from misdemeanor to felony, in which case the officer could arrest on probable cause and the offense need not be committed in his presence.

Because of the transitory nature of alcohol in the blood, obtaining a search warrant is impossible. Therefore the search inside the body for blood is constitutionally justified, in the absence of an arrest or consent, only as an emergency search to prevent disappearance of evidence. The general rule is that the results of the test are admissible in evidence and not the product of an unlawful search.[6]

The importance of obtaining a blood sample, or other body specimen which will reflect the presence of alcohol, is not as critical as some believe. If the suspected intoxicated driver refuses to submit to the test, his refusal may be used as evidence against him at trial. That same refusal may be commented on by the prosecutor as evidence of consciousness of guilt. Evidence of refusal to submit to a blood sample does not violate the privilege against self-incrimination, a privilege that affects only testimonial compulsion.[7]

Moreover, under "implied consent" laws, the driver of an automobile is deemed to consent to provide a blood, breath, or urine sample if he drives on the highway. If he refuses to consent when arrested for driving under the influence of alcohol, his driving privilege may be revoked in an administrative hearing. Of course, evidence of the alcoholic content of the body is clearly desirable, but failure to obtain a sample is not crucial to successful court or administrative proceedings. (See also chapter 13, Force to Obtain Evidence.)

---

6. One state court has held that the search must still be incidental to arrest, and if no arrest is made the search is unreasonable. The court reasoned that the disappearance of the evidence did indeed create an emergency. But the emergency only dispensed with the need for a warrant, not the arrest; *People* v. *Superior Court* (Hawkins), 6 C 3d 757, 493 P. 2d 1145.

7. Compare this reasoning with the rule that evidence of a refusal to answer police questions is inadmissible because a suspect does have an absolute right not to incriminate himself, and his refusal to talk is a lawful exercise of that right. To allow comment on his refusal would penalize the exercise of that right.

Probation Searches

Regarded by many as the single most important function of the judiciary, probation is the conditional judicial release of a criminal offender back into society under certain terms and conditions. Failure to comply with these conditions results in the possible revocation of probation and incarceration in jail. Normally the revocation proceedings are instituted if the probationer is arrested for commission of another crime. Can the court go further, though, and impose as a condition of probation that the probationer consent to a search even if the officer lacks probable cause for an arrest?

The issue is whether the court can demand a waiver of Fourth Amendment rights as a condition of probation. Policy issues of the Fourth Amendment emerge again. Probationers who are conditionally released into society may have a reduced expectation of privacy, thereby rendering reasonable certain intrusions by governmental authorities that would otherwise be invalid under traditional constitutional concepts. Moreover, probationary terms can be imposed that reasonably relate to the conditions of release in an attempt to prevent the commission of another crime. Presumably, a probationer subject to search at any time would exercise considerably more caution than if the condition were not imposed. Under these circumstances, waiver of Fourth Amendment rights in advance would be reasonable, depending to some extent on the type of crime involved, but most frequently the condition is imposed on probationers convicted of violating the narcotic laws.

Those who would refuse to approve diminution of Fourth Amendment rights argue that imposing such a condition in no way relates to the objectives of probation. Total denial of Fourth Amendment rights is a serious matter, and, assuming a probationer must accept some dilution of Fourth Amendment protection, any modification of protection against unreasonable searches and seizures should be carefully tailored to the nature of the original offense and not imposed indiscriminately. Law enforcement officers can question or arrest a probationer just as they could anyone else—if adequate grounds exist. The role of the peace officer in the rehabilitative process is marginal, and probationary violations should be the responsibility of the probation officer.

These two divergent theories can be argued plausibly in every state. Some states might require a statute authorizing such a procedure; in others the court could impose the condition as an exercise of judicial authority. If a state does sanction a probationary search, the danger of harassment is ever present. Use of the probationary search should be carefully exercised.

Specialized Searches

Because the Fourth Amendment protects people—not places—from unreasonable searches and seizures, the scope of constitutional protection cannot be judged solely by the area in which a search takes place. For obvious reasons, however, one cannot discuss search and seizure without reference to places, and in some cases the place will affect searching authority. The Fourth Amendment is a guarantee of personal security that follows a citizen no matter where he travels. The degree of protection, or privacy, to which he is entitled varies, however, as he moves from place to place. Searches of houses are measured by the same rules as are searches of vehicles, but their application differs according to the amount of privacy expected in each of these places. But the vehicle is not talismanic, and Fourth Amendment protection does not disappear merely because a car is involved. Yet certain places have been singled out for special Fourth Amendment treatment because of their unique characteristics.

School Searches

Because children and young people depend heavily on their parents and others for most of their needs, the law recognizes this unique relationship in many ways. In the context of the Fourth Amendment, however, the courts have generally regarded parents as supervisors of their children who are empowered to make decisions on their behalf. For example, parents are authorized to consent to a search of quarters occupied by their son or daughter as long as there is evidence that the child has not established an independent status as an adult.[8]

When a minor child attends school, courts still hold the school to accountability for his safety and welfare. Standing in the place of parents, though, the schools also exercise similar parental powers over the child as student. Certainly this power extends to students at the elementary and high school level and, to some extent, at college and university campuses.

In a typical case, school officials will be informed that a student is in possession of contraband or that the contraband is concealed in his locker. If school officials attempt to search the student's person, they may fear possible resistance or violence and request police assistance. If the police search reveals contraband, the student will argue insufficient probable cause for his arrest, calling into question the entire range of law on probable cause.

---

8. For example, if the minor were eighteen and could prove he was fully employed, paid room, board, and laundry costs to his parents, owned his own car, and in no way depended financially on his parents, his independent status might not allow his parents with whom he lived to authorize consent any more than if he were a tenant.

The court must determine whether to apply the usual rules of search and seizure, or else subordinate a full application of Fourth Amendment principles to the need for the school to maintain discipline. Alternatively, the court might conclude that the purpose of the search was not police-initiated; their assistance was requested to prevent a possible eruption of violence in the school office. In which case, the search would be classified as a citizen search and not within the scope of the Fourth Amendment (see Citizen Arrest and Search, this chapter). If school officials were informed that contraband was concealed in a locker, the validity of their search would be tested by a similar analysis, although school officials could argue that school lockers are provided only for the convenience of students, and that although school property was made available to the students, the school had authority to consent to their search.

Increasingly vocal demands for student rights might persuade some courts to increase Fourth Amendment protection. Yet the special nature of a school-student relationship argues strongly for the continued flexible use of searching authority of students and their "effects" as long as the student is an enrolled pupil and on school property.

Border Searches

Responsibility for preventing the unauthorized entry of aliens, contraband, stolen property, and foreign goods into the United States is vested in the federal government, and state laws do not control. Border detention and search of people and automobiles is of the widest possible scope, although probable cause is still a factor. Strip searches, which involve substantial invasions of privacy, are allowable as long as there is some suggestion that such a search is necessary. A search may even be conducted inland and at some distance from the border, if the government can establish that seized items were carried across the border within a reasonable time before the actual search took place. But searches for aliens remote from the borders (or functional equivalents of the border) cannot be indiscriminate. Probable cause still remains a factor in evaluating the lawfulness of the detention. At a minimum, officers must offer evidence of probable cause to believe the car contained aliens or at least probable cause to believe the car made a border crossing: *Condrado Almeida-Sanchez* v. *U.S.*, 41 Law Week, 4970 (June 1973).

Citizen Arrest and Search

The authority of a private citizen to arrest is usually defined by statute, but usually his power to arrest is narrower than that of a peace officer. The validity of arrests, which can be made for misdemeanors committed in a citizen's presence or felonies based on probable cause, can be tested by the same theories that are applied to peace officers. Perhaps the only difficult question is the power of the citizen to delegate his arresting authority when the peace officer arrives. Other arrest issues involving citizens usually emerge from policy decisions adopted by all police departments. Different questions do arise when a police agency requires a citizen to adopt certain procedures before the law enforcement agency takes custody of the arrestee. Frequently the civil aspects of a case supersede any question of criminal responsibility. Because the practice varies widely, no general rules can be stated.

On the other hand, a search by a private citizen involves a more serious invasion of the right of privacy, and questions have arisen as to the power of a citizen to search. In *Burdeau* v. *McDowell,* decided by the U.S. Supreme Court in 1921, the Court held that the Fourth Amendment prohibited only governmental action, i.e., state action, and could not be applied to searches by private individuals. Thus, if the citizen search was unreasonable within the meaning of the Fourth Amendment, the exclusionary rule will not be invoked, and any seized evidence will be admitted in a subsequent criminal prosecution. Because the exclusionary rule exists to deter unlawful acts by state and federal officials, the purpose of the rule is not served by applying it to those who do not regularly enforce the law and whose conduct is not likely to be repeated.

The general rule allowing citizen searches without reference to the Fourth Amendment has some limitations. If a state statute defines the searching authority of a citizen, a state court could apply the stricter provisions of the statute to prevent searches that would otherwise be lawful under the Fourth Amendment. Nothing prevents a state from imposing a stricter standard of search and seizure than that required by the Fourth Amendment. Thus a search incidental to a citizen arrest might be limited by statute to authorize only the removal of weapons, not evidence.

Second, any search by a private citizen must have been instigated on his own initiative in order to come within the general rule allowing such searches without reference to the Fourth Amendment. If the citizen acts as an agent of the police to carry out their directions, any search would be judged by standards applicable to governmental searches. A similar result would follow if the citizen and police were acting jointly. Because the line between agency, or some form of joint operation, may not always be drawn clearly, the court may impose a duty on the police to prevent unlawful searches by private citizens, rather than allow officers to stand idly by and tacitly consent to a search they could not conduct themselves.

This latter rule has emerged in recognition of widespread cooperation between police departments and private investigative agencies whose sole function is the investigation, detection, and apprehension of people suspected of committing crimes, usually against large commercial companies. Private security agencies differ widely in objectives, ranging from in-house security personnel employed by large department stores to nationwide detective firms. In the former category, personnel are employed to prevent the theft of goods from the store; in the latter case, personnel are hired to locate and apprehend those suspected of committing theft or fraud from the client. Because the conduct of these agencies closely resembles conventional law enforcement, the courts may reexamine the rules that allow these full-time investigative officials to escape the restrictions of the Fourth Amendment. And closely allied to this issue is the scope of arrest and search authority held by a regularly salaried peace officer who works off-duty on an investigative assignment for a private employer. Serious Fourth Amendment issues arise when the officer merely removes his uniform to engage in a slightly different type of police work.

Cases and Materials

1. The guest of a hotel deposited a package with the hotel clerk for safekeeping. When the package was not requested by the guest for several days, the clerk opened it. Inside he found a loaded revolver. The police were contacted and, subsequently, when the guest returned and claimed his package, he was arrested for carrying a loaded firearm in a public place. The search of the package by the officer revealed a gun.

Assuming that the officer had sufficient probable cause to search the bag, was a warrant required? Is the deposit of a package for safekeeping in a hotel analogous to the carton consigned for shipment to a common carrier? (*People* v. *Garcia,* 29 Cal. App. 3d 430.)

2. The sudden increase of skyjacking led the U.S. Congress to enact heavy penalties for the commission of this crime. In an effort to focus on deterrence, a federal task force developed a preflight apprehension system, which consists of the following features:

a) Notice to the Public.

Signs in English and Spanish are posted at the boarding gates where passengers' tickets are checked reading as follows:

AIRCRAFT HIJACKING IS A FEDERAL CRIME
PUNISHABLE BY DEATH

CARRYING CONCEALED WEAPONS ABOARD
AIRCRAFT IS PUNISHABLE BY PRISON
SENTENCES & FINES

PASSENGERS AND BAGGAGE
SUBJECT TO SEARCH

These signs are eleven by fourteen inches with half-inch-high letters. Warnings of the same or larger dimensions are posted conspicuously at other parts of the air terminal.

While probably not required to give notice of the applicable law and penalties, these signs fill that function. They serve to deter and to reduce the possibility of embarrassment should a passenger's boarding progress be interrupted.

b) Profile.

If a passenger meets a prescribed "profile," airline employees focus on him. The details of the profile and its use are set out below.

c) Magnetometer.

A magnetometer is installed in the passageway leading to the plane so that all passengers must pass through it. It is set to flash a warning light when metal equal to or greater than an average .25-caliber gun in magnetic force deflecting power is carried by. This device is described in more detail below.

d) Interview by Airlines Personnel.

A person who triggers the magnetometer and meets the profile requirements is "interviewed" by airlines personnel. If he provides satisfactory identification, he is permitted to proceed unimpeded. Otherwise he is designated a "selectee" and is denied boarding until a deputy United States marshal is summoned.

e) Interview by Marshal.

The Marshal again requests identification of those designated as selectees. If a person furnishes satisfactory identification, it is suggested that he go through the magnetometer once more. Before walking through, he is asked if he has any metal on his person or in any baggage he is carrying. If he replies in the negative and still sets off the magnetometer, he is requested to submit to a "voluntary" search. It is explained that this search is part of an attempt by the government to prevent hijacking.

f) Frisk.

The Marshal pats down the external clothing of the subject in order to discover whether he is carrying any weapons. Depending on what is found as a result of the frisk, boarding is permitted or the person is detained.

The program is designed to speed passengers who are unlikely to present danger and to isolate, with the least possible discomfiture or delay, those presenting a substantial probability of danger. At each successive screening stage, an attempt is made to permit as many as possible to complete boarding.

While no single screening technique can by itself completely protect the flying public—without creating an objectionable level of disturbance and inconvenience—probabilities are increased by combining several approaches, thus sufficiently reducing the size of the population that must ultimately be physically interfered with to a practicable and socially acceptable level.

Obviously, the use of the magnetometer and subsequent frisk for weapons raises Fourth Amendment issues. In the usual cases of stop and frisk on the street, the officer must observe some unusual activity relating to crime and inconsistent with innocent activity. If the officer's observations justify detention, the frisk is justified only if there is some reasonable basis to believe that the person whom he is confronting is armed and dangerous.

Assuming now that the act of a person passing through the magnetic device designed to detect the presence of metal on boarding aircraft passengers is not "detention," what occurs when the magnetometer reacts positively? For Fourth Amendment purposes, when some governmental agent detains the passenger to determine whether he is carrying a prohibited metal object, the agent will subject the passenger to a limited search—a frisk—for weapons. There is no objective evidence, however, that the person detained poses any danger to the officer absent any testimony by the officer that he believed the person was armed or dangerous. And if the frisk reveals a hard object, may the officer conduct a second search to remove it? If the search reveals no weapons but, rather, a closed metal container, may the officer open (i.e., search) it without probable cause? If the officer feels a possibly dangerous object on a person whom he frisks on the street, he is justified in removing it. But once the officer is satisfied the object is not lethal, he cannot open it. Can the airport security officer be given more latitude?

Finally, suppose that the officer removes contraband, instead of a weapon, from the passenger. Should such evidence be admitted or should it be excluded, even though the initial search was lawful?

For a discussion of these problems see: *United States* v. *Lopez*, 328 F. Supp. 1077; *United States* v. *Epperson*, 454 F. 2d 769; *United States* v. *Lindsey*, 451 F. 2d 701; and *People* v. *Lacey*, 30 Cal. App. 3d 170.

3. Mrs. K. was the owner of a building containing two flats. She occupied the downstairs unit; the defendant rented the upstairs unit where she lived with her daughter, who was approximately six years old.

"Mrs. K. returned from a shopping trip and heard defendant's daughter crying, and saw the girl sitting on the steps outside the upstairs flat. The girl told Mrs. K. she had hurt her knee while dancing, but no injury could be seen. She also told Mrs. K. she was alone in her apartment, and did not want to stay there because she was 'lonesome.' Mrs. K. took the girl into her own flat, consoled her, and gave her some food. After about an hour, however, Mrs. K. decided she could not continue to assume responsibility for the girl, and therefore called the police.

"An officer came in response to the call, and questioned the girl for 10 or 15 minutes. He learned she had been left alone in her apartment, had apparently fallen down and begun crying, and had been taken in by Mrs. K.

"According to his testimony, the officer then decided to ascertain whether the girl's mother had returned home in the interim. Accompanied by Mrs. K., he went upstairs and knocked on defendant's door, announcing his identification. There was no response. He nevertheless directed Mrs. K. to unlock the door with her key. He stepped inside and called defendant's name. Again there was no response. Yet the officer 'continued to go through the apartment,' entering each room in turn. On a nightstand in the bedroom he found a jar containing marijuana, and additional marijuana on a newspaper on the dresser.

"The officer looked through the rest of the flat, then confiscated the marijuana and returned downstairs. When the defendant arrived he placed her under arrest." (*People* v. *Smith,* 7 Cal. 3d 282.)

Was there an emergency, and if so, did the officer's act in entering and seeking the mother exceed the scope of an emergency entry?

4. An officer went to the defendant's home and found the latter's wife slumped in a chair with blood on her face, hands, and clothing. Defendant volunteered that "she fell down" and that "she hemorrhaged." The defendant was taken into custody, but no charges were filed. On the following day, the police made a complete and thorough search of the entire house and basement and found the murder weapon, a whiskey bottle, concealed under paper and trash in a barrel in the garage. (*State* v. *Chapman*, 250 A. 2d 203.)

Was this search lawful?

5. In the following two examples, the court came to different conclusions on whether a search was reasonable. Can you see a distinction?

a) Burglars broke into a medical center and stole money, stamps, retail sales items, a radio, hypodermic needles, barbiturates, and amphetamines. The officers developed probable cause to arrest the defendant for the burglary. The defendant had also registered as a narcotics offender and was on probation for the possession of marijuana. The officers noted that one of the conditions of the defendant's probation required him to "submit his person, place of residence, vehicle, to search and seizure at any time of the day or night, with or without a search warrant, whenever requested to do so by the Probation Officer or any law enforcement officer."

The officers went to the defendant's residence and saw his car parked in front. An officer knocked on the door of the house, identified himself, and announced he wanted to search the apartment. When defendant opened the door, the officer informed him that he had reason to believe that the defendant had participated in a burglary and that he was subject to search and seizure by court order as a condition of probation. The defendant admitted he was subject to such a condition. Thereupon, the officers entered the house, searched, and found evidence of the burglary.

b) The defendant, in the company of another young woman, was stopped by an officer for a speeding violation and for driving with one headlight only. When asked for identification, she produced a driver's license. Then, as the officer testified: "A. When I received the driver's license from the young lady, I went back to the radio car and ran a warrant check, and while I was waiting for the warrant check, I issued a citation for speeding. Q. What was the result of the warrant check? A. I was advised by radio that there were no outstanding warrants; however, the subject had a prior arrest for sales of dangerous drugs and that she was on probation and that the stipulation of the probation was that she was open to search and seizure.

"The officer returned to defendant's car, requested her to step out, and inquired if she had been previously arrested. She replied she had. He then asked if she were 'open to search and seizure,' and when she answered that so far as she knew she still was, he said he was going to search the vehicle and her handbag. Inside her handbag he found a change purse containing contraband." (*People* v. *Bremmer*, 30 Cal. App. 3d 1058.)

Would this search be lawful?

Motor Vehicles

Chambers v. *Maroney*, 399 U.S. 42, 90 S. Ct. 1975, 26 L. Ed. 2d 419.

Coolidge v. *New Hampshire*, 403 U.S. 443, 91 S. Ct. 2022, 29 L. Ed. 2d 564.

Johnson v. *State*, 238 Md. 528, 209 A. 2d 765 (Maryland).

People v. *Teale*, 70 Cal. 2d 497, 450 P. 2d 564.

Emergency

McDonald v. *United States*, 335 U.S. 451, 69 S. Ct. 191, 93 L. Ed. 153.

People v. *Smith*, 63 Cal. 2d 779, 409 P. 2d 222.

Schmerber v. *United States,* 384 U.S. 757, 86 S. Ct. 1826, 16 L. Ed. 2d 908.

Warden v. *Hayden*, 387 U.S. 294, 87 S. Ct. 1642, 18 L. Ed. 2d 782.

Goods in Transit

People v. *McKinnon*, 7 Cal. 3d 899, 103 Cal. R. 897.

Parole Searches

People v. *Kanos,* 14 Cal. App. 3d 642, 92 Cal. R. 613 (n. 3).

Student Searches

In re Thomas G., 11 Cal. App. 3d 1193, 90 Cal. R. 361.

People v. *Jackson*, 65 M. 2d 909, 319 NYS 2d 731 (New York).

See articles collected in *People* v. *Lanthier,* 5 Cal. 3d 751 (n. 3), 488 P. 2d 625.

"The Fourth Amendment and High School Students," 6 *Willamette Law Journal*, 567.

Citizen Searches

Burdeau v. *McDowell*, 256 U.S. 465, 41 S. Ct. 574, 65 L. Ed. 1048.

Stapleton v. *Superior Court*, 70 Cal. 2d 97 (n. 2), 447 P. 2d 967.

Chapter Nine

Quasi-Criminal Proceedings

Fourth Amendment principles arise most often in the context of the criminal courtroom when the defendant objects to the introduction of evidence seized by police officers. But the constitutional guarantee of personal security extends to all governmental invasions of privacy, not just police-initiated searches. Or, even if the search was police-initiated, but subsequent proceedings took a form other than a criminal trial, the Fourth Amendment still applies. Only in one major area—revocation of parole—does the Fourth Amendment surrender to overriding social goals. Elsewhere, the courts afford constitutional protection against unlawful governmental action.

That the rules of search and seizure apply to proceedings technically civil, but essentially criminal in nature, can be seen from several examples.

Car Forfeitures

Car forfeitures, which result from the arrest of the driver for possession of contraband in a vehicle, depend on the validity of the original search. In some cases, depriving a person of his car is a heavier penalty than he might expect from criminal proceedings against him personally. Because the driver has an ownership interest in his vehicle that cannot be disposed of without reference to constitutional protection, the lawful seizure of his car depends on the reasonableness of the search. That the proceeding to forfeit the vehicle for carrying contraband is labeled *civil* is immaterial.

Addict Commitment

Addict-commitment proceedings are also denominated *civil* in many jurisdictions because addiction is regarded as a disease rather than a crime. But an addict cannot be deprived unlawfully of his personal security any more than someone else. If an addict could be unlawfully searched and the product of that search introduced in a commitment hearing, the Fourth Amendment would be quickly eroded. The civil commitment for addiction cannot be substituted for a criminal trial—even if the evidence is essentially the same—in order to escape the requirements of probable cause. As a practical matter, commitment results in a form of confinement not unlike jail. Thus, the addict can urge Fourth Amendment protection in the context of civil proceedings.

Administrative Searches

In each of the preceding examples, the courts have refused to permit the civil action to replace the Fourth Amendment merely because of labels. But in both cases the initial search was probably police-initiated, and the subsequent proceedings arose out of a governmental act. There is another category of search, however, which is initiated by governmental employees rather than by police officers, and the evidence seized thereby may be offered either in a criminal trial or in administrative proceedings to revoke a license.

The U.S. Supreme Court has ruled that health inspectors cannot enter a residence to search for housing code violations if the owner refuses entry, unless an emergency exists. In *Camara* v. *Municipal Court*, the Court held that if police officers could not enter a house without a search warrant, why should health inspectors be afforded power to enter without a warrant. Yet the Court concluded that a search warrant for each individual home was unnecessary; enforcement officers need only demonstrate probable cause in appraising the area as a whole. Needless to say, the requirement of a detailed form of general search warrant for areas to be inspected by nonpolice personnel has left the validity of such entries and searches unclear.[1]

---

1. A search warrant will also be required for the search of commercial premises, absent consent, unless the inspector sees that which is open to public view, or if the issuance of a license is conditioned on consent to enter; *People* v. *White*, 259 Cal. App. 2d 936, 65 Cal. R. 923. For an example of inspection warrants, see California Code of Civil Procedure, sections 1822.50–57.

Parole Revocation

Parole revocation is the major exception to the rule that all people shall be secure against unreasonable searches and seizures. The courts have considered two categories of cases involving parolees: the search of the parolee, his car, or his house; and the use of such evidence against him in administrative proceedings to violate his parole.

Generally speaking, a parolee is deemed to be in constructive custody when he is released from prison. Arguably he should not be entitled to any more freedom from search than he would enjoy if he were in prison. Yet part of the parole process assumes that the parolee has demonstrated some basis for society to risk his temporary freedom from total incarceration. As a result, the parolee ought to be entitled to some kind of protection from unreasonable governmental interference. Where to draw the line between these two points of view is not always easy, but generally the courts have acknowledged the potential danger a prison inmate poses to society and have diluted full Fourth Amendment protection accordingly.

As one dispossessed of full civil rights protection, the parolee, his car, and his premises may be searched without probable cause as long as the parole officer initiates the search. This rule prevents police officers from initiating a search motivated by their own desire to enforce the criminal law rather than the needs of effective parole administration. Nothing is improper about a parole officer seeking the assistance of peace officers in effecting the search of a parolee. He can delegate his authority if necessary. But authority to arrest may not necessarily include authority to search. Cooperation between parole authorities and the police is laudable and desirable. But arrest and searching authority must be related to the legitimate demands of the parole process. To the extent that arrests and searches of parolees deviate from that goal, the reasonableness of the search will be called into question.

Even though Fourth Amendment protection has been diluted, arrest or search of a parolee is not automatically reasonable. Governmental authorities have sometimes abandoned the criminal proceedings either because the arrest and search were tenuous, or because revoking the parolee's released status was deemed an adequate substitute. Revocation of parole is not a criminal trial; rather, the proceedings are essentially administrative. Because in other contexts the Fourth Amendment is available in civil or administrative proceedings, a question arises whether unlawfully seized evidence is permissible in revocation proceedings. The dilemma is apparent: if the arrest and search are, by everyone's standards, unreasonable within the meaning of the Fourth Amendment, the evidence should not be admitted regardless of the parolee's status.[2] On the other hand, parolees pose a risk to society, and the protection of personal security enjoyed by most people cannot be used as a shield to allow someone who has already demonstrated a previous criminal history to remain at large. To allow the exclusionary rule to prevent the admission of otherwise relevant and truthful evidence in a proceeding designed to evaluate the risk of a parolee's release back into society is too heavy a price to pay.

The latter view will no doubt prevail. But the ferment in the correctional system in general may spill over to the parole process. Revocation proceedings themselves have been under attack, and some courts may look more closely at the statutory procedures relating to parole revocation. Courts may insist on more strict compliance with statutes affecting parole, or they may refuse to enforce their provisions if violations of due process or equal protection are established. And, as the role of the criminal law in society fluctuates and different systems of incarceration are attempted, the Fourth Amendment may be invoked more often. For example, addicts on outpatient status may enjoy Fourth Amendment protection unavailable to parolees. But the debate resembles the argument for revocation of probation. Although probation and parole are clearly distinct, analysis of them tends to be similar. In both cases, however, the courts are likely to continue an attempt toward favorably balancing the interests of society against those of the offender.

Cases and Materials

Camara v. *Municipal Court,* 387 U.S. 523, 87 S. Ct. 1727, 18 L. Ed. 2d 930 (health inspection).

Carroll v. *United States,* 267 U.S. 132, 45 S. Ct. 280, 69 L. Ed. 543.

Colonnade Catering Corp. v. *United States,* 397 U.S. 72, 90 S. Ct. 774, 25 L. Ed. 2d 60.

Dyke v. *Taylor, etc.,* 391 U.S. 216, 88 S. Ct. 1472, 20 L. Ed. 2d 538.

One 1958 Plymouth Sedan v. *Pennsylvania,* 380 U.S. 693, 85 S. Ct. 1246, 14 L. Ed. 2d 170 (vehicle forfeitures).

People v. *Moore,* 69 Cal. 2d 674, 446 P. 2d 800 (civil commitments).

See v. *Seattle,* 387 U.S. 541, 87 S. Ct. 1737, 18 L. Ed. 2d 943 (business inspection).

United States v. *Biswell,* 406 U.S. 311, 92 Sup. Ct. 1593, 32 L. Ed. 2d 87.

---

2. For example: Police, lacking probable cause, stop a parolee without knowledge of his status. A search reveals seizable evidence and an arrest follows. If such an arrest and search were approved, everyone could be stopped and searched and an occasional parolee might be turned up. Thus, the rule is that the status of the parolee must be known prior to the search.

Chapter Ten

Exploiting Unlawful Arrest or Search

The "right of the people to be secure against unreasonable searches and seizures" is not limited to direct violations of the Fourth Amendment, but extends to indirect violations as well. Police may not exploit illegal conduct by insulating an otherwise lawful act from constitutional scrutiny. Both the direct unlawful act and the fruits of that act are within the scope of the Fourth Amendment.

The classic expression of this doctrine was stated in *Wong Sun* v. *United States,* decided in 1963 by the U.S. Supreme Court. Evidence obtained unlawfully may not be introduced, nor may any evidence seized as a consequence of an unlawful act be used. This doctrine has been called the "fruit of the poisoned tree," i.e., the ripened fruit is tainted by the poisoned tree.

With Unlawful Entry or Arrest

How does this doctrine apply? Under conventional rules of search and seizure, the product of a search conducted pursuant to an arrest made without probable cause is excluded from evidence as a direct result of the unlawful arrest. The lawfulness of the search incident to arrest depends on the validity of the arrest. Similarly, a search conducted pursuant to a warrant, or consent, depends on the validity of the warrant or the voluntariness of the consent. In other words, the search itself is an act that may be ratified only if its underlying justification is lawful. Normally, these rules govern most violations of the Fourth Amendment. But suppose that prior to the search in question, the following occurs:

An inspector of the narcotics detail testified that he received unverified information that the defendant had narcotics at a house on Army Street. He went to the house with other officers. They had no warrant. He testified that he "knocked and rang the bell but received no answer. The door was open about two inches, and he could see defendant through a hallway in the kitchen at the back of the house. Defendant was sitting at a table. The inspector pushed the door open, displayed his badge, and said, 'Police officer. I would like to talk to you.' He entered the house and defendant said, 'What do you want?' I said, 'I am a narcotic officer.' They went into the living room and the other officers then entered the house.

"The inspector questioned defendant about narcotics. The officer examined defendant's arm and saw puncture marks. He searched him and found a key in his pocket with no identifying marks. Defendant told him it was a key to his hotel room." The officers took the defendant to the hotel. One of the officers opened the door with the key, and they all entered. The officers found marijuana in the pocket of a coat in the closet. The court said:

"The right to seek interviews with suspects or witnesses at their homes does not include the right to walk in uninvited merely because there is no response to a knock or a ring. In the present case it clearly appears that the inspector entered the house before the defendant had any opportunity to object, and it seems most probable that he was in the house before he was even aware of his presence. There is no evidence whatever that the defendant consented to the entry of the other officers a few minutes later.

"Since the officers' presence in the house was unlawful, they could not rely on defendant's consent to search. The defendant was suddenly confronted by five officers who had entered without right or permission, and it was equivocal at best whether his apparent consent to being searched was voluntary. The substantial probability that the unlawful entry was essential to securing consent and the inescapable uncertainty whether the consent was voluntary preclude treating the consent as an independent valid basis for the ensuing search of defendant's person. Accordingly, the consent, the search, the finding of the key, and the resulting discovery of the marijuana in the hotel room were all products of the officers' unlawful entry and cannot be relied upon to sustain the judgment." (*People* v. *Haven.*) In other words, even if the consent was voluntary, the officers' prior illegal entry voided the consent. The "consent" was the "fruit" of the prior illegal act of unlawful entry.

Compare this case: An informant told officers that one Curtis Cooper was selling heroin in his room at a named hotel. That night the officers went to the hotel to talk to Cooper, who had previously admitted being "a user." As the officers approached, "Cooper came out of his room and walked down the hall towards them. They stopped Cooper in the hallway and questioned him as to possible sales of heroin. The officers searched Cooper and found that he was carrying approximately $100 in small bills. No heroin was found on Cooper. They then asked Cooper if they could search his room, and Cooper said they could and gave the officers the key to the room. The officers went to the hotel room, inserted the key into the lock and were attempting to open the door, when it was opened by the defendant. On seeing the officers, defendant appeared surprised, backed away, turned his back to the officers, bowed his head, and put his hand toward his face. One of the officers asked him to turn around and open his mouth, and, when defendant did so, the officer saw a balloon in defendant's mouth. The officer told defendant to spit it out, and he did so." The balloon contained a powder, which later proved to be heroin. (*People* v. *Johnson.*)

Absent probable cause to arrest Cooper, the arrest was unlawful. This unlawful arrest directly contributed to seeking Cooper's consent to search his room. Thus, the prior unlawful arrest voided the subsequent arrest of the defendant.

With Search Warrants

The fruit-of-the-poisoned-tree doctrine applies to search warrants as well.

Defendant was registered at a motel. "While cleaning his room a maid saw what appeared to be an empty cigarette package on a nightstand. She opened it to see if it was in fact empty and should be discarded and discovered a plastic sandwich bag containing a green leafy substance. She had previously attended a drug demonstration class conducted by the police department at which she saw and smelled marijuana. On the basis of that experience she believed that she had discovered marijuana. She replaced the bag in the cigarette package, put the package back on the nightstand, and told the motel manager of her discovery. The manager inspected the items and then telephoned the police.

"A police officer went to the motel in response to the call, and the maid told him that she believed there was marijuana in defendant's room. With the manager's permission the officer entered the room with the two women. He inspected the cigarette package and the plastic bag and saw the substance, which was later identified as marijuana. He then put the cigarette package and its contents back on the nightstand as he had found them." (*Krauss* v. *Superior Court.*)

That afternoon the officer obtained a warrant to search defendant's room. He returned to the motel that evening with the search warrant and properly served it on defendant, who was then in his room, seized the marijuana, and arrested defendant.

Assuming that the maid was a sufficiently reliable informant, her information would have formed the basis for a search warrant to enter the room. Instead, the officer's prior entry without a warrant was an unlawful act that jeopardized the validity of the subsequently issued search warrant.

If the court only examined the voluntariness of a consent without reference to a prior unlawful arrest, the judge would confine his inquiry only to the issue of voluntariness. Similarly, if he reviewed an affidavit for probable cause, his decision to issue a warrant would not include reviewing the possible previous unlawful search upon which the affidavit was based. In both instances, the "fruit" of earlier illegal conduct taints the subsequent search. Thus the courts have concluded that a defendant is entitled to offer evidence of illegal conduct prior to the search at issue. If, in the first example, the court found that the consent came after an earlier illegal arrest, or, in the second example, if the search warrant was based on prior unlawful conduct, any fruit of that conduct would be excluded.

With Unlawful Searches

Just as prior unlawful conduct taints a subsequent search, any acts *after* an unlawful search cannot be used in exploitation of the earlier conduct. For example, if peace officers unlawfully search a passenger in a car, a subsequent search of the car itself may be tainted. And the "fruits" doctrine is not limited only to searches conducted after a prior unlawful search. The rule can be invoked to exclude fingerprints or handwriting samples obtained from an arrestee; testimony of a witness whose identity was learned from an unlawful search; and identification testimony by a witness who observed a police lineup in which the arrestee wore articles of clothing seized after his unlawful arrest.

Kinds of Evidence Excluded

As in the case of evidence seized as a direct result of an unlawful act, evidence seized indirectly will be excluded from evidence. The unlawful act does not immunize the defendant from arrest or prosecution, however, and if otherwise admissible evidence is offered, the defendant may be convicted. But because evidence seized is usually tangible, i.e., physical evidence, the exclusion of such evidence is damaging to the prosecution's case.

The fruit-of-the-poisoned-tree doctrine reaches further than exclusion of tangible evidence. In *Wong Sun,* the U.S. Supreme Court said that although "The exclusionary rule has traditionally barred from trial physical, tangible materials obtained either during or as a direct result of an unlawful invasion, but the Fourth Amendment may also protect against the overhearing of verbal statements as well as against the more traditional seizure of papers and effects. Similarly, testimony as to matters observed during an unlawful invasion has been excluded in order to enforce basic constitutional policies. . . . Thus, verbal evidence which derives so immediately from an unlawful entry and an unauthorized arrest . . . is no less the 'fruit' of official illegality than the more common tangible fruits of the unwarranted intrusion."

The verbal evidence to which the court refers usually is a confession. Thus, an unlawful search that directly results in a confession may taint the confession and exclude an otherwise voluntary statement from evidence. Nothing more clearly illustrates the reach of the fruits doctrine back to the original search. If the original search was unlawful, the investigators' painstaking attempts to obtain a voluntary confession may be wasted.

Yet a fundamental distinction exists between a prior unlawful arrest and a prior unlawful search in determining whether to admit a subsequent confession. Evidence seized in violation of search-and-seizure provisions and voluntary statements during an illegal detention are tested differently. The voluntary admission is not a necessary product of an illegal detention; the evidence obtained by an illegal search or by a coerced confession is the necessary product of the search or of the coercion. "Cases where a confession follows an unlawful arrest, and those where the confession follows a confrontation of the defendant with illegally seized evidence, are distinguishable. In the latter case, the illegality induces the confession by showing the suspect the futility of remaining silent. Where a confession follows a false arrest, the custodial environment is merely one factor (though a significant one) to be considered in determining whether the confession is inadmissible." (*Rogers* v. *Superior Court.*) Voluntariness of the confession remains as the test of admissibility.

Modifications of the Doctrine

Not all evidence is fruit of the poisonous tree simply because it would not have come to light but for the illegal action of the police. Rather, the more apt question in such a case is "whether granting establishment of the primary illegality, the evidence to which instant objection is made has been come at by exploitation of that illegality or instead by means sufficiently distinguishable to be purged of the primary taint." (*Wong Sun* v. *United States.*) In other words, even if the prior illegal act is proven, not all evidence obtained thereafter is tainted. The question is whether the police exploited the illegal act or not. The line between the illegal act and the subsequent lawful act can be so thin that the prior conduct is only remotely related; or, some other intervening lawful act can break the chain between the two acts. For example, a voluntary confession obtained after an unlawful arrest, and preceded by a fully adequate *Miranda* admonition, might be an independent act by the defendant sufficient to break the chain.

Another modification of the doctrine: If knowledge is gained from a source independent of the unlawful act, this evidence may be admitted without reference to evidence seized unlawfully. In other words, if evidence is obtained lawfully during the course of an investigation, the similar product of an exploited unlawful search will not affect admissibility of the evidence.

Closely allied to this rule is another restriction on the "fruits" doctrine. If the illegally obtained evidence would have been discovered "in any event," then evidence which was obtained unlawfully may be admitted. This rule assumes, however, that the evidence may be admitted if it *would have* been discovered, not merely if it *could have* been discovered. The burden is on the prosecution to establish this condition.

Cases and Materials

Alderman v. *United States*, 394 U.S. 165, 89 S. Ct. 961, 22 L. Ed. 2d 176.

Commonwealth v. *Perez*, 357 Mass. 290, 258 NE 2d 1 (Massachusetts).

Davis v. *Mississippi*, 394 U.S. 721, 89 S. Ct. 1394, 22 L. Ed. 2d 676.

Lockridge v. *Superior Court*, 3 Cal. 3d 166, 474 P. 2d 683.

McGuire, "How to Unpoison the Fruit, the Fourth Amendment and the Exclusionary Rule," 55 *Journal of Criminal Law, Criminology, and Police Science* 307.

Nardone v. *United States*, 308 U.S. 338, 60 S Ct. 266, 84 L. Ed. 307.

People v. *Bilderbach*, 62 Cal. 2d 757, 401 P. 2d 921.

People v. *Johnson*, 70 Cal. 2d 541, 450 P. 2d 865.

Rogers S. Ruffin, "Out on a Limb of the Poisonous Tree: The Tainted Witness," 15 *U.C.L.A. Law Review* 32.

Silverthorne Lumber Co. v. *United States*, 251 U.S. 385, 40 S. Ct. 182, 64 L. Ed. 319.

United States v. *Williams*, 436 F. 2d 1166.

Walder v. *United States*, 347 U.S. 62, 74 S. Ct. 354, 98 L. Ed. 503.

Wong Sun v. *United States*, 371 U.S. 471, 83 S. Ct. 407, 9 L. Ed. 2d 441.

Chapter Eleven

Entry

Although the courts have modified rules of search and seizure pertaining to automobiles, the dwelling house continues to enjoy maximum constitutional protection. The phrase "a man's home is his castle" continues to reflect a judicial consensus of the right of privacy in dwelling houses. *Chimel* v. *California* (see chapter 6, Search Incident to Arrest), which restricted the scope of a search incidental to an arrest effected inside a dwelling house, is an example. Requiring a search warrant to search a house even if probable cause exists to search the interior provides another example. Any invasion of personal security inside a dwelling house is rigorously scrutinized by the courts to assure an entry and search consistent with strict constitutional construction.

Entry on the Premises

Before discussing entry into a dwelling house, some consideration needs to be given to entry on the premises themselves. Officers must often enter the land prior to approaching a house, and the property adjoining the house enjoys constitutional protection, too. Entry on the land may be necessitated by several purposes: response to a complaint; desire to interview an occupant as a potential witness or as a possible suspect; or desire to obtain visual surveillance. In the latter case, a minor trespass may be involved. Is this element important?

The U.S. Supreme Court has said that open fields are not entitled to constitutional protection, but that land adjoining a residence does not fall within this category. And there is a difference between entry onto the front yard of a dwelling house and entry through a closed gate into a backyard. Obviously, the degree of trespass in the latter case is more substantial. Although the Fourth Amendment says nothing about prohibiting trespass, surely a householder expects a greater degree of privacy in his fenced backyard than he does in the front yard adjoining a public street. This degree of privacy may be significant in determining whether a particular governmental intrusion unreasonably invaded the occupant's reasonable expectation of privacy. No firm rule can be drafted because of the infinite variety of factors, i.e., location of the house; presence or absence of fences, gates, or shrubs; proximity of neighbors, etc. If an officer enters the land, he must be able to present some reasonable basis for his presence on the property. Often a crime report or a report from an informant will suffice. Normally this requirement will be routinely fulfilled. (See chapter 3, Search.)

Visual Entry

Assuming that some reasonable basis exists for entry onto the land, the next issue often involves the visual entry of the premises as distinct from a physical entry. Surveillance frequently is conducted from neighboring locations, and often a physical entry is preceded by a visual entry through the doors or windows. The officer's personal safety often motivates his peering inside a home prior to entry, but if the officer observes criminal conduct or seizable evidence inside, what legal implications are involved?

Under the "plain view" rule, the officer would be observing evidence concealed from view and not within the classic definition of a search. But if the boundaries of the plain-view rule are respected, as expressed in *Coolidge* v. *New Hampshire*, the evidence must have been discovered inadvertently. Can entry on the land followed by an intentional observation of the interior of the house be inadvertent? And what about the defendant's right of privacy? Assuming that there is a reasonable basis for entering the land, has the officer unreasonably invaded the defendant's right of privacy by looking through the windows? If the defendant elects to leave his windows open or the drapes undrawn, the prosecutor can argue waiver of privacy. If, on the other hand, the officer needs to move an object away from the window in order to see inside, or push back shrubbery, or stand on a box to improve his view, then the defendant can argue that such affirmative acts cannot be guarded against, and that he should not be required to build a shell over his house to maintain privacy. In any event, the defendant will muster a strong argument for privacy if he can establish such evidence.

Another method of effecting visual entry prior to physical entry is the use of subterfuge. Suspects may be induced to open the door when police officers falsely represent themselves or misrepresent themselves as guests, deliverymen, or the landlord. Or, the police may request someone to induce the occupant to open the door on their behalf. The rule is well established that, although strategy is not always impermissible, entry may not be obtained by subterfuge unless probable cause to arrest exists prior to the visual entry. Evidence observed from visual entry alone cannot form the sole basis for probable cause. If probable cause to arrest already exists, officers may use strategy to induce the occupant to open the door or to encourage him to flee the premises so they can effect arrest outside.[1]

Unlawful Entry

Apart from judicial solicitude for the house, the consequences of an unlawful visual or physical entry result in the possibility of exclusion of any evidence discovered inside. An unlawful entry voids a subsequent search or seizure of evidence inside the house. Thus a lawful entry is indispensable to a lawful search, although an unlawful entry does not insulate the defendant from trial if otherwise competent evidence may be introduced. Most often, however, the only evidence seized is obtained at the time of arrest. Even if mere "leads" are discovered inside, a subsequent lawful search at a later time and place may be tainted by an original unlawful entry.

Consensual Entry

Aside from entries to effect arrest, officers may request consent of the householder to enter. If the occupant is a potential witness or someone with knowledge concerning a crime, the consent usually is granted. If, however, the occupant is a possible suspect, he may not so readily admit the officer. In such event, the court will determine the free and voluntary nature of any alleged consensual entry. If the entry was obtained by subterfuge or by submission to authority (see chapter 7, Consent Searches), any evidence obtained inside the house will be excluded. Consent to enter does not authorize consent to search. Just as the defendant may revoke his consent to search, he may revoke his permission to enter. These issues are resolved under the same questions presented in the section on consensual searches.

Emergency Entry

Officers can also enter a dwelling house pursuant to an emergency. Necessity often justifies a trespass, but the entry must be based on

---

1. In one celebrated case, the officers telephoned the occupants of the house and misrepresented themselves as third parties. They informed the person who answered the phone that the "heat" would be there shortly and to remove the contraband quickly. The occupants fled, carrying the contraband, whereupon they were arrested outside. The court held that no unlawful entry was involved.

evidence involving a substantial and immediate danger to the life or welfare of the occupant. Absent such evidence, the entry is authorized only if officers can demonstrate some compelling need for immediate entry, i.e., the need to quickly identify a fleeing suspect.

Entry to Arrest

Entering to effect an arrest is no less a judicial concern than are other entries. Even if the justification for entry is stronger when an arrest is anticipated, the U.S. Supreme Court has noted a "grave constitutional question" in allowing a warrantless entry of a home at night. Most arrests are made on probable cause alone, without a warrant, regardless of the location of the arrest. But if an entry of a home to seize evidence cannot be executed without a search warrant—even if probable cause to search exists—why should not an entry to seize the person require an arrest warrant? As yet that issue remains unresolved, but cautious police practice suggests the advisability of an arrest pursuant to a warrant if the circumstances allow.

On the assumption that officers have developed probable cause to arrest prior to entry, and that there is some reasonable basis to believe the arrestee is inside, federal and state law require the officers to alert the occupant to their presence and demand entry prior to any forcible entry.[2] If the occupant voluntarily answers the door, the entry is not forcible. Or if the officer tricks the occupant into opening the door, the entry is not forcible. But the requirement of prior notice of authority and purpose before forcing entry into a home is deeply rooted in our heritage, often codified from tradition imbedded in Anglo-American law that declares the reverence of the law for the individual's right of privacy in his house.

Announcement Statutes

The purpose and policy of "knock and notice" statutes is fourfold: "(1) the protection of the privacy of the individual in his home; (2) the protection of innocent persons who may also be present on the premises where an arrest is made; (3) the prevention of situations that are conducive to violent confrontations between the occupant and individuals who enter his home without proper notice; and (4) the protection of police who might be injured by a startled and fearful householder." (*Duke* v. *Superior Court.*)

In most cases, a similar policy also relates to entries pursuant to the forcible execution of search warrants, and the analysis is essentially the same whether the object is arrest, search, or both. Because these "knock and notice" statutes are closely related to the purposes of the

---

2. State statutes requiring notice and demand are collected in *Miller* v. *United States*, footnote 8.

Fourth Amendment in its protection against unlawful entries, any entry in violation thereof is unlawful and results in the exclusion of any evidence seized inside the dwelling house.

Although literal compliance with statutory requirements is the norm, an entry can be lawful if officers substantially comply with the statute. But substantial compliance requires at least some notice to the occupants that it is the police who are seeking entry. Moreover, failure to announce the purpose for which entry is demanded is excusable only if the surrounding circumstances make the officers' purpose clear to the occupant. But in the absence of some reasonable basis for excused compliance, officers are well advised to comply strictly. The entry announcement does not normally exceed five seconds, and eliminating part of the announcement could only be justified by circumstances rapidly evolving in front of the officers.

Not all entries can safely be preceded by compliance with the announcement statutes. In some instances, to announce the presence of peace officers would signal the advent of gunfire or assault. Compliance with "knock and notice" statutes is excused, therefore, if there is some reason to believe that an announcement would jeopardize the safety of officers or others, or if there is a substantial danger of a suspect's escape, or a belief that evidence will be destroyed. But these reasons cannot be generalized in every case. Officers must be able to articulate the reasons for noncompliance in each particular case. The defendant's criminal history or the circumstances of the crime for which he is being sought are relevant.

Nor is compliance excused on a blanket basis that some classes of offenders will automatically destroy evidence on confrontation with the police. Noncompliance must be based on the facts of each case, such as: information from an informant that an occupant has specifically planned to effect disposal of evidence or made specific preparations in that regard; or the fact that, immediately prior to entry, officers observe conduct indicating that the occupants are engaged in the destruction or concealment of evidence.

The statutes of each state may vary in wording, but generally they require officers to identify themselves before they enter forcibly, i.e., "break open the doors." What constitutes a "breaking"? A number of appellate decisions have struggled with entries through open doors, screen doors, closed but unlocked doors, and doors ajar that swing open. Most of these issues could be resolved by reference to the common-law requirement of "breaking" in house burglaries, i.e., any unconsented unlawful entry across the threshold. Absent evidence that the occupant knew of police presence and purpose, and assuming no basis for noncompliance, officers intending to enter a dwelling house to arrest should fully notify the occupants regardless of the position of the door. If someone other than the prospective arrestee opens the door, notice can still be provided. If the arrestee opens the door, the prosecution could argue no "breaking." Yet the better practice is to comply in all cases. If no one responds to knocking and notice, officers should have some basis to believe the occupants are inside and not responding to the knock before a forcible entry occurs.

Compliance with announcement statutes becomes important if evidence is seized inside the house. But even if the entry is unlawful, the arrestee may still be tried and convicted on other evidence obtained independent of the arrest.

Cases and Materials

Coolidge v. *New Hampshire*, 403 U.S. 443, 91 S. Ct. 2022, 29 L. Ed. 2d 564.

Duke v. *Superior Court*, 1 Cal. 3d 314, 461 P. 2d 628.

Grevan v. *Superior Court*, 71 Cal. 2d 287, 455 P. 2d 432.

Miller v. *United States*, 357 U.S. 301, 78 S. Ct. 1190, 2 L. Ed. 2d 1332.

People v. *Gastello*, 67 Cal. 2d 586, 432 P. 2d 706.

People v. *Lujan*, 484 P. 2d 1238 (Colorado).

People v. *Rosales*, 68 Cal. 2d 299, 437 P. 2d 489.

1. Based on unverified information of criminal activity, officers approach a home surrounded by a high wall. On opening the unlocked gate, they enter a landscaped courtyard containing garden furniture, tables, and other outdoor furnishings. They cross the courtyard, ascend a few stairs to the house and knock. Subsequent events culminate in an arrest.

Question: Does the unannounced entry into the courtyard violate the defendant's reasonable expectation of privacy (a major consideration in requiring announcement), thereby requiring compliance with the knock-and notice statutes? Are entries for investigation measured by the same rule as entries to arrest?

2. Officers have positive information that there is a reasonable basis for forcibly entering a dwelling house without announcing their authority and purpose. Although there is ample time to appear before a magistrate, officers enter forcibly without an arrest warrant and without announcement.

At trial, the defendant objects to the introduction of evidence seized inside his dwelling house on the grounds that the officers should have obtained a magistrate's approval for unannounced entry. Is this objection valid? What difference exists between obtaining a magistrate's warrant to search and seeking judicial authority to enter and arrest?

See *New York Code of Criminal Procedure*, section 799; *People* v. *De-Lago*, 16 N.Y. 2d 289, 213 N.E. 2d 659 (New York); *Parsley* v. *Superior Court*, 28 Cal. App. 3d 372, n. 3.

Chapter Twelve

Wiretapping
and Eavesdropping

When the Fourth Amendment was adopted, and for many years thereafter, none of the sophisticated methods of communications now current existed in the United States. Not surprisingly, therefore, the U.S. Supreme Court early held that Fourth Amendment protection only embraced tangible "things" rather than the seizure of communications. The only protection afforded against seizure of communications was a federal statute prohibiting the unlawful interception of wire communications. But absent any "interception" within the meaning of the statute, no other constitutional or statutory provision prevented overhearing a third party's conversation and subsequently repeating it in court.

The *Katz* Decision

In 1967, the Supreme Court was confronted by the following facts in *Katz* v. *United States*:

"The defendant was convicted under an eight-count indictment charging him with transmitting wagering information by telephone from Los Angeles to Miami and Boston. At trial, the Government was permitted to introduce evidence of the defendant's end of telephone conversations, overheard by FBI agents who had attached an electronic listening and recording device to the outside of the public telephone booth from which he had placed his calls."

The Court began by explaining that the Fourth Amendment protects people, not places. "What a person knowingly exposes to the public, even in his own home or office, is not a subject of Fourth Amendment protection. But what he seeks to preserve as private, even in an area accessible to the public, may be constitutionally protected. . . .

"What defendant sought to exclude when he entered the booth was not the intruding eye—it was the uninvited ear. He did not shed his right to do so simply because he made his calls from a place where he might be seen. No less than an individual in a business office, in a friend's apartment, or in a taxicab, a person in a telephone booth may rely upon the protection of the Fourth Amendment. One who occupies it, shuts the door behind him, and pays the toll that permits him to place a call is surely entitled to assume that the words he utters into the mouthpiece will not be broadcast to the world. To read the Constitution more narrowly is to ignore the vital role that the public telephone has come to play in private communication."

The government argued that the activities of its agents in this case should not be tested by Fourth Amendment requirements, for the surveillance technique involved no physical penetration of the telephone booth from which the defendant placed his calls. "The absence of such penetration was at one time thought to foreclose further Fourth Amendment inquiry, for that Amendment was thought to limit only searches and seizures of tangible property. The premise that property interests control the right of the Government to search and seize has been discredited." At this point the Court departed from the earlier view that the Fourth Amendment governs only the seizure of tangible items, and extended its protection as well to the recording of "oral statements overheard without any technical trespass under . . . local property law. Once this much is acknowledged, and once it is recognized that the Fourth Amendment protects people—and not simply 'areas'—against unreasonable searches and seizures, it becomes clear that the reach of that Amendment cannot turn upon the presence or absence of a physical intrusion into any given enclosure. . . .

"The Government's activities in electronically listening to and recording the petitioner's words violated the privacy upon which he justifiably relied while using the telephone booth and thus constituted a 'search and seizure' within the meaning of the Fourth Amendment. The fact that the electronic device employed to achieve that end did not happen to penetrate the wall of the booth can have no constitutional significance.

"The question remaining for decision, then, is whether the search and seizure conducted in this case complied with constitutional standards.

"The surveillance in this case was so narrowly circumscribed that a duly authorized magistrate, properly notified of the need for such investigation, specifically informed of the basis on which it was to proceed, and clearly apprised of the precise intrusion it would entail, could constitutionally have authorized, with appropriate safeguards, a limited search and seizure.

"Under sufficiently precise and discriminate circumstances, a federal court may empower government agents to employ a concealed electronic device for the narrow and particularized purpose of ascertaining the truth of the . . . allegations of a detailed factual affidavit alleging the commission of a specific criminal offense.

"The order authorizing the use of the electronic device affords similar protections to those . . . of conventional warrants authorizing the seizure of tangible evidence. Through those protections, no greater invasion of privacy was permitted than was necessary under the circumstances.

"It was apparent that the agents in this case acted with restraint. Yet the inescapable fact is that this restraint was imposed by the agents themselves, not by a judicial officer. They were not required, before commencing the search, to present their estimate of probable cause for detached scrutiny by a neutral magistrate. They were not compelled, during the conduct of the search itself, to observe precise limits established in advance by a specific court order. Nor were they directed, after the search had been completed, to notify the authorizing magistrate in detail of all that had been seized. In the absence of such safeguards, this Court has never sustained a search upon the sole ground that officers reasonably expected to find evidence of a particular crime and voluntarily confined their activities to the least intrusive means consistent with that end. Searches conducted without warrants have been held unlawful notwithstanding facts unquestionably showing probable cause, for the Constitution requires that the deliberate, impartial judgment of a judicial officer be interposed between the citizen and the police.

"Over and again this Court has emphasized that the mandate of the [Fourth] Amendment requires adherence to judicial processes, and that searches conducted outside the judicial process, without prior approval by judge or magistrate, are per se unreasonable under the Fourth Amendment—subject only to a few specifically established and well-delineated exceptions.

"It is difficult to imagine how any of those exceptions could ever apply to the sort of search and seizure involved in this case. Even electronic surveillance substantially contemporaneous with an individual's arrest could hardly be deemed an 'incident' of that arrest. Nor could the use of electronic surveillance without prior authorization be justified on grounds of 'hot pursuit.' And of course, the very nature of electronic surveillance precludes its use pursuant to the suspect's consent."

The government argued for the creation of a new exception to cover this case; that surveillance of a telephone booth should be exempted from the usual requirement of advance authorization by a magistrate upon a showing of probable cause. The Court disagreed. Omission of such authorization "bypasses the safeguards provided by an objective predetermination of probable cause, and substitutes instead the far less reliable procedure of an after-the-event justification for the . . . search, too likely to be subtly influenced by the familiar shortcomings of hindsight judgment. And bypassing a neutral predetermination of the *scope* of a search leaves individuals secure from Fourth Amendment violations only in the discretion of the police.

"These considerations do not vanish when the search in question is transferred from the setting of a home, an office, or a hotel room to that of a telephone booth. Wherever a man may be, he is entitled to know that he will remain free from unreasonable searches and seizures. The government agents here ignored the procedure of antecedent justification . . . that is central to the Fourth Amendment, a procedure indispensable to a constitutional precondition of the kind of electronic surveillance involved in this case." Because the surveillance here had failed to meet that condition, and because it had led to the defendant's conviction, the judgment was reversed.

The *Hoffa* Decision (Reviewed in *United States* v. *White*)

Katz involved no revelation to the government by a party to conversations with the defendant nor did the Court indicate in any way that a defendant has a justifiable and constitutionally protected expectation that a person with whom he is conversing will not then or later reveal the conversation to the police.

Hoffa v. *United States*, which was left undisturbed by *Katz*, held that "however strongly a defendant may trust an apparent colleague, his expectations in this respect are not protected by the Fourth Amendment when it turns out that the colleague is a government agent regularly communicating with the authorities. In these circumstances, no interest legitimately protected by the Fourth Amendment is involved, for that amendment affords no protection to a wrongdoer's misplaced belief that a person to whom he voluntarily confides his wrongdoing will not reveal it. No warrant to search and seize is required in such circumstances, nor is it when the Government sends to defendant's home a secret agent who conceals his identity and makes a purchase of narcotics from the accused or when the same agent, unbeknown to the defendant, carries electronic equipment to record the defendant's words and the evidence so gathered is later offered in evidence. . . .

"Concededly a police agent who conceals his police connections may write down for official use his conversations with a defendant and testify concerning them, without a warrant authorizing his encounters with the defendant and without otherwise violating the latter's Fourth Amendment rights. For constitutional purposes, no different result is required if the agent instead of immediately reporting and transcribing his conversations with defendant, either (1) simultaneously records them with electronic equipment which he is carrying on his person; (2) or carries radio equipment which simultaneously transmits the conversations either to recording equipment located elsewhere or to other agents monitoring the transmitting frequency. If the conduct and revelations of an agent operating without electronic equipment do not invade the defendant's constitutionally justifiable expectations of privacy, neither does a simultaneous recording of the same conversations made by the agent or by others from transmissions received from the agent to whom the defendant is talking and whose trustworthiness the defendant necessarily risks . . .

The Court stated that its problem is not what the "privacy expectations of particular defendants in particular situations may be or the extent to which they may in fact have relied on the discretion of their companions. Very probably, individual defendants neither know nor suspect that their colleagues have gone or will go to the police or are carrying recorders or transmitters. Otherwise, conversation would cease and the problem with these encounters would be nonexistent or far different. . . . The problem, in terms of the principles announced in *Katz*, is what expectations of privacy are constitutionally 'justifiable'— what expectations the Fourth Amendment will protect in the absence of a warrant. So far, the law permits the frustration of actual expectations of privacy by permitting authorities to use the testimony of those associates who for one reason or another have determined to turn to the police, as well as by authorizing the use of informants. If the law gives no protection to the wrongdoer whose trusted accomplice is or becomes a police agent, neither should it protect him when that same agent has recorded or transmitted the conversations which are later offered in evidence to prove the State's case.

"Inescapably, one contemplating illegal activities must realize and risk that his companions may be reporting to the police. If he sufficiently doubts their trustworthiness, the association will very probably end or never materialize. But if he has no doubts, or allays them, or risks what doubt he has, the risk is his. In terms of what his course will be, what he will or will not do or say . . . he would probably not distinguish between probable informers on the one hand and probable informers with transmitters on the other. Given the possibility or probability that one of his colleagues is cooperating with the police, it is only speculation to assert that the defendant's utterances would be substantially different or his sense of security any less if he also thought it possible that the suspected colleague is wired for sound. At least there is no persuasive evidence that the difference in this respect between the electronically equipped and the unequipped agent is substantial enough to require discrete constitutional recognition, particularly under the Fourth Amendment which is ruled by fluid concepts of 'reasonableness.' "

The Court stated that it "should not be too ready to erect constitutional barriers to relevant and probative evidence which is also accurate and reliable. An electronic recording will many times produce a more reliable rendition of what a defendant has said than will the unaided memory of a police agent. It may also be that with the recording in existence it is less likely that the informant will change his mind, less chance that threat or injury will suppress unfavorable evidence and less chance that cross-examination will confound the testimony. Considerations like these obviously do not favor the defendant, but a defendant who has no constitutional right to exclude the informer's unaided testimony should not have a Fourth Amendment privilege against a more accurate version of the events in question.

"It is thus untenable to consider the activities and reports of the police agent himself, though acting without a warrant, to be a 'reasonable' investigative effort and lawful under the Fourth Amendment but to view the same agent with a recorder or transmitter as conducting an 'unreasonable' and unconstitutional search and seizure. . . .

"No different result should obtain where the informer disappears and is unavailable at trial; for the issue of whether specified events on a certain day violate the Fourth Amendment should not be determined by what later happens to the informer. His unavailability at trial and proffering the testimony of other agents may raise evidentiary problems or pose issues of prosecutorial misconduct with respect to the informer's disappearance, but they do not appear critical to deciding whether prior events invaded the defendant's Fourth Amendment rights." (*United States* v. *White.*)

Personal Privacy and the Fourth Amendment

In *Katz* v. *United States* and later in *Berger* v. *New York,* the Court concluded that the seizure of an intangible, i.e., conversation, is entitled to as much protection against unreasonable search and seizure as the seizure of tangible things. Further, the trespass doctrine was disapproved, and the Court held that the Fourth Amendment is not confined solely to the protection of places against trespass, but that, rather, it protects people.

Although a person is entitled to more or less Fourth Amendment protection depending on the place searched, the factors of location or area searched are not dispositive. The true rationale of the Fourth Amendment, said the Court, is the protection of personal privacy from unreasonable governmental interference. For the first time, the Court held that privacy is a legitimate factor in evaluating Fourth Amendment protection. The rule now seems to be that all people who would reasonably expect their communications to be private are entitled to be secure against an unreasonable governmental invasion of privacy. Any governmental invasion, therefore, must be accomplished by warrant.

Up until 1968, when Congress passed U.S.C. 2210, a defendant in a federal court could object to the introduction of any evidence seized by wiretapping or electronic eavesdropping obtained by trespass. In state courts, no wiretapping evidence could be admitted even if the telephone communication did not cross state lines, because the U.S. Supreme Court had held that under the old federal statute the distinction between intrastate and interstate conversations is only marginal. Of course, state courts could still admit wiretapping evidence if no exclusionary rule had been adopted in their jurisdiction. After the U.S. Supreme Court imposed the exclusionary rule on state courts, such flexibility was no longer available, and wiretapping evidence was inadmissible in all courts absent a warrant. As to electronic eavesdropping, the *Katz* case placed federal and state officers on the same footing regarding the scope of constitutional protection.

In some states, notably New York, a statute authorized electronic eavesdropping pursuant to the issuance of a warrant.[1] New York avoided the holding of the Katz case, which merely required a warrant to eavesdrop if there was evidence of probable cause. New York officials could comply with *Katz* by furnishing a state court with an affidavit of probable cause. In the Berger case, the U.S. Supreme Court held that the New York statute was overly broad. The Court found the statute lacking in several respects. First, the statute did not require a description of the conversation sought to be seized, or even a showing of belief that a crime had been or was being committed. These omissions violated the requirement of the Fourth Amendment that warrants describe with particularity the place to be searched and the things to be seized. Second, the sixty-day listening period authorized by the statute was the equivalent of a series of searches and seizures pursuant

1. New York Code of Civil Procedure, section 813A.

to a single showing of probable cause. Third, there was no requirement
for prompt execution. Fourth, renewal of this authorization could be
obtained without a new showing of probable cause. Fifth, no provision
was made for termination of the surveillance once the conversation
sought had been obtained. Sixth, the statute contained no provision for
a return on the warrant. Seventh, there was no requirement that notice
be given to the subject of surveillance or a showing of exigent circumstances be made in lieu thereof.

In response to the *Berger* and *Katz* cases, the Congress enacted
comprehensive national legislation embracing all electronic surveillance
and wiretapping.[2] The Act permits surveillance by law enforcement
officials under a warrant system that attempts to meet the requirements
of *Berger* and *Katz*. It provides for judicial issuance of warrants based
on probable cause in describing the person whose conversations are to
be seized, the location where the surveillance is to take place, and the
nature of the offense for which evidence is sought. The warrants can
be issued for a period of thirty days, with renewals available for
additional thirty-day periods, to expire upon obtaining the desired conversations. There are also other provisions dealing with emergency
authorization, notice to the suspect, and authentication of the recordings.

Because of the wide sweep of the new act, all previous state
statutes and court decisions affecting electronic eavesdropping must
now be reexamined. But some eavesdropping may not be within the
scope of the new act. For example, if one party consents to another
overhearing the conversation of a third party, such evidence should be
admissible. Anyone who confides in another runs a risk that his conversation will be repeated. That a recording device attached to the
phone reports the conversation more accurately should make no
constitutional difference. The new act, on the other hand, prohibits
nonconsensual eavesdropping.

Recordings and the Fifth Amendment

Although the use of recordings in reproducing statements of two
parties in a face-to-face conversation does not violate the Fourth
Amendment, other constitutional objections to this practice can be
raised. For example, a defendant could argue that he was not informed
of his right to remain silent prior to his statements to an undercover
officer. But this Fifth Amendment objection lacks merit because no
admonition under the well-known *Miranda* case needs to be made until
the suspect is in *custody*, a condition that does not exist on the public
streets. That the agent deceived the suspect as to his true identity is
immaterial.

---

2. Omnibus Crime Control and Safe Streets Act of 1968; 82 Stats. 197.

On the other hand, if the defendant is in custody, different problems arise. If officers were to place a recording in a jail facility to overhear conversations between prisoners, the defendant could urge that custody had attached and that he should have been warned. But *Miranda* also requires an admonition only if the *officer* intends to ask incriminating questions; voluntary statements are not within *Miranda*'s prohibition. If two prisoners voluntarily converse with each other, no constitutional objection exists to prevent overhearing or recording their statements. Conversely, though, if an officer enters the cell disguised as a prisoner and initiates a conversation with an inmate, a *Miranda* admonition would be required prior to the conversation. As a practical matter, therefore, such a practice is only useful to serve an intelligence function.

If an officer interviews a suspect in an attempt to question him about a crime, must he advise the suspect that their conversation is being recorded? No, on the theory that the officer is consenting to the conversation as a party. If the defendant's statements are voluntary and preceded by an adequate *Miranda* admonition, the recording, or a transcript of the recording, may be introduced at trial.[3]

Investigators should note a potential trial problem if, in the recorded confession, one suspect implicates a cosuspect. As to the cosuspect, the suspect's confession is hearsay and inadmissible. If both suspects are tried jointly, the nonconfessing suspect can object to the introduction of the recording as hearsay and thereby prevent the evidence from being admitted even against the confessing subject. In *Bruton* v. *New York*, the U.S. Supreme Court held that an instruction to the jury to disregard the confession as to the nonconfessing suspect is too difficult of a task for a juror to undertake. Therefore, said the Court, all references by the suspect in his confession concerning the nonconfessing suspect must be deleted or else the confession may be excluded entirely. If the officer testifies to the confession orally and without reference to the recording, he can exclude all references to the nonconfessing suspect. The loss of a sound recording, though, weakens the force of prosecution evidence.

One remedy for this dilemma is to take two confessions from a suspect. In the first, no restrictions are placed on the questions and answers. In the second, the investigator should caution the suspect to discuss only his own responsibility for the crime and remove all references to other suspects. Of course, this task cannot always be successful, but, where possible, investigators should employ it.

---

3. The admissibility of a recording may also depend on whether a state statute prohibits certain conversations from being recorded, i.e., attorney-client conversations.

Cases and Materials

Alderman v. *United States,* 394 U.S. 165, 89 S. Ct. 961, 22 L. Ed. 2d 176.

Berger v. *New York,* 388 U.S. 41, 87 S. Ct. 1873, 18 L. Ed. 2d 1040.

Bruton v. *New York,* 391 U.S. 123, 88 S. Ct. 1620, 20 L. Ed. 2d 476.

Goldman v. *United States,* 316 U.S. 129, 62 S. Ct. 993, 86 L. Ed. 1322.

Hoffa v. *United States,* 385 U.S. 293, 87 S. Ct. 408, 17 L. Ed. 2d 374.

Katz v. *United States,* 389 U.S. 347, 88 S. Ct. 507, 19 L. Ed. 2d 576.

Lanza v. *New York,* 370 U.S. 139, 82 S. Ct. 1218, 8 L. Ed. 2d 384.

Lee v. *Florida,* 392 U.S. 378 88 S. Ct. 2096, 20 L. Ed. 2d 1166.

Lopez v. *United States,* 373 U.S. 427, 83 S. Ct. 1381.

Olmstead v. *United States,* 277 U.S. 438, 48 S. Ct. 564, 72 L. Ed. 944.

Rathbun v. *United States,* 355 U.S. 107, 78 S. Ct. 161, 2 L. Ed. 2d 134.

Schwartz v. *Texas,* 344 U.S. 199, 73 S. Ct. 232, 97 L. Ed. 231.

United States v. *White,* 401 U.S. 745, 91 S. Ct. 1122, 28 L. Ed. 453.

Some of the principal requirements of the new federal wiretapping statute are as follows:

1. The application must be made by the principal prosecuting attorney of the state or the principal prosecuting attorney of a political subdivision. 18 U.S.C. 2516(2).

2. An eavesdropping affidavit can be obtained only for certain specified crimes. 18 U.S.C. 2516(2).

3. The application (or affidavit) must include:
  a) the identity of the officer and the identity of the prosecutor; 18 U.S.C. 2518(1)(a).
  b) a statement of probable cause that a crime has been committed which gives details of the offense, a description of the place where the communication is to be intercepted, a description of the type of communication involved, and the identity of the person who is committing the offense and whose communication is to be intercepted; 18 U.S.C. 2516(1)(b).
  c) whether or not other investigative procedures have been tried and whether or not it seems likely that they might succeed; 18 U.S.C. 2518(1)(c).
  d) the time for which the interceptions will be required; 18 U.S.C. 2518(1)(d).
  e) a statement about previous applications for wiretaps and the action taken on them; 18 U.S.C. 2518(1)(e).
  f) if the application is for an extension of the order, the court must be told the results thus far; 18 U.S.C. 2518(1)(f).

4. Other requirements are:

a) the warrant must contain the identity of the person whose communications are to be intercepted, the place where the interception will be made, the kind of communication to be intercepted, and the offense to which it relates, the agency authorized to intercept, and the person authorizing the application, the period of time during which communications will be intercepted, and whether interception will terminate when the described communication has been obtained;

b) the interception must be recorded, if possible; 18 U.S.C. 2518(8).

c) after a period of time not to exceed ninety days, the judge must be given an inventory of the parties to the communication; 18 U.S.C. 2518(8)(d).

d) the tape cannot be introduced in evidence unless the order and application are given the defendant ten days prior to trial; 18 U.S.C. 2518(9).

e) the authorization must contain a provision that the interceptions will be conducted in such a way as to minimize the interception of other communications; 18 U.S.C. 2518(9).

Chapter Thirteen

Force to Obtain Evidence

The use of force to extract a confession has long been condemned by American courts. Part of the rationale for excluding such evidence stems from the obvious unreliability of coerced statements. But even if a coerced confession were demonstrably truthful, the means to such an end are inconsistent with the American concept of due process. Brutality is simply intolerable as a means of obtaining evidence.

In those cases where force is used to obtain physical evidence, as distinct from oral statements, different considerations are at stake. The principal distinction between coerced confessions and coerced physical evidence is that the latter is always credible. For example, suppose that officers physically restrain and then choke a suspect in order to compel him to spit out narcotics he has attempted to swallow. The evidence he discharges will be relevant and inherently credible—there is no question about its truthfulness.

What objections do exist to removing evidence forcibly from a person? Under the due process clause of the Fourteenth Amendment,[1] every arrestee must be arrested, tried, and convicted in accordance with lawful procedures. These procedures must be complied with prior to any deprivation of personal liberty. Part of the "due process of law"

---

1. ". . . nor shall any State deprive any person of life, liberty, or property, without due process of law. . . ."

requires that the procedures used to convict a person must be in harmony with the Anglo-Saxon tradition of "fair trial." And a fair trial cannot include the admissibility of evidence seized by brutal means. Despite the truthfulness of the evidence, and even assuming compliance with the Fourth Amendment in its acquisition, the due process clause of the Fourteenth Amendment remains as a judicial technique to exclude evidence obtained brutally.

Perhaps the most well-known judicial expression of this doctrine is stated in *Rochin* v. *California*, decided by the U.S. Supreme Court in 1952. Rochin had been arrested and, over his objection, his stomach had been pumped. His conviction was based on evidence subsequently removed from his stomach contents. The Supreme Court reversed the conviction. The Court said that such methods "shocked the conscience of the court" and violated due process. "Illegally breaking into the privacy of the [defendant], the struggle to open his mouth and remove what was there, the forcible extraction of his stomach's contents—this course of proceeding by agents of government to obtain evidence is bound to offend even hardened sensibilities. They are methods too close to the rack and the screw to permit of constitutional differentiation."

Despite the due process limitation, officers are not powerless to use some force to obtain physical evidence. In each case the approach may vary, and several examples may best serve to illustrate the solution.

Choking Cases

Narcotic suspects routinely attempt to swallow contraband when confronted by officers. The problem for the officer is clear: prevent the swallowing of evidence otherwise unretrievable. Choking, i.e., an act which prevents breathing, is an impermissible use of force and violates due process. But officers can employ limited forcible techniques to prevent swallowing. Because the line between the two acts is thin, the issue is principally a question of fact. The officer's testimony and that of the defendant will often conflict sharply, and the trier of fact must determine whether choking was employed or whether the defendant was merely prevented from swallowing.

One court summed up the problem this way: "Not every display of force or trespass to the person is unreasonable. . . . Lack of consent and physical resistance by the suspect or accused are not enough in of themselves to create or constitute illegality. . . . The defendant had no constitutional right to swallow or destroy the evidence of his crime. . . . The police should not be required to be subjected to beatings by arrestees any more than arrestees should be subjected to beatings by the police." (*People* v. *Tahtinen*.)

Emetics

Once a suspect has swallowed contraband the ability to retrieve the substance still exists. Forcible extraction of stomach contents is prohibited, but some courts have approved methods designed to induce vomiting i.e., emetics. Of course, this rule may not be universally followed, and some attempt needs to be made in planning whether to employ such methods. If a particular jurisdiction approves the use of emetics in general, officers should have the services of a medical doctor and medical personnel to administer the emetic; testimony on the need for induced vomiting must be elicited, i.e., the danger of death from swallowing an undetermined amount of heroin and the absence of any covering over the narcotic which would prevent its digestion; and testimony on the normal use to which emetics are put, i.e., disgorge poison accidentally swallowed.

Blood Samples

Blood samples are routinely taken from a person suspected of being under the influence of alcohol. Insertion of a needle under the surface of the skin is a "search" within the meaning of the Fourth Amendment, but it is reasonable if incidental to a lawful arrest. Removal of blood samples, performed in a medically approved manner, is commonplace in the United States, involves only slight and fleeting pain, and does not offend due process.

Similar reasoning would apply to breathalizer or saliva tests.

Cases and Materials

Breithaupt v. *Abram,* 352 U.S. 432, 77 S. Ct. 408, 1 L. Ed. 2d 448.

"Constitutional Limitations on the Taking of Body Evidence," 78 *Yale Law Journal* 1074.

Lane v. *United States,* 321 F. 2d 573.

People v. *Bass,* 214 Cal. App. 2d 742, 29 Cal. R. 778.

People v. *Tahtinen,* 210 Cal. App. 2d 755, 26 Cal. R. 864.

Rivas v. *United States,* 368 F. 2d 703.

Rochin v. *California,* 342 U.S. 165, 72 S. Ct. 205, 96 L. Ed. 183.

Schmerber v. *California,* 384 U.S. 757, 86 S. Ct. 1826, 16 L. Ed. 2d 908.

Chapter Fourteen

Arrest and Confessions

Just as the Fourth Amendment prohibits the court from admitting evidence seized in violation of its prohibition against unreasonable searches and seizures, the Fifth Amendment to the U.S. Constitution excludes evidence obtained in violation of its command that "no person shall be compelled to be a witness against himself." The U.S. Supreme Court has construed this phrase to mean that any statement of a suspect in custody is inadmissible in evidence in a criminal trial if obtained in violation of the Fifth Amendment. Because confessions are heavily incriminating, their admissibility in evidence may be crucial to the prosecution case. To understand the current law on the admissibility of confessions, some background is necessary.

History

In early American legal history, involuntary confessions were excluded on the ground of their presumed untrustworthiness, i.e., not because any wrong was done to the accused in using them, but because he may have been induced by the pressure of hope or fear to admit facts unfavorable to him, without regard to their truth, in order to obtain promised relief or avoid threatened danger. Because of this rule, evidence of physical facts discovered by means of involuntary confession was uniformly held to be admissible since it tended to "corroborate" or prove the trustworthiness of the confession.

Since that time, the courts have evolved a new concept of the nature and scope of the constitutional guarantee of "due process of law" as provided by the Fourteenth Amendment. In 1936, the U.S. Supreme Court set aside a conviction on the grounds that the due process clause of the Fourteenth Amendment is "grievously breached when an involuntary confession is obtained by officers and introduced into evidence in a criminal prosecution."

More recently, the U.S. Supreme Court declared that the older "trustworthiness" test of admissibility is not a permissible standard under the due-process clause of the Fourteenth Amendment. The court held that admission into evidence of confessions that are involuntary, i.e., the product of coercion, either physical or psychological, is prohibited regardless of their truth or falsity. This is so not because such confessions are unlikely to be true, said the Court, but because the methods used to extract them offend an underlying principle in the enforcement of criminal law; that ours is an accusatorial and not an inquisitorial system—a system in which the state must establish guilt by evidence independently and freely secured, and may not prove the charge against an accused by coercing it out of his own mouth.

Under this reasoning, the justification for the old rule permitting the introduction of real evidence discovered by means of an involuntary confession, i.e., that such evidence tends to prove the "trustworthiness" of the confession, is now constitutionally indefensible. The issue now is whether the introduction of the challenged evidence—the confession itself or its asserted product—in the particular circumstances of the case denied the accused any essential element of a fair trial or due process of law. Thus, any threat, promise, or reward made by an officer to the defendant voids any subsequent confession regardless of the truthfulness of the confession or any corroborating facts.

The line to be drawn between permissible police conduct and conduct deemed to induce, or to tend to induce, an involuntary statement does not depend on the bare language of inducement, but rather on the nature of the benefit to be derived by the defendant if he speaks the truth, as represented by the police. Advice or exhortation by a police officer to an accused to "tell the truth," or that "it would be better to tell the truth," unaccompanied by either a threat or promise, does not render a subsequent confession involuntary. When the benefit pointed out by the police to a suspect is merely that which flows naturally from a truthful and honest course of conduct, there is nothing improper. On the other hand, if in addition to the foregoing benefit or in place of it, the defendant is given to understand that he might reasonably expect benefits in the nature of more lenient treatment at the hands of the police, prosecution, or court in consideration for making a statement, even a truthful one, such motivation is deemed to render the statement involuntary and inadmissible. The offer or promise of such benefit need not be expressed, but may be implied from equivocal language not otherwise made clear.

With these guidelines, the courts attempted to resolve questions of voluntariness. But the frequency with which defendants challenged the voluntariness of a confession motivated the court in *Miranda* v. *Arizona* to formulate a rule that attempted to avoid resolution of disputed questions of voluntariness.

Often a suspect attempts to exonerate himself or minimize his responsibility for a criminal act. His offer to talk may be preceded by queries as to the benefit which will flow to him if he confesses. At this point, the interrogating officer is on dangerous legal ground. Any temptation to promise a benefit—other than that of telling the truth—must be avoided.

Aside from the *Miranda* admonition, officers questioning suspects eighteen years of age or under must do so with "special caution," according to the U.S. Supreme Court. Immaturity and inexperience weigh heavily in determining whether a juvenile can intelligently and knowingly give a voluntary confession within the meaning of that term. Courts are alert to the subtle psychological coercion that can be exerted on a minor that would be ineffective for adults.

But the California Supreme Court has held that age alone will not disable a minor from confessing voluntarily. The general rule is that a minor has the capacity to make a voluntary confession without the presence or consent of counsel or other responsible adult, and that the admissibility of such a confession depends, not on his age alone, but on a combination of that factor with others such as intelligence, education, experience, and ability to comprehend the meaning and effect of his statements. Among the circumstances considered by the courts as tending to show that the minor possessed the capacity required to make a voluntary confession are his prior experience with the police and the courts; whether advice as to his legal rights was given to him before he confessed; his level of intelligence. As a result, a minor may seek to exclude his confession on two grounds: that his age disabled him from making a truly voluntary statement; that his age disabled him from understanding his rights to counsel and silence.

The *Miranda* Decision

The Supreme Court held in *Miranda* that a suspect in custody, or a person deprived of his freedom of action in a significant way, must be advised that he has a right to counsel before any questions are asked, that he has a right to remain silent at any time before or during questioning, and that if he does answer questions, any response he makes may be used in evidence against him. The suspect, having been informed of these rights, must then waive both rights in order for interrogation to proceed. If a suspect knew he could foreclose questioning, or discontinue an interrogation, the Court thought such knowledge would correct the psychological imbalance created by official questioning in an alien environment. If the suspect refused to discuss the case, knowing he could not be penalized for his refusal, no promises or threats would be availing. It is of course the responsibility of the police to inform the defendant of these rights. Failure to advise a suspect of his right to silence and counsel renders any subsequent confession inadmissible.

The principal legal issue in *Miranda* v. *Arizona* was the admissibility in evidence of pretrial statements obtained from the defendant by law enforcement officers. The Supreme Court was required to decide whether the admissibility of the defendant's confession was in violation of the defendant's Fifth Amendment rights. Under the Fifth Amendment, no person in a criminal case can be compelled to be a witness against himself. Most of the legal issues regarding the Fifth Amendment prior to *Miranda* involved prohibiting compulsory testimony from a defendant as a witness—unless he waived his Fifth Amendment right and elected to testify as a witness.

In *Miranda,* the Court held that the Fifth Amendment privilege extends beyond testimony at trial and protects the witness from incriminating himself prior to trial. This rule was not really novel, because suspects in criminal cases have always had the right to remain silent when confronted by official questioning. Suspects who knew of their Fifth Amendment rights—probably because of past experience with law enforcement—exercised their rights. But if a suspect was unaware of his right to silence, his ignorance prevented him from intelligently choosing whether or not to exercise his Fifth Amendment privilege. The Court in *Miranda* concluded that everyone should be informed of his Fifth Amendment rights in order to be advised of the alternatives available to him. The fourfold admonition of *Miranda* adequately serves that function.

Yet the admonition itself is only the first step. The next question is: When must the admonition be given? The *Miranda* admonition must be given whenever two conditions arise: (1) the suspect is *in custody, or deprived of his freedom of action in a significant way;* and (2) the officer intends to *question* him, as a suspect, about the crime.

Determining whether a suspect is in "custody" generally is not difficult. Anyone under arrest for a specific crime, whether questioned after his arrest by patrol officers in the street or by detectives at the police station, is in "custody" for purposes of the *Miranda* admonition. Generally speaking, "custody implies an arrest for a particular charge and advice by the arresting officer of his intention to arrest, of the cause of arrest, and of his authority to make it. A subsequent complaint stating the charge against the arrested person is normally required. Thus, custody implies an arrest on a particular charge, followed by an accusation initiating the criminal process." But what is the meaning of the term "deprived of freedom of action in a significant way"? How do we determine at what stage a person is deprived of his freedom of action? (*People* v. *Manis.*)

What the Court sought to do in *Miranda* was avoid those situations where a person cannot effectively exercise an intelligent decision whether to talk to law enforcement officers or remain silent. The Court wants to eliminate what it calls an "atmosphere of coercion" that precludes such a choice. Of course, the phrase "atmosphere of coercion" is not particularly precise but, in essence, a court will review all the circumstances of a detention and the attendant questioning in an attempt to resolve the issue. By being aware of several critical factors in this reviewing process, officers can avoid unfavorable court rulings.

Depriving a person of his freedom of action, as that term is used in the *Miranda* case, occurs whenever an atmosphere of coercion exists. What are some of the relevant factors in this determination? One of the key elements in determining whether an atmosphere of coercion exists is the character of questioning the officer undertakes.

Questioning is the great engine of investigation and clearly merits the most judicial attention. As officers well know, questioning can assume a variety of forms. The questioner can ask investigatory questions, or he can ask accusatory questions. Nothing in *Miranda* precludes asking witnesses or suspects questions in an investigatory manner as officers seek to sort out the facts and reconstruct the crime. But once the character of that questioning shifts to accusatory, and the questioner attempts to corroborate already known incriminating facts, or challenges the suspect's statement, or contradicts his statements, the stage shifts, and the suspect now becomes the accused. But as long as officers assume an investigatory posture, rather than an accusatory one, no *Miranda* warnings need precede questioning.

Since the Fifth Amendment privilege against self-incrimination applies only to verbal communications, the key element is the questions asked by the officers. The kind of questions the officer asks depends largely on the amount of information and knowledge he possesses about the person he questions. Suppose an officer confronts someone under one of the following situations:

1. He is uncertain whether any crime has been committed. Most frequently this situation occurs during detentions by patrol officers—based either on information given by someone else or on their own personal observations. Thus, the questions asked during the detention may vary depending on the extent of the officer's observations, whether

lengthy or cursory; the credibility of any informant, whether reliable or untested; and the officer's own experience and knowledge.

2. A crime has been committed, but the identity of the suspect is uncertain. Under these circumstances, the officer will have already acquired knowledge of the commission of the crime, and his focus is on the culprit. The officer's ability to verify or dispel incriminating facts is considerably greater than when he is uncertain whether any crime has been committed at all.

3. A crime has been committed, and the suspect has been identified. Under these circumstances, the officer will clearly place the suspect in custody.

In the first and second examples, the character of the questioning, i.e., whether investigatory or accusatory, will be critical. The time of the questioning, the length of the questioning, the nature of the questions, the tone of the questioning, and the place where the questioning took place will all be added up judicially to determine whether the questioning was investigatory or accusatory. The shift from one stage to another can be subtle, but it is often identifiable.

The second factor is the place of the interrogation. If the questioning is done in the isolated surroundings of an interrogation room, the atmosphere of coercion is clear. But if the person were invited down to the police station and questioned in an investigatory manner, the result might be different.

Contrast these with situations in which a person is involuntarily detained while driving his car. On the one hand, the questioning takes place on a public street while the person remains inside his own vehicle, possibly accompanied by companions. The fact of involuntary detention is important because the detention itself involves a certain element of coercion. Yet the questioning is not done in private but in public—and in proximity to possible witnesses. Here the length and character of the questioning will also be important.

If detectives interview a person at his own home, the element of coercion is substantially diminished. Although the location of the questioning may not be ideal from the officer's standpoint, the home yields less readily to an atmosphere of coercion—absent any sustained or accusatory questioning. Thus, the location plus the questioning itself are critical factors.

Although the phrase "atmosphere of coercion" is perhaps not the exact equivalent of "depriving a person of his freedom of action in a significant way," the term illustrates what the Court is trying to prevent: accusatory questioning of a person under circumstances where he feels compelled to answer. If the detective involuntarily detains a person on the street or in his car, he is not necessarily depriving him of his freedom of action in a significant way. Temporary detention for a brief period of time for questioning is not the legally significant deprivation of freedom of action that the Court is concerned about. The legally significant "freedom of action" the Court discusses is that stage in a criminal investigation when the officer confronts the person with questions of a character that, combined with the time and place of questioning, deprives a person of his ability to freely exercise his right to remain silent.

Deciding whether a suspect is in custody, or deprived of his freedom of action in any significant way, is only the first stage in determining when the *Miranda* admonition must be given. The second stage is deciding whether the officer intends to question the suspect, at that time, about the crime. If the officer intends to question the suspect, the admonition is required preceding the interrogation. If the officer intends to defer questioning, or does not intend to question a suspect at all, no admonition is necessary. Merely because a person is in custody, or deprived of his freedom of action, does not automatically require that he be advised of his constitutional rights. Only if questioning is undertaken is the admonition necessary.[1]

If the officer asks the suspect to perform certain *acts,* the admonition is not required. Under the judicial interpretation of the Fifth Amendment privilege against self-incrimination, only verbal communication is included. Thus, officers may request a suspect to supply a handwriting sample or fingerprints; perform a sobriety test; participate in a lineup; submit to a naline test—all without advising him of his Fifth Amendment rights.

Although the *Miranda* admonition may not be necessary in the preceding examples, a different admonition may still be necessary. Thus, a suspect must be admonished of his Sixth Amendment right to counsel prior to his participation in a lineup if judicial proceedings have commenced; and if a state has an "implied consent" statute,[2] a suspected intoxicated driver must be informed that his license will be suspended if he refuses to participate in a sobriety test.

That the *Miranda* admonition is required before interrogation begins is best illustrated by the rule that voluntary statements from a suspect are admissible regardless of *Miranda.* In fact, in the *Miranda* case itself the Court stated that voluntary statements need not be interrupted by an admonition. Whether a suspect is in custody or not, if he voluntarily discloses incriminating facts implicating himself, no

---

1. In California, under Welfare & Institutions Code §625, an abbreviated *Miranda* admonition must be given to any minor who is in custody regardless of whether or not he is to be questioned. Nothing in the statute provides for excluding statements obtained from minors in violation of the statute.

2. A statute that presumes every driver of a motor vehicle on a public highway consents to a removal of a sample of his blood, breath, or urine for chemical analysis of alcoholic content if there is probable cause to arrest him for driving under the influence of alcohol.

Miranda admonition is necessary. Whether the statement is indeed voluntary is a question for the court to decide. In any event, spontaneous statements should always be written down.

A companion rule is that a suspect in custody who has initially refused to answer questions may elect to discuss his case with the officer at a later time. If the suspect initiates the conversation (assuming no pressure has been exerted to achieve that result), the legal effect is similar to a voluntary statement, and no admonition is required. The circumstances are not entirely the same as a voluntary statement, however, and caution dictates a readvisement.

Lastly, the courts realize that informing suspects of their right to remain silent may thwart a valuable source of information. But under the judicial interpretation of the Fifth Amendment, no other course is possible. For this reason, whenever officers believe that someone's life or welfare is in danger, no admonition need precede the questioning if it is reasonably likely that the person in question can provide information to save a life or prevent injury.

Assuming that the stage is now set to recite the fourfold *Miranda* admonition, officers must be aware that not only must the defendant knowingly and intelligently be advised of his right to counsel and silence, and that he must understand those rights, but also that he must waive these rights. The burden is on the prosecution to establish the element of waiver. In every case, this determination must be judicially resolved after the Court hears testimony on the issue.

Although an express waiver is not legally required, it is nevertheless the strongest evidence available to establish waiver. Many departments ask the suspect specifically whether he wants an attorney or whether he wants to discuss the case. The answers to those questions reflect whether a waiver was obtained. But the courts may imply a waiver if, after having been informed of his Fifth Amendment rights, the suspect responds to questions. Mere response to questioning alone may not automatically assure a valid waiver. The age of the person, his previous experience with law enforcement, his educational background, his general mental ability—all are factors to be considered.

Suppose a subject is under the influence of drugs or alcohol at the time he is questioned? The defendant will later argue that his ability to intelligently understand and waive his Fifth Amendment privilege was impaired. The courts have indicated that both these elements are factors in determining an intelligent waiver. But neither factor necessarily invalidates a waiver. The kind of drug, or degree of intoxication, will be relevant.

A few final notes: A written waiver is not required; corroboration of the waiver is not required.

In determining whether a waiver has been obtained, the Court stated in *Miranda* that once a suspect has indicated by word or conduct that he refuses to discuss the case, all questioning must cease. Or if he has indicated that he desires the presence of counsel before he discusses the case, all questioning must cease until counsel is present. The refusal to discuss the case may be voiced by the suspect initially or at any time during the questioning.

Of course, a decision by the suspect to discontinue questioning is not always explicit. In some cases, the court has indicated that a general statement by the suspect about the possible need for a lawyer, or even a desire to call a lawyer on the phone—followed thereafter by a valid waiver and confession—is an invocation of the privilege. Or, a refusal to sign a written waiver of rights—as distinct from a written statement of facts—is conduct that effectively implies a desire to remain silent and thereby invokes the privilege. And, in the case of a minor, a request to see his parents has been interpreted as the substantial equivalent of a desire to have counsel. Because of the possibility that waiver will not be implied when a suspect unclearly or indirectly desires silence or counsel, officers should clarify the facts and develop a clear understanding of the suspect's desire.

Whenever an admonition is necessary, officers should clearly state that counsel will be provided immediately and prior to questioning, rather than at some future unspecified time. Any ambiguity will be resolved in the defendant's favor. If the suspect does request counsel, officers are under no obligation to comply; their responsibility is to discontinute the questioning until—or unless—counsel is present.

Officers must also exercise caution in not diluting the *Miranda* admonition with expressions of personal opinion as to the desirability of counsel's presence. If a suspect requests advice from the officers, any response must not reflect the officers' personal judgment as to the best course of action, but as clearly as possible should explain the options available to the suspect and require him to decide.

If a suspect is not admonished, and questioning proceeds nevertheless, such conduct is not unlawful. Any suspect may be questioned without prior warnings. The penalty is the exclusion of his statements at his trial. But those same statements may be used for other purposes: to impeach, i.e., contradict the defendant's testimony at trial if he elects to testify as a witness; to establish probable cause to arrest a third party (assuming the sum total of all information qualifies as probable cause); to clear up other cases; or to recover additional stolen property. Of course, failure to admonish in no way affects the right of the People to try the defendant. The principal penalty is the exclusion of the officers' testimony relating the suspect's statements.

Cases and Materials

Miranda v. *Arizona*, 384 U.S. 436, 86 S. Ct. 1602, 16 L. Ed. 2d 694.

Appendix

Search Warrant Check List

A. Participants

Judge_____

Superior Court (   )   Municipal Court (   )

Judicial District_____

Prosecutor_____

Assignment_____

Affiant_____

Occupation_____ No. of yrs._____

Assignment_____ No. of yrs._____

Identification No._____

Employer_____

Monitor (if telephone search warrant)

(name)_____

B. Description of *person* to be searched

Name_____ Age_____

Address_____ Sex_____

Height_____Weight_____Race_____

Color hair_____Color eyes_____Complexion_____

Other distinguishing features_____

_____

Place where person believed to be_____

_____

_____

C. Description of *place* to be searched

House (   )   Apartment (   )   Office (   )

Number_____Floor_____

Other structure (i.e., garage, carport)_____

Address_____City_____

Side of street_____Nearest intersection_____

If no address, describe location_____

_____

Name of business or building_____

Location_____

General description of building_____

Number of floors_____

Primary type of construction_____

D. Description of *vehicle* to be searched

Make_____Year_____No. of doors_____

License number and state_____

Registered to_____

Primary color_____Secondary color_____

Other marks of identification_____

E. Description of property

Enter description of property to be seized

1. Narcotics (example)

   a) Heroin

   "Heroin, a narcotic, and narcotic paraphernalia including, but not limited to: hypodermic syringes, spoons, cotton, milk sugar, weighing devices, measuring devices; containers of various types commonly associated with the storage or use of said narcotic; and articles of personal property tending to establish the identity of persons in control of areas where narcotics are found."

   b) Marijuana

   "Marijuana, and paraphernalia including, but not limited to: pipes, alligator clips and other devices used to assist in the smoking of marijuana; containers of various types commonly associated with the storage or use of said contraband and articles of personal property tending to establish the identity of persons in control of areas where contraband is found."

2. Drugs (example)

   "Amphetamine and barbituric acid, LSD, and derivatives of same, consisting in part of and including, but not limited to: Benzedrine, Seconal, and drug paraphernalia, including, but not limited to: containers of various types, commonly associated with the storage, use, or manufacture of said drugs; and articles of personal property tending to establish the identity of persons in control of areas where restricted dangerous drugs are found."

3. Bookmaking (example)

   "Papers, pencils, racing information, bet registrations, and all other bookmaking property and paraphernalia used or capable of being used for the purpose of recording or registering bets and wagers upon race horses and sporting events, and other property tending to establish the identity of persons in control of areas where bookmaking paraphernalia are found."

4. Other (describe)_____

F. Grounds for search warrant (check one or more)
  1. (   ) Stolen or embezzled property
  2. (   ) Property used to commit a felony
  3. (   ) Property in possession of a person who intends to use it to commit
              a felony, or
              Property in the possession of another to whom it has been given by
              the felon for the purpose of concealment.
  4. (   ) Property tending to show that a felony was committed, or
              Property which tends to show a particular person committed a
              felony.

G. Facts establishing probable cause for issuance
  1. Observations of affiant
      Give specific facts, including reliable hearsay, which standing alone or in
      conjunction with other information establish probable cause to believe
      that the property to be seized is at the location to be searched. Give time
      and date observations made.
  2. Opinion of affiant
      Give specific facts upon which affiant bases his opinion which standing
      alone or in conjunction with other information establishes probable cause
      to believe that the property to be seized is at the location to be searched.
      Describe expert qualifications.
  3. Information received from reliable informant
      a) Date information received_____
          Approximate time_____
      b) Name of informant_____
      c) If confidential
          (   ) Disclosure endangers safety
          (   ) Disclosure impairs future usefulness
          (   ) Identity is unknown
      d) Reliability based on information given by him in the past
          1) Which resulted in the arrest of_____person(s) under
              circumstances which verified the information received in that

              _____

              _____

          2) Which resulted in_____person(s) being held to answer
              at preliminary hearing
          3) Which resulted in_____person(s) being convicted
          4) Which resulted in no arrest but verified the information given in
              that_____

              _____

e) Observations of informant

Give specific facts, including reliable hearsay, which standing alone or in conjunction with other information establish probable cause to believe that the property to be seized is at the location to be searched. Give time and date observations made. Informant must express his personal knowledge.

4. Information received from untested informant

a) Date information received_____

Approximate time_____

b) Name of informant_____

c) If confidential

( ) Disclosure endangers safety

( ) Disclosure impairs future usefulness

d) Observations of informant

Give specific facts, including reliable hearsay, which in conjunction with corroborating information establish probable cause to believe that the property to be seized is at the location to be searched. Give time and date observations made.

e) Where corroboration not required

1) In case of emergency, no corrobative facts are required. Detail the existence of an emergency_____

_____

_____

_____

2) Observations of informant who gives information while not in custody to affiant and is unaware of affiant's official position need not be corroborated.

Give specific facts, including reliable hearsay, which standing alone or in conjunction with other information establish probable cause to believe that the property to be seized is at the location to be searched. Establish informant speaks from personal knowledge, implicates himself and statement made under circumstances when he had no opportunity or apparent reason to fabricate a false story.

5. Information received from citizen informant

a) Date information received_____

Approximate time_____

b) Name of informant_____

c) Status of informant

( ) Citizen informant is a victim of a crime

( ) Citizen informant has no personal interest in the matter and is openly acting to assist law enforcement in that_____

_____

_____

d) Employment of informant_____

e) Observations of informant

Give specific facts, including reliable hearsay, which standing alone or in conjunction with other information establish probable cause to believe that the property to be seized is located at the place to be searched. Give time and date observations made. Information must be based on citizen's personal knowledge.

6. Information received through official channels

a) Describe with particularity the official sources which affiant used to gain the information and the content of what he learned.

_____

_____

b) State the *underlying source* which gave information to the "official channel."

_____

_____

H. Request for nighttime service

Describe reasons for good faith belief that property to be seized may be destroyed or taken from the jurisdiction if search is delayed until daytime.

_____

_____

I. Basis for excuse from giving notice (not applicable in all states)

Describe in detail why there is a good faith belief that giving notice to occupants of place to be searched would result in destruction or concealment of property sought or would expose the officers to physical peril.

_____

_____

_____

Affidavit for Search Warrant

On the basis of his personal knowledge, as set forth in the attachments hereto, and on the basis of the information contained in those attachments,

being duly sworn deposes and

(name)

says, that the property described hereinafter falls within those grounds indicated below by "x"(s) in that it:

_____was stolen or embezzled

_____was used as the means of committing a felony

_____is possessed by a person with the intent to use it as a means of committing a public offense or is possessed by another to whom he may have delivered it for the purpose of concealing it or preventing its discovery

_____is evidence which tends to show that a felony has been committed or a particular person has committed a felony;

and requests the issuance of a warrant to SEARCH

for the following property:

The following attachments are incorporated by reference as though set forth herein:

Probable cause for search (see attached_____)

Nighttime service request (see attached_____)

Request that announcement prior to entry be excused (see attached_____)

_____

Affiant

Subscribed and sworn to before me

this _____ day of _____ , 197   .

_____

Magistrate

Judge of the_____Court_____

Superior/Municipal   Judicial District

WHEREFORE, it is prayed that a Search Warrant be issued.

By_____

Observations of Affiant

Your affiant, a peace officer, employed by
states that he has been a peace officer for   years, and that his present
assignment is

That on   at   .m., your affiant

                (date)   (time)

observed the following:

Opinion of Affiant

Your affiant, a peace officer, employed by
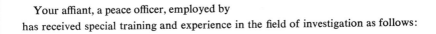
has received special training and experience in the field of investigation as follows:

Based on the following facts contained in this affidavit,

your affiant has formed the expert opinion that

Reliable Informant

Your affiant, a peace officer, employed by

on _____ at _____ .m., received information
          (date)   (time)

from an informant who has previously given truthful information to affiant
(affiant's fellow officer _____).
                          (name)

The name of the informant is

Your affiant wishes to keep the identity of the informant confidential for the
following reason(s):

Your affiant believes the informant to be a reliable person because:

Your affiant was informed by the said informant that he observed (heard)
the following facts:

Untested Informant

Your affiant, a peace officer, employed by
received information from an informant whose reliability has not been tested.

The name of the informant is

Your affiant wishes to keep the identity of the informant confidential for the
following reason(s):

Your affiant was informed on   by the
                                         (date)

said informant that on   at   .m.:
                               (date)   (time)

Citizen Informant

Your affiant, a peace officer, employed by
received information from a citizen whose name is
                        , and who is a victim of the crime for which
this search warrant is being sought (a citizen who observed a crime or has
information regarding a crime, and appears to have no personal interest in the
matter except to assist law enforcement in that):

Your affiant was informed on   by the said
                                        (date)
informant who spoke from personal knowledge that on
                                                (date)
        at   .m.:
            (time)

Official Channels

Your affiant, a peace officer, employed by
has obtained information from the following official sources which he believes
to be reliable:

The sources supplied the following information:

Request for Nighttime Service

Your affiant requests that this warrant contain a direction that it may be served at any time of the day or night, good cause appearing therefor in that:

Excuse from Giving Notice

Your affiant requests that this warrant contain a direction that it be served without notice to the occupants for the following reasons which it is believed will remain in effect at the time the warrant is served in that the occupants if given notice

_____will likely destroy the property described in the warrant because your affiant has the following information:

_____will likely direct violent and deadly force against the officer(s) serving the warrant because your affiant has the following information:

_____will likely attempt to escape with the property described in the warrant because your affiant has the following information:

Search Warrant

PEOPLE OF THE STATE OF CALIFORNIA to any sheriff, policeman or peace officer in the County of Los Angeles: PROOF by affidavit having been made before me by

(name)

that there is probable cause to believe that the property described herein may be found at the locations set forth herein and that it falls within those grounds indicated below by "x" (s) in that it:

————————was stolen or embezzled

————————was used as the means of committing a felony

————————is possessed by a person with the intent to use it as a means of committing a public offense or is possessed by another to whom he may have delivered it for the purpose of concealing it or preventing its discovery

————————is evidence which tends to show that a felony has been committed or a particular person has committed a felony;

you are therefore COMMANDED TO SEARCH

for the following property:

and to SEIZE it if found and bring it forthwith before me, or this court, at the courthouse of this court.

Good cause having been shown by affidavit, you may do such of the following as bear my initials.

————————You may serve this Warrant at any time of the day or night,

————————You need not comply with requirement of notice to occupants.

GIVEN under my hand and dated
this   day of   , 197   .

_____
                                          Magistrate

Judge of the_____Court_____
                  Superior/Municipal   Judicial District

Return to Search Warrant

The personal property listed below (listed on the inventory attached hereto) was taken from the premises located and described as

and from the vehicle(s) described as

and from the person(s) of

by virtue of a search warrant dated the   day of
197   , and executed by Judge
of the below-entitled court:

I,

by whom this Warrant was executed, do swear that the above (attached) inventory contains a true and detailed account of all the property taken by me under the warrant, on   , 197   .

All of the property taken by virtue of said warrant will be retained in my custody subject to the order of this court or of any other court in which the offense in respect to which the property or things taken, is triable.

_____

Affiant

Subscribed and sworn to before me
this   day of   , 197   .

_____

Magistrate

Judge of the_____Court_____
            Superior/Municipal   Judicial District

P.C. § 806.   (Felony Complaint)

A proceeding for the examination before a magistrate of a person on a charge of an offense originally triable in a superior court must be commenced by written complaint under oath subscribed by the complainant and filed with the magistrate. . . .

P.C. § 813.   (Felony Warrant)

When a complaint is filed with a magistrate charging a public offense originally triable in the superior court of the county in which he sits, if such magistrate is satisfied from the complaint that the offense complained of has been committed and that there is reasonable ground to believe that the defendant has committed it, he must issue a warrant for the arrest of the defendant; provided, that when the magistrate is a judge of the justice court, he may issue such a warrant only upon the concurrence of the district attorney of the county in which he sits or the Attorney General of the State of California.

P.C. § 814.   (Form of Arrest)

A warrant of arrest issued under Section 813 may be in substantially the following form:

County of_____

The people of the State of California to any peace officer of said State:

Complaint on oath having this day been laid before me that the crime of_____(designating it generally) has been committed and accusing_____
(naming defendant) thereof, you are therefore commanded forthwith to arrest the above named defendant and bring him before me at _____(naming the place), or in case of my absence or inability to act, before the nearest or most accessible magistrate in this county.

Dated at_____(place) this _____day of_____, 19_____.

_____
(Signature and full official title
of magistrate)

P.C. § 815.   (Contents of Warrant)

A warrant of arrest * * * shall specify the name of the defendant or, if it is unknown to the magistrate, judge * * *, justice, or other issuing authority, the defendant may be designated therein by any name. It * * * shall also state the time of issuing it, and the city * * * or county where it is issued, and shall be signed by the magistrate, judge * * *, justice, or other issuing authority issuing it with the title of his office and the name of the court or other issuing agency.

P.C. § 825.   (Arraignment)

The defendant must in all cases be taken before the magistrate without unnecessary delay, and, in any event, within two days after his arrest, excluding Sundays and holidays; provided, however, that when the two days prescribed herein expire at a time when the court in which the magistrate is sitting is not in session, such time shall be extended to include the duration of the next regular court session on the judicial day immediately following.

After such arrest, any attorney at law entitled to practice in the courts of record of California, may, at the request of the prisoner or any relative of such prisoner, visit the person so arrested. Any officer having charge of the prisoner so arrested who willfully refuses or neglects to allow such attorney to visit a prisoner is guilty of a misdemeanor. Any officer having a prisoner in charge, who refuses to allow any attorney to visit the prisoner when proper application is made therefor, shall forfeit and pay to the party aggrieved the sum of five hundred dollars ($500), to be recovered by action in any court of competent jurisdiction.

P.C. § 1427.   (Misdemeanor Warrant)

(a) When a complaint is presented to a judge of an inferior court of the commission of a public offense appearing to be triable in his court, he must, if satisfied therefrom that the offense complained of has been committed and that there is reasonable ground to believe that the defendant has committed it, issue a warrant, for the arrest of the defendant.

(b) Such warrant of arrest and proceedings upon it shall be in conformity to the provisions of this code regarding warrants of arrest, and it may be in the following form:

County of_____

The people of the State of California, to any peace officer in this state:

Complaint upon oath having been this day made before me that the offense of_____(designating it generally) has been committed and accusing_____

_____(name of defendant) thereof you are therefore commanded forthwith to arrest the above-named defendant and bring him forthwith before the_____

court of_____(stating full title of court)

at_____(naming place).

Witness my hand and the seal of said court this_____

day of_____, 19_____.

(Signed).

_____

Judge of said court

If it appears that the offense complained of has been committed by a corporation, no warrant of arrest shall issue, but the judge must issue a summons substantially in the form prescribed in Section 1391. Such summons must be served at the time and in the manner designated in Section 1392 except that if the offense complained of is a violation of the Vehicle Code or a local ordinance adopted pursuant to the Vehicle Code, such summons may be served by deposit by the clerk of the court in the United States mail of an envelope enclosing the summons, which envelope shall be addressed to a person authorized to accept service of legal process on behalf of the defendant, and which envelope shall be mailed by registered mail or certified mail with a return receipt requested. Promptly upon such mailing, the clerk of the court shall execute a certificate of such mailing and place it in the file of the court for that case. At the time stated in the summons the corporation may appear by counsel and answer the complaint. If it does not appear, a plea of not guilty must be entered, and the same proceedings had therein as in other cases.